Durham's

Place-Names
of

California's Old Wine Country

Durham's Place-Names of California Series

- Fourteen volumes cover the state of California by region

- The most complete California place-name series

- *Durham's Place-Names of California's Gold Country Including Yosemite National Park:* **Includes Madera, Mariposa, Tuolumne, Calaveras, Amador, El Dorado, Placer, Sierra & Nevada Counties** ISBN 1-884995-25-X

- *Durham's Place-Names of the California North Coast:* **Includes Del Norte, Humbolt, Lake, Mendocino & Trinity Counties** ISBN 1-884995-26-8

- *Durham's Place-Names of California's Old Wine Country:* **Includes Napa & Sonoma Counties** ISBN 1-884995-27-6

- *Durham's Place-Names of Greater Los Angeles:* **Includes Los Angeles, Orange & Ventura Counties** ISBN 1-884995-28-4

- *Durham's Place-Names of California's Central Coast:* **Includes Santa Barbara, San Luis Obispo, San Benito, Monterey & Santa Cruz Counties** ISBN 1-884995-29-2

- *Durham's Place-Names of California's Eastern Sierra:* **Includes Alpine, Inyo & Mono Counties** ISBN 1-884995-30-6

- *Durham's Place-Names of California's Desert Counties:* **Includes Imperial, Riverside & San Bernadino Counties** ISBN 1-884995-31-4

- *Durham's Place-Names of* **San Diego County** ISBN 1-884995-32-2

- *Durham's Place-Names of Central California:* **Includes Madera, Fresno, Tulare, Kings & Kern Counties** ISBN 1-884995-33-0

- *Durham's Place-Names of California's North Sacramento Valley:* **Includes Butte, Glenn, Shasta, Siskiyou & Tehama Counties** ISBN 1-884995-34-9

- *Durham's Place-Names of The San Francisco Bay Area:* **Includes Marin, San Francisco, San Mateo, Contra Costa, Alameda , Solano & Santa Clara Counties** ISBN 1-884995-35-7

- *Durham's Place-Names of California's South Sacramento Valley:* **Includes Colusa, Sacramento, Sutter, Yuba & Yolo Counties** ISBN 1-884995-36-5

- *Durham's Place-Names of California's North San Joaquin Valley:* **Includes San Joaquin, Stanislaus & Merced Counties** ISBN 1-884995-37-3

- *Durham's Place-Names of Northeastern California:* **Includes Lassen, Modoc & Plumas Counties** ISBN 1-884995-38-1

The above titles are available at better bookstores, on-line bookstores or by calling 1-800-497-4909

Durham's

Place-Names
of

California's Old Wine Country

Includes Napa and Sonoma Counties

David L. Durham

Clovis, California

Published by
Quill Driver Books/Word Dancer Press, Inc.
8386 N. Madsen
Clovis, CA 93611
559-322-5917
800-497-4909

Word Dancer Press books may be purchased at special prices
for educational, fund-raising, business or promotional use. Please
contact Special Markets, Quill Driver Books/Word Dancer Press,
Inc. at the above address or phone number.

To order another copy of this book or another book in the
Durham's Place-Names of California series, please call
1-800-497-4909.

Quill Driver Books/Word Dancer Press, Inc. project cadre:
Doris Hall, Dave Marion, Stephen Blake Mettee

ISBN 1-884995-27-6

Library of Congress Cataloging-in-Publication Data

Durham, David L., 1925-
  [Place names of California's old wine country]
  Durham's place names of California's old wine country : includes Napa & Sonoma
counties / David L. Durham.
    p. cm.
  Includes bibliographical references (p.).
  ISBN 1-884995-27-6 (trade paper)
    1. Names, Geographical--California--Napa County. 2. Napa County (Calif.)--History,
Local. 3. Names, Geographical--California--Sonoma County. 4. Sonoma County
(Calif.)--History, Local. I. Title: Place names of California's old wine country. II. Title:
California's old wine country. III. Title.

F868.N2D87   2001
917.94'18003--dc21

                                                                    00-069261

Cover photograph, "Knights Valley Vineyard," by Peter B. Hickey, courtesy of Beringer
Vineyards, St. Helena, California.

Contents

CALIFORNIA
OLD WINE COUNTRY
COUNTIES SHADED

INTRODUCTION

Purpose, organization and scope

This gazetteer, which lists geographic features of Napa and Sonoma counties, California, is one of a series of fourteen books that cover the whole state. This series is derived from *California's Geographic Names: A Gazetteer of Historic and Modern Names of the State,* David L. Durham's definitive gazetteer of California. Each book contains all the entries for the counties covered that are included in the larger volume. United States government quadrangle maps, which are detailed, somewhat authoritative, and generally available, are the primary source of information. Included are features that are named on quadrangle maps, or that can be related to features named on the maps. The books list relief features, water features, and most kinds of cultural features, but omit names of streets, parks, schools, churches, cemeteries, dams and the like. Some names simply identify a person or family living at a site because such places are landmarks in sparsely settled parts of the state.

The listing of names is alphabetical, and multiword names are alphabetized as one word. Terms abbreviated on maps are given in full in the alphabetical list, and numerals in names are listed in alphabetical order rather than in numerical order. In addition to the principal entries, the list includes cross references to variant names, obsolete names and key words in multiword English-language names. For each principal entry, the name is followed by the name of the county or counties in which the feature lies, a classifying term, general and specific locations, identification of one or more quadrangle maps that show the name and other information. All features named in an entry generally belong to the same county. The classifying terms are defined under the heading "Geographic Terms" beginning on page *xi.*

Locations and measurements are from quadrangle maps, distances and directions are approximate, and latitude and longitude generally are to the nearest five seconds. Distances between post offices are measured by road, as the mail would be carried. Other distances are measured in a straight line unless the measurement is given with a qualifying expression such as "downstream" or "by road." For streams, the location given generally is the place that the stream joins another stream, enters a body of water, or debouches into a canyon or valley. For features of considerable areal extent, the location given ordinarily is near the center, except for cities and towns, for which the location given is near the center of the downtown part, or at the city hall or civic center. Measurements to or from areal features usually are to or from the center. Specific locations are omitted for some very large or poorly defined places. Books, articles, and miscellaneous maps are listed under "References Cited." The references identify sources of data and provide leads to additional information. If a name applies to more than one feature in a county, the features are numbered and identified elsewhere in the list by that number in parentheses following the name.

SETTING

This book concerns geographical features of Napa and Sonoma counties, California, the heart of California's early wine-growing region. The map on page *vi* shows the location of the counties. Townships (T) and Ranges (R) refer to Mount Diablo Base and Meridian.

Napa County.—Napa County lies north of San Francisco Bay along Napa River. The first state legislature created Napa County in 1850; the north part of the original county territory was lost in 1861 with the creation of Lake County; other boundary changes were made mainly to remedy deficiencies in the first county-boundary description (Coy, p. 187-193). The city of Napa has always been the county seat (Hoover, Rensch, and Rensch, p. 239).

Sonoma County.—Sonoma County extends from the sea to San Pablo Bay. The first state legislature created the county in 1850; some redefinition of county boundaries in the 1850's were made largely to rectify difficulties in the original boundary descriptions (Coy, p. 262-268). Sonoma was the county seat until 1854, when the county government moved to Santa Rosa (Hoover, Rensch, and Rensch, p. 525). The county name is from the town of Sonoma.

GEOGRAPHIC TERMS

Area —A tract of land, either precisely or indefinitely defined.

Bay —A body of water connected to a larger body of water and nearly surrounded by land.

Beach —An expanse of sandy or pebbly material that borders a body of water.

Bend —A pronounced curve in the course of a stream, and the land partly enclosed therein.

Canyon —A narrow elongate depression in the land surface, generally confined between steep sides and usually drained by a stream.

City —An inhabited place that has a population greater than about 25,000 in an urban setting.

District —Part of an inhabited place, either precisely or indefinitely defined.

Embayment —An indentation in the shoreline of a body of water.

Hill —A prominent elevation on the land surface that has a well-defined outline on a map, and that rises less than 1000 feet above its surroundings.

Intermittent lake —A lake that ordinarily contains water only part of the time.

Island —A tract of normally dry land, or of marsh, that is surrounded by water.

Lake —A body of standing water, either natural or artificial.

Land grant —A gift of land made by Spanish or Mexican authority and eventually confirmed by the United States government.

Locality —A place that has past or present cultural associations.

Marsh —A poorly drained wet area.

Military installation —Land or facility used for military purposes.

Pass —A saddle or natural depression that affords passage across a range or between peaks.

Peak —A prominent high point on a larger elevated land surface.

Peninsula —An elongate tract of land nearly surrounded by water.

Promontory —A conspicuous, but not necessarily high, elevation of the land surface that protrudes into a body of water or into a lowland.

Range —An elevated land surface of ridges and peaks.

Relief feature —A general term for a recognizable form of the land surface produced by natural causes.

Ridge —A prominent elongate elevation on the land surface; occurs either independently or as part of a larger elevation.

Rock —A rocky mass that lies near or projects above the surface of a body of water.

Settlement —An informal inhabited place.

Shoal —A shallow place in a body of water.

Spring —A natural flow of water from the ground.

Stream —A body of water that moves under gravity in a depression on the land surface; includes watercourses that have intermittent flow and watercourses that are modified by man.

Town —An inhabited place that has a population of about 500 to 25,000 in an urban setting.

Valley —A broad depression in the land surface, or a wide place in an otherwise narrow depression.

Village —An inhabited place that has a compact cluster of buildings and a population less than about 500.

Waterfall —A perpendicular or very steep descent of the water in a stream.

Water feature —A general term for something or some place involving water.

Well —A hole sunk into the ground to obtain water.

Place-Names
of
California's
Old Wine Country

– A –

Ababais Creek: see **Ebabias Creek** [SONOMA].

Adams Creek [NAPA]: *stream,* flows 6.5 miles to Eticuera Creek 5 miles northeast of Walter Springs (lat. 38°41'50" N, long. 122°17'15" W; sec. 22, T 10 N, R 4 W); the stream is south of Adams Ridge. Named on Walter Springs (1959) 7.5' quadrangle.

Adams Flat [NAPA]: *valley,* 9 miles northwest of Mount Vaca along Capell Creek (lat. 38°28'30" N, long. 122°14'05" W; on S line sec. 6, T 7 N, R 3 W). Named on Capell Valley (1951) 7.5' quadrangle.

Adams Ridge [NAPA]: *ridge,* generally northwest-trending, 2 miles long, 5 miles south of Knoxville (lat. 38°45' N, long. 122°20' W). Named on Knoxville (1958) and Walter Springs (1959) 7.5' quadrangles.

Adelante: see **Napa Junction** [NAPA].

Adobe Canyon [SONOMA]: *canyon,* 4.5 miles long, along Sonoma Creek above a point 1.25 miles north-northwest of Kenwood (lat. 38°26' N, long. 122°33'10" W). Named on Kenwood (1954) and Rutherford (1951) 7.5' quadrangles. Called Sonoma Canyon on Santa Rosa (1916) 15' quadrangle.

Adobe Creek [SONOMA]: *stream,* flows 7.5 miles to Petaluma River 2 miles east-southeast of downtown Petaluma (lat. 38°13'25" N, long. 122°36'15" W); the stream goes past Petaluma Adobe state historical monument. Named on Glen Ellen (1954) and Petaluma River (1954) 7.5' quadrangles.

Aetna Springs [NAPA]: *locality,* 10 miles north of Saint Helena (lat. 38°39'10" N, long. 122°29' W; near SW cor. sec. 1, T 9 N, R 6 W). Named on Aetna Springs (1958) 7.5' quadrangle. Crawford (1894, p. 341) used the form "Etna Springs" for the name. Postal authorities established Phoenix Mine post office, named for a quicksilver mine, in 1873 and discontinued it in 1880, when they moved the service 1 mile west to Lidell (Salley, p. 170). They established Lidell post office in 1880, moved it and changed the name to Aetna Springs in 1915, and discontinued it in 1945; the name "Lidell" was for William H. Lidell, first postmaster (Salley, p. 2, 122). The property at Aetna Springs post office belonged to Ætna Quicksilver Mining Company; after the company stopped mining in one of the tunnels, mineralized water from that tunnel was the basis of a resort as early as 1878 (Waring,

p. 156-157). United States Board on Geographic Names (1991, p. 7) approved the name "Upper Bohn Lake" for a reservoir, 1 mile long, located 6 miles north-northeast of Aetna Springs on Napa-Lake county line (lat. 38°43'48" N, long. 122°26'28" W), and rejected the name "Eaton H. Magoon Lake" for the feature.

Agua Caliente [SONOMA]:
(1) *land grant,* at Agua Caliente (2) and Glen Ellen in Valley of the Moon. Named on Glen Ellen (1954), Kenwood (1954), and Sonoma (1951) 7.5' quadrangles. Lazaro Piña received 11 leagues in 1840; C.P. Stone claimed 212 acres patented in 1880; Mariano Guadalupe Vallejo claimed 1864 acres patented in 1880; T. M. Leavenworth claimed 592 acres patented in 1880; Joseph Hooker claimed 551 acres patented in 1866 (Cowan, p. 12).
(2) *locality,* nearly 3 miles northwest of Sonoma (lat. 38°19'25" N, long. 122°29'10" W); the place is on Agua Caliente grant. Named on Sonoma (1951) 7.5' quadrangle. Postal authorities established Agua Caliente post office in 1886 and discontinued it in 1951 (Frickstad, p. 193). Naturally occurring hot water at the place was the basis for a resort called Agua Caliente Springs (Bradley, p. 334). Postal authorities established Cave Dale post office 3 miles northeast of Agua Caliente (2) in 1913 and discontinued it in 1925 (Salley, p. 40).

Agua Caliente: see **Calistoga** [NAPA].

Agua Caliente Canyon [SONOMA]: *canyon,* 4 miles long, along Agua Caliente Creek above a point 1.5 miles northwest of Sonoma (lat. 38°18'35" N, long. 122°28'25" W). Named on Sonoma (1951) 7.5' quadrangle.

Agua Caliente Creek [SONOMA]: *stream,* flows nearly 5 miles to Sonoma Creek 1.5 miles west-northwest of Sonoma (lat. 38°18'10" N, long. 122°28'55" W); the stream goes through Agua Caliente Canyon. Named on Sonoma (1951) 7.5' quadrangle.

Agua Caliente Springs: see **Agua Caliente** [SONOMA] (2).

Agua Rica Hot Sulphur Springs: see **Boyes Hot Springs** [SONOMA].

Albany: see **Knights Valley** [SONOMA].

Alder Creek [SONOMA]:
(1) *stream,* heads in Mendocino County and flows 3.5 miles to Squaw Creek 5 miles north-northwest of Geyser Peak (lat. 38°50'05" N, long. 122°52' W; sec. 4, T 11 N, R 9 W). Named on Asti (1959) and The Geysers (1959) 7.5' quadrangles.

(2) *stream,* flows less than 1 mile to Dutch Bill Creek nearly 2 miles north-northwest of Occidental (lat. 38°25'50" N, long. 122° 57'40" W; near SW cor. sec. 22, T 7 N, R 10 W). Named on Camp Meeker (1954) 7.5' quadrangle.

Alderglen Springs [SONOMA]: *locality,* 3 miles northwest of Cloverdale (lat. 38°50'05" N, long. 123°03'15" W; sec. 2, T 11 N, R 11 W). Named on Cloverdale (1960) 7.5' quadrangle. Called Alder Glen Sps. on Hopland (1944) 15' quadrangle. In 1909, a resort at the place had a hotel, cottages, and tents that provided accommodations for 75 guests (Waring, p. 166).

Alexander: see **Alexander Valley** [SONOMA].

Alexander Valley [SONOMA]: *valley,* along Russian River from Cloverdale southeast for 20 miles to the latitude of Healdsburg. Named on Asti (1959), Cloverdale (1960), Geyserville (1955), Healdsburg (1955), and Jimtown (1955) 7.5' quadrangles. The name commemorates Cyrus Alexander, a trapper and trader who came to California in 1833 and later owned land in the valley (Hoover, Rensch, and Rensch, p. 534). Postal authorities established Alexanderville post office 7 miles southeast of Geyserville in 1871 and discontinued it in 1872; They established Alexander post office at or near the site of Alexanderville post office in 1879 and discontinued it in 1880 (Salley, p. 4). They established Soda Rock post office 6 miles east of Healdsburg in 1889 and discontinued it in 1892, when they moved it 1 mile northwest and renamed it Alexander Valley; they discontinued Alexander Valley post office in 1903 (Salley, p. 4, 207).

Alexanderville: see **Alexander Valley** [SONOMA].

Alfalfa Patch Reservoir [NAPA]: *lake,* 150 feet long, nearly 3 miles south-southeast of Berryessa Peak (lat. 38°37'30" N, long. 122°10'30" W). Named on Brooks (1959) 7.5' quadrangle.

Alice Rock [SONOMA]: *relief feature,* 2.25 miles north-northwest of the village of Bodega Bay (lat. 38°21'55" N, long. 122°03'05" W). Named on Bodega Head (1942) 7.5' quadrangle.

Allen Creek [SONOMA]: *stream,* flows 2.5 miles to House Creek 7 miles southwest of Big Mountain (lat. 38°38'10" N, long. 123°13'40" W; sec. 7, T 9 N, R 12 W). Named on Tombs Creek (1978) 7.5' quadrangle.

Alliance Redwood [SONOMA]: *locality,* 2.25 miles northwest of Occidental (lat. 38°26' N, long. 122°58'20" W; sec. 21, T 7 N, R 10 W). Named on Camp Meeker (1954) 7.5' quadrangle.

Altamont Medical Springs: see **Occidental** [SONOMA].

Alta Vista [SONOMA]: *locality,* 2 miles north-northeast of Sonoma (lat. 38°19'15" N, long. 122°26'30" W). Named on Sonoma (1942) 15' quadrangle.

Alten [SONOMA]: *locality,* 1.5 mile southeast of Sebastopol along Petaluma and Santa Rosa Railroad (lat. 38°23' N, long. 122°48'25" W; sec. 12, T 6 N, R 9 W). Named on Sebastopol (1942) 15' quadrangle.

Altruria: see **Fulton** [SONOMA].

America: see **Santa Rosa** [SONOMA].

American Canyon [NAPA]: *canyon,* 2.25 miles long, opens into lowlands 2 miles south-southeast of Napa Junction (lat. 38°09'50" N, long. 122°13'55" W); the canyon heads opposite the head of American Canyon in Solano County. Named on Cordelia (1951) 7.5' quadrangle, where the name "American Canyon" applies to American Canyon in Napa County, and to American Canyon in Solano County together. Postal authorities established American Canyon post office 5 miles north of Vallejo in the canyon in 1956 (Salley, p. 7).

American Canyon Creek [NAPA]: *stream,* flows 2.25 miles to lowlands nearly 2 miles south-southeast of Napa Junction (lat. 38°09'50" N, long. 122°13'55" W); the stream drains American Canyon. Named on Cordelia (1951) and Cuttings Wharf (1949) 7.5' quadrangles.

Americano Creek [SONOMA]: *stream,* forms part of Marin-Sonoma county line, heads in Sonoma County and flows 11 miles to Estero Americano 4.5 miles north-northwest of Tomales in Marin County (lat. 38°18'45" N, long. 122°55'40" W). Named on Two Rock (1954) and Valley Ford (1954) 7.5' quadrangles. United States Board on Geographic Names (1943, p. 9) rejected the names "Ebabias Creek," "Estero Americano," and "Estero Americano Creek" for the stream, or for any part of it.

Analy: see **Freestone** [SONOMA].

Analy Valley: see **Freestone** [SONOMA].

Anchor Creek [SONOMA]: *stream,* heads in Mendocino County and flows 1.5 miles to Cherry Creek 4.5 miles west-northwest of Cloverdale (lat. 38°49'30" N, long. 123°05'50" W; near SW cor. sec. 4, T 11 N, R 11 W). Named on Cloverdale (1960) 7.5' quadrangle.

Anderson Canyon [NAPA]: *canyon,* drained by a stream that flows 2.5 miles to lowlands along Lake Berryessa nearly 3 miles west-southwest of Berryessa Peak (lat. 38°39'20" N, long. 122°14'15" W); the canyon is south of Anderson Mountain. Named on Brooks (1959) 7.5' quadrangle.

Anderson Mountain [NAPA]: *peak,* 1.25 miles west-southwest of Berryessa Peak (lat. 38°39'35" N, long. 122°12'45" W); the peak is north of Anderson Canyon. Altitude 1807 feet. Named on Brooks (1959) 7.5' quadrangle.

Angel Creek [SONOMA]: *stream,* flows 1.25 miles to Mill Creek (1) 7 miles north of Guerneville (lat. 38°36'20" N, long. 122°58'45" W; near NW cor. sec. 28, T 9 N,

R 10 W). Named on Guerneville (1955) 7.5' quadrangle.

Angwin [NAPA]: *town,* 5 miles north-northeast of Saint Helena (lat. 38°34'45" N, long. 122°26'45" W); the town is on La Jota grant. Named on Saint Helena (1960) 7.5' quadrangle. Postal authorities established Angwin post office in 1883 and discontinued it in 1910; they established La Jota post office 7 miles northeast of Saint Helena in 1923 and discontinued it in 1925, when they moved it and changed the name to Angwin (Salley, p. 8, 115). The name "Angwin" commemorates Edwin Angwin, who operated a summer resort at the site (Gudde, 1949, p. 11).

Anna Belcher Creek [SONOMA]: *stream,* flows 1.25 miles to Little Sulphur Creek 10 miles north-northeast of Healdsburg at Pine Flat (lat. 38°44'30" N, long. 122°46'15" W; sec. 5, T 10 N, R 8 W). Named on Jimtown (1955) 7.5' quadrangle. Called Florence Cr. on Healdsburg (1940) 15' quadrangle. Anne Belcher quicksilver mine was situated near the stream about 1.75 miles north of Pine Flat (Bailey, p. 228).

Annadel [SONOMA]: *locality,* 3.25 miles west-northwest of Kenwood along Southern Pacific Railroad (lat. 38°26'25" N, long. 122° 36' W). Named on Santa Rosa (1916) 15' quadrangle. Postal authorities established Annadel post office in 1892 and discontinued it in 1893 (Frickstad, p. 194). The name was derived from the first name of Annie Hutchinson, the daughter of a landowner at the place (Higgins, p. 235).

Annapolis [SONOMA]: *settlement,* 5 miles north-northeast of the village of Stewarts Point (lat. 38°43'15" N, long. 123°22'05" W). Named on Annapolis (1977) 7.5' quadrangle. Postal authorities established Annapolis post office in 1901 and moved it 0.5 mile east in 1940; the name is from Annapolis Orchards, started in the 1880's (Salley, p. 8).

Appleby Bay [NAPA]: *marsh,* 5 miles west of Napa Junction along Napa Slough (lat. 38°11'30" N, long. 122°20'20" W; sec. 18, T 4 N, R 4 W). Named on Cuttings Wharf (1949) 7.5' quadrangle.

Apple Tree Canyon [NAPA]: *canyon,* drained by a stream that flows 1 mile to Gosling Canyon 7 miles south-southeast of Berryessa Peak (lat. 38°34'05" N, long. 122°09'10" W; sec. 2, T 8 N, R 3 W). Named on Lake Berryessa (1959) 7.5' quadrangle.

Arched Rock [SONOMA]:
(1) *island,* 400 feet long, 1.25 miles south-southwest of Jenner, and 1250 feet offshore (lat. 38°26' N, long. 123°07'35" W). Named on Arched Rock (1977) 7.5' quadrangle.
(2) *rock,* 3 miles north-northwest of the village of Bodega Bay, and 150 feet offshore (lat. 38°22'10" N, long. 123°04'25" W). Named on Bodega Head (1972) 7.5' quadrangle.

Arched Rock Beach [SONOMA]: *beach,* nearly 3 miles north-northwest of the village of Bodega Bay along the coast (lat. 38°22'05" N, long. 123°04'20" W); the beach is southeast of Arched Rock (2). Named on Bodega Head (1972) 7.5' quadrangle.

Arrowhead Mountain [NAPA-SONOMA]: *ridge,* northwest-trending, 2 miles long, 3 miles east-southeast of Sonoma on Napa-Sonoma county line (lat. 38°16'35" N, long. 122°24'10" W). Named on Sonoma (1951) 7.5' quadrangle.

Arroyo Creek: see **Holmes Canyon** [SONOMA].

Arroyo de los Guilicos: see **Calabazas Creek** [SONOMA].

Arroyo de Permanente: see **Santa Rosa Creek** [SONOMA].

Arroyo de San Antonio: see **San Antonio Creek** [SONOMA].

Arroyo de Santa Rosa: see **Santa Rosa Creek** [SONOMA].

Arroyo Grande: see **Sonoma Creek** [SONOMA].

Arroyo Seco [SONOMA]: *stream,* flows 6.5 miles to Schell Creek 5.25 miles south-southeast of Sonoma (lat. 38°14'55" N, long. 122°26' W). Named on Sears Point (1951) and Sonoma (1951) 7.5' quadrangles.

Arroyo Verde [SONOMA]: see **Salmon Creek** [SONOMA] (1).

Asbury Creek [SONOMA]: *stream,* flows 2.5 miles to Sonoma Creek 0.5 mile south of Glen Ellen (lat. 38°21'20" N, long. 122° 31'25" W). Named on Glen Ellen (1954) 7.5' quadrangle.

Asti [SONOMA]: *village,* 4 miles southeast of Cloverdale (lat. 38°45'45" N, long. 122°58'20" W). Named on Asti (1959) 7.5' quadrangle. Postal authorities established Asti post office in 1888 (Frickstad, p. 194). Andrea Sbarboro founded a cooperative enterprise in 1881 that he called Italian-Swiss Colony; Asti was part of the venture and was named for a city in northern Italy (Hansen and Miller, p. 56).

Asylum Slough: see **Tulucay Creek** [NAPA].

Atascadero Creek [SONOMA]: *stream,* flows 8.5 miles to Green Valley Creek 4.25 miles northeast of Occidental (lat. 38°26'55" N, long. 122°53'10" W). Named on Camp Meeker (1954) and Sebastopol (1954) 7.5' quadrangles.

Atlas [NAPA]: *locality,* 8 miles west-northwest of Mount Vaca (lat. 38°25'45" N, long. 122°14'50" W; sec. 25, T 7 N, R 4 W); the place is 1.5 miles south-southeast of Atlas Peak. Named on Capell Valley (1951) 7.5' quadrangle. Postal authorities established Atlas post office in 1893, moved it 1 mile south in 1894, and discontinued it in 1934; the place was a resort community named for nearby Atlas Peak (Salley, p. 11).

Atlas Peak [NAPA]: *peak,* 6.25 miles east-northeast of Yountville (lat. 38°27'05" N, long. 122°15'45" W; near SW cor. sec. 14, T 7 N, R

4 W). Altitude 2663 feet. Named on Yountville (1951) 7.5' quadrangle.

Aurora Creek: see **Stemple Creek** [SONOMA].

Austin: see **Cazadero** [SONOMA].

Austin Creek [SONOMA]: *stream,* flows 15 miles to Russian River 3.5 miles southwest of Guerneville (lat. 38°27'55" N, long. 123°02'55" W). Named on Cazadero (1978), Duncans Mills (1979) and Fort Ross (1978) 7.5' quadrangles. Called Big Austin Creek on Cazadero (1943) and Fort Ross (1943) 7.5' quadrangles. On Healdsburg (1940) 15' quadrangle, present Gilliam Creek is called East Br. Austin Cr.

Austin Creek: see **East Austin Creek** [SONOMA]; **Little Austin Creek**, under **Gray Creek** [SONOMA].

Austin Gap [SONOMA]: *pass,* nearly 3 miles southwest of Guerneville (lat. 38°28'45" N, long. 123°02'20" W); the pass is east of Austin Creek. Named on Duncans Mills (1979) 7.5' quadrangle.

– B –

Bacon Flat [SONOMA]: *area,* 5.5 miles northwest of Mount Saint Helena (lat. 38°43'35" N, long. 122°42'10" W; sec. 11, T 10 N, R 8 W). Named on Mount Saint Helena (1959) 7.5' quadrangle.

Bahia de San Pablo: see **San Pablo Bay** [SONOMA].

Bahia de Sonoma: see **San Pablo Bay** [SONOMA].

Bahia Redondo: see **San Pablo Bay** [SONOMA].

Bailhache [SONOMA]: *locality,* 1 mile southeast of Healdsburg along Northwestern Pacific Railroad (lat. 38°36'15" N, long. 122° 51'15" W). Named on Healdsburg (1955) 7.5' quadrangle.

Bak [SONOMA]: *locality,* 2.5 miles east-northeast of downtown Santa Rosa along Southern Pacific Railroad (lat. 38°27'30" N, long. 122°40'15" W). Named on Santa Rosa (1916) 15' quadrangle. Bradley (p. 358) referred to Baku switch, located 2 miles east of Santa Rosa.

Baku: see **Bak** [SONOMA].

Bald Hill [NAPA]: *peak,* 2.5 miles north-northeast of Calistoga (lat. 38°36'35" N, long. 122°33'30" W; near SE cor. sec. 19, T 9 N, R 6 W). Named on Calistoga (1958) 7.5' quadrangle.

Bald Hill [SONOMA]: *peak,* 3.25 miles west-southwest of Big Mountain (lat. 38°41'45" N, long. 123°12' W; near SE cor. sec. 20, T 10 N, R 12 W). Named on Tombs Creek (1978) 7.5' quadrangle. Called Hayfield Hill on Tombs Creek (1943) 7.5' quadrangle.

Bald Hills [SONOMA]: *ridge,* southeast- to south-trending, 1 mile long, 3.5 miles north of Mark West Springs (lat. 38°36'05" N, long.

122°42'35" W). Named on Mark West Springs (1958) 7.5' quadrangle. California Division of Forestry's (1945) map shows Patty Clark Springs situated on the northeast side of the ridge.

Bald Mountain [NAPA-SONOMA]:

(1) *peak,* 3.5 miles northeast of Kenwood on Napa-Sonoma county line (lat. 38°27'25" N, long. 122°30'30" W; sec. 15, T 7 N, R 6 W). Altitude 2729 feet. Named on Kenwood (1954) 7.5' quadrangle.

(2) *peak,* 4.25 miles west-southwest of Rutherford on Napa-Sonoma county line (lat. 38°25'45" N, long. 122°29'35" W; near N line sec. 26, T 7 N, R 6 W). Altitude 2275 feet. Named on Rutherford (1951) 7.5' quadrangle.

Baldy: see **Old Baldy** [NAPA].

Baldy Mountain [NAPA]: *peak,* 8.5 miles east-northeast of Saint Helena (lat. 38°33'05" N, long. 122°19'30" W). Altitude 2114 feet. Named on Chiles Valley (1958) 7.5' quadrangle.

Bale [NAPA]: *locality,* 4.25 miles east-southeast of Calistoga along Southern Pacific Railroad (lat. 38°33'15" N, long. 122°30'35" W); the place is on Carne Humana grant. Named on Calistoga (1945) 15' quadrangle. The name commemorates Edward F. Bale, who came to California in 1837 and received Carne Humana grant in 1841 (Gudde, 1949, p. 21).

Bale Slough [NAPA]: *water feature,* joins Napa River 0.5 mile northeast of Rutherford (lat. 38°27'50" N, long. 122°24'50" W). Named on Rutherford (1951) 7.5' quadrangle.

Barcal Spring: see **Preston** [SONOMA].

Barlow [SONOMA]: *locality,* 2.5 miles northwest of Sebastopol along Petaluma and Santa Rosa Railroad (lat. 38°25'25" N, long. 122°51'30" W). Named on Sebastopol (1954) 7.5' quadrangle.

Barns Creek [SONOMA]: *stream,* flows 2.25 miles to Brooks Creek 6 miles east-southeast of Healdsburg (lat. 38°35'10" N, long. 122° 45'45" W; sec. 32, T 9 N, R 8 W). Named on Healdsburg (1955) and Mark West Springs (1958) 7.5' quadrangles.

Barrelli Creek [SONOMA]: *stream,* flows 3 miles to Russian River less than 1 mile northwest of Asti (lat. 38°46'05" N, long. 122°58'45" W). Named on Asti (1959) and Warm Springs Dam (1978) 7.5' quadrangles.

Barro [NAPA]: *locality,* 2 miles northwest of Saint Helena along Southern Pacific Railroad (lat. 38°31'35" N, long. 122°29'30" W). Named on Saint Helena (1960) 7.5' quadrangle.

Barton Hill [NAPA]: *peak,* 2.5 miles east-northeast of Walter Springs (lat. 38°40' N, long. 122°18'50" W; near E line sec. 32, T 10 N, R 4 W). Altitude 1041 feet. Named on Walter Springs (1959) 7.5' quadrangle.

Bateman Creek [NAPA]: *stream,* flows 2 miles to James Creek 7 miles north-northeast of Calistoga (lat. 38°40'10" N, long. 122°31'40"

W; sec. 33, T 10 N, R 6 W). Named on Detert Reservoir (1958) 7.5' quadrangle.

Batto [SONOMA]: *locality,* 1.25 miles east-southeast of Sonoma along Northwestern Pacific Railroad (lat. 38°17' N, long. 122°26'05" W). Named on Sonoma (1951) 7.5' quadrangle.

Baumert Springs [SONOMA]: *spring,* 1.25 miles northwest of Occidental (lat. 38°25'10" N, long. 122°57'50" W; sec. 28, T 7 N, R 10 W). Named on Camp Meeker (1954) 7.5' quadrangle.

Bay: see **Bodega Bay** [SONOMA] (2).

Bear Canyon [NAPA]: *canyon,* drained by a stream that flows 3 miles to Napa Valley 1 mile southwest of Rutherford (lat. 38°27'05" N, long. 122°26'15" W). Named on Rutherford (1951) 7.5' quadrangle.

Bear Canyon [SONOMA]:
(1) *canyon,* drained by a stream that flows 1.25 miles to Squaw Creek 4.5 miles north-northeast of Geyser Peak (lat. 38°49'40" N, long. 122°48'55" W; sec. 1, T 11 N, R 9 W). Named on The Geysers (1959) 7.5' quadrangle.
(2) *canyon,* drained by a stream that flows nearly 1.5 miles to Sausal Creek 6.5 miles northeast of Healdsburg (lat. 38°41'15" N, long. 122°47'45" W; sec. 30, T 10 N, R 8 W). Named on Jimtown (1955) 7.5' quadrangle.

Bear Creek [SONOMA]:
(1) *stream,* flows 3.25 miles to McDonnell Creek nearly 6 miles west-northwest of Mount Saint Helena (lat. 38°41'35" N, long. 122°44'10" W; near N line sec. 27, T 10 N, R 8 W). Named on Mount Saint Helena (1959) 7.5' quadrangle.
(2) *stream,* flows 1 mile to Warm Springs Creek 1 mile west of Skaggs Springs (lat. 38°41'50" N, long. 123°02'35" W; sec. 23, T 10 N, R 11 W). Named on Warm Springs Dam (1978) 7.5' quadrangle.
(3) *stream,* flows 2.5 miles to Sonoma Creek 2 miles north-northeast of Kenwood (lat. 38°26'35" N, long. 122°31'50" W; near N line sec. 21, T 7 N, R 6 W). Named on Kenwood (1954) 7.5' quadrangle.

Bear Flat [NAPA]: *area,* 10 miles northwest of Mount Vaca along Capell Creek (lat. 38°29'15" N, long. 122°14'40" W; near E line sec. 1, T 7 N, R 4 W). Named on Capell Valley (1951) 7.5' quadrangle.

Bear Flat [SONOMA]: *area,* nearly 7 miles north-northeast of Guerneville along Mill Creek (1) (lat. 38°35'50" N, long. 122°57'50" W). Named on Guerneville (1955) 7.5' quadrangle.

Bear House Creek: see **Bearpen Creek** [SONOMA] (1).

Bearpen Creek [SONOMA]:
(1) *stream,* flows 3 miles to Austin Creek 3.5 miles north-northwest of Cazadero (lat. 38°34'40" N, long. 123°06'55" W; sec. 31, T 9 N, R 11 W). Named on Cazadero (1978) and Fort Ross (1978) 7.5' quadrangles. Called

Bear House Cr. on California Division of Forestry's (1945) map.
(2) *stream,* flows 1.25 miles to Warm Springs Creek 4 miles west-southwest of Skaggs Springs (lat. 38°39'55" N, long. 123°05'25" W; at SW cor. sec. 33, T 10 N, R 11 W). Named on Warm Springs Dam (1978) 7.5' quadrangle.

Bear Ridge [SONOMA]: *ridge,* west- to northwest-trending, 2.5 miles long, 10 miles northeast of the village of Stewarts Point (lat. 38°45'10" N, long. 123°16' W). Named on Ornbaun Valley (1960) 15' quadrangle, and on Annapolis (1977) and Tombs Creek (1978) 7.5' quadrangles.

Bear Valley [NAPA]: *valley,* 5 miles north-northeast of Calistoga along Van Ness Creek (lat. 38°38'50" N, long. 122°33'15" W; near NW cor. sec. 8, T 9 N, R 6 W). Named on Detert Reservoir (1958) 7.5' quadrangle.

Beatty Ridge [SONOMA]: *ridge,* west- to west-northwest-trending, 5 miles long, 5 miles north of the village of Stewarts Point (lat. 38°43'20" N, long. 123°23'45" W). Named on Annapolis (1977) and Stewarts Point (1978) 7.5' quadrangles.

Bedrock Spring [SONOMA]: *spring,* 3 miles northeast of the village of Bodega Bay (lat. 38°22' N, long. 123°00'30" W). Named on Bodega Head (1942) 7.5' quadrangle.

Bee Flat [SONOMA]: *area,* 4.5 miles west-southwest of Big Mountain along Wheatfield Fork Gualala River (lat. 38°41'40" N, long. 123°13'40" W; sec. 19, T 10 N, R 12 W); the place is 0.5 mile southwest of Bee Knoll. Named on Tombs Creek (1978) 7.5' quadrangle.

Beehive: see **The Beehive** [NAPA].

Bee Knoll [SONOMA]: *peak,* 4.25 miles west of Big Mountain (lat. 38°42' N, long. 123°13'20" W; sec. 19, T 10 N, R 12 W). Altitude 861 feet. Named on Tombs Creek (1978) 7.5' quadrangle. On Tombs Creek (1943) 7.5' quadrangle, Bee Knoll is the high point on a ridge called Bee Tree Ridge.

Bee Tree Ridge: see **Bee Knoll** [SONOMA].

Belcher: see **Anna Belcher Creek** [SONOMA].

Bell Canyon [NAPA]: *canyon,* drained by a stream that flows 7.5 miles to Napa River 2.5 miles north-northwest of Saint Helena (lat. 38°32'05" N, long. 122°29'30" W). Named on Saint Helena (1960) 7.5' quadrangle.

Bell Canyon Reservoir [NAPA]: *lake,* behind a dam in Bell Canyon 3.5 miles north of Saint Helena (lat. 38°33'20" N, long. 122°28'55" W; sec. 12, T 8 N, R 6 W). Named on Saint Helena (1960) 7.5' quadrangle. Saint Helena (1942) 15' quadrangle shows Bell Valley at the site.

Bellevue [SONOMA]: *locality,* 2.5 miles south of downtown Santa Rosa (lat. 38°24'05" N, long. 122°43' W). Named on Santa Rosa (1954) 7.5' quadrangle.

Bell Mountain [SONOMA]: *peak,* 4.25 miles

north-northwest of Mark West Springs (lat. 38°36'20" N, long. 122°45' W; near S line sec. 21, T 9 N, R 8 W). Named on Healdsburg (1955) and Mark West Springs (1958) 7.5' quadrangles.

Bell Station: see **Zinfandel** [NAPA].

Bell Valley: see **Bell Canyon Reservoir** [NAPA].

Beltane [SONOMA]: *locality,* 2 miles southeast of Kenwood along Southern Pacific Railroad (lat. 38°23'20" N, long. 122°31'25" W). Named on Santa Rosa (1916) 15' quadrangle.

Bennett Mountain [SONOMA]: *peak,* 4 miles west of Kenwood (lat. 38°24'50" N, long. 122°37'25" W; sec. 34, T 7 N, R 7 W); the peak is northeast of Bennett Valley. Altitude 1887 feet. Named on Kenwood (1954) and Santa Rosa (1954) 7.5' quadrangles.

Bennett Valley [SONOMA]: *valley,* along Matanzas Creek above a point 2 miles east of downtown Santa Rosa (lat. 38°26' N, long. 122°40'20" W). Named on Kenwood (1954) and Santa Rosa (1954) 7.5' quadrangles. The name commemorates James N. Bennett, who was a squatter in the valley (LeBaron and others, p. 21).

Berkeley Camp: see **Berkeley Music Camp** [SONOMA].

Berkeley Music Camp [SONOMA]: *locality,* 0.5 mile south of Cazadero (lat. 38°31'20" N, long. 123°05'05" W; sec. 21, T 8 N, R 11 W). Named on Cazadero (1978) 7.5' quadrangle. Called Berkeley Camp on Cazadero (1943) 7.5' quadrangle.

Berryessa: see **Lake Berryessa** [NAPA].

Berryessa Marina [NAPA]: *locality,* 6.5 miles south-southwest of Berryessa Peak on the west side of Lake Berryessa (lat. 38°34'50" N, long. 122°14'55" W). Named on Lake Berryessa (1959) 7.5' quadrangle.

Berryessa Peak [NAPA]: *peak,* 18 miles northeast of Saint Helena on Napa-Yolo county line near the southeast end of Blue Ridge (lat. 38°39'50" N, long. 122°11'20" W). Altitude 3057 feet. Named on Brooks (1959) 7.5' quadrangle.

Berryessa Valley [NAPA]: *valley,* 15 miles northeast of Saint Helena along Putah Creek (lat. 38°37' N, long. 122°15' W); the valley is on Las Putas grant. Named on Capay (1945) and Saint Helena (1942) 15' quadrangles. The name is for Joe Jesus Berryessa and Sixto Berryessa, who received Las Putas grant in 1843 (Gudde, 1949, p. 30). Water of Lake Berryessa now covers a large part of the valley.

Bidwell Creek [SONOMA]: *stream,* flows 4.5 miles to Franz Creek 4.25 miles north-northeast of Mark West Springs (lat. 38°36'30" N, long. 122°41'35" W). Named on Mark West Springs (1958) 7.5' quadrangle.

Big Austin Creek: see **Austin Creek** [SONOMA].

Big Basin [NAPA]: *valley,* 7.5 miles north-northeast of Aetna Springs along Putah Creek (lat. 38°45' N, long. 122°25' W). Named on Aetna

Springs (1958) and Jericho Valley (1958) 7.5' quadrangles.

Big Basin [SONOMA]: *relief feature,* 5.25 miles west-northwest of Mount Saint Helena along Bear Creek (1) (lat. 38°42'45" N, long. 122°42'45" W; sec. 14, T 10 N, R 8 W). Named on Mount Saint Helena (1959) 7.5' quadrangle.

Big Bend [SONOMA]: *village,* 6 miles north of Sears Point (lat. 38°14'10" N, long. 122°27'35" W). Named on Sears Point (1951) 7.5' quadrangle.

Big Brush: see **The Big Brush** [SONOMA].

Big Hill [SONOMA]: *peak,* 6 miles west-northwest of Mount Saint Helena (lat. 38°42' N, long. 122°44'05" W; sec. 22, T 10 N, R 8 W). Altitude 1075 feet. Named on Mount Saint Helena (1959) 7.5' quadrangle.

Big Mountain [SONOMA]: *peak,* 15 miles north-northeast of Fort Ross (lat. 38°42'35" N, long. 122°08'35" W; near SW cor. sec. 13, T 10 N, R 12 W). Altitude 2675 feet. Named on Tombs Creek (1978) 7.5' quadrangle.

Big Oat Creek [SONOMA]: *stream,* flows 1.5 miles to Ward Creek 6.5 miles east-northeast of Fort Ross (lat. 38°32'25" N, long. 123°07'30" W; near E line sec. 13, T 8 N, R 12 W); the stream is east of Big Oat Mountain. Named on Fort Ross (1978) 7.5' quadrangle.

Big Oat Mountain [SONOMA]: *peak,* 6.5 miles east-northeast of Fort Ross (lat. 38°32'45" N, long. 123°07'55" W; near S line sec. 12, T 8 N, R 12 W); the peak is west of Big Oat Creek. Named on Fort Ross (1978) 7.5' quadrangle.

Big Pepperwood Creek [SONOMA]: *stream,* heads in Mendocino County and flows 3.5 miles to South Fork Gualala River 8.5 miles north-northwest of the village of Stewarts Point (lat. 38°45'45" N, long. 123°28'40" W; near NW cor. sec. 31, T 11 N, R 14 W). Named on Ornbaun Valley (1960) 15' quadrangle.

Big Ridge [SONOMA]: *ridge,* east-southeast-to southeast-trending, 3 miles long, 6 miles south-southwest of Geyserville (lat. 38°37'30" N, long. 122°56'15" W). Named on Geyserville (1955) and Guerneville (1955) 7.5' quadrangles.

Big Spring [SONOMA]: *spring,* 5.5 miles east of Mark West Springs (lat. 38°32'25" N, long. 122°36'55" W; near SE cor. sec. 15, T 8 N, R 7 W). Named on Calistoga (1958) 7.5' quadrangle.

Big Sulphur Creek [SONOMA]: *stream,* flows 21 miles to Russian River 1 mile north-northeast of Cloverdale (lat. 38°49'05" N, long. 123°00'35" W). Named on Asti (1959), Cloverdale (1960), The Geysers (1959), and Whispering Pines (1958) 7.5' quadrangles. Called Sulphur Cr. on Calistoga (1945) and Lower Lake (1945) 15' quadrangles. Called Pluton R. on Goddard's (1857) map. Shepherd (p. 153) used the name "Pluton valley" for the canyon of the stream in the vicinity of The Geysers, and Goodyear (1890b, p. 674) used the name "Pluton Cañon" for the same feature.

Bihler Landing: see **Black Point Landing** [SONOMA].

Bihler Point: see **Black Point** [SONOMA].

Bismark Knob [NAPA-SONOMA]: *peak,* 4.5 miles north of Sonoma on Napa-Sonoma county line (lat. 38°21'30" N, long. 122°26'20" W; on N line sec. 20, T 6 N, R 5 W). Named on Sonoma (1951) 7.5' quadrangle. The feature also was known as Mount Nebo (Gudde, 1949, p. 32). Eddy's (1854) map has the name "Carnero Mt." for the ridge where Bismark Knob lies.

Bitter Creek [NAPA]: *stream,* flows 2.25 miles to lowlands 3.25 miles east of Calistoga (lat. 38°34'40" N, long. 122°30'55" W). Named on Calistoga (1958) 7.5' quadrangle.

Black Mountain [SONOMA]:
(1) *peak,* 4.5 miles east of Fort Ross (lat. 38°30'05" N, long. 123° 09'35" W). Altitude 1632 feet. Named on Fort Ross (1978) 7.5' quadrangle.
(2) *peak,* 12 miles north-northeast of the village of Stewarts Point (lat. 38°47'40" N, long. 123°16'05" W; near S line sec. 14, T 11 N, R 13 W). Altitude 2646 feet. Named on Ornbaun Valley (1960) 15' quadrangle.
(3) *peak,* 4.25 miles east-northeast of Guerneville (lat. 38°31'30" N, long. 122°55'20" W; sec. 24, T 8 N, R 10 W). Named on Guerneville (1955) 7.5' quadrangle.
(4) *range,* 9.5 miles north-northeast of Healdsburg (lat. 38°44'40" N, long. 122°48'15" W). Named on Jimtown (1955) and The Geysers (1959) 7.5' quadrangles.

Black Mountain: see **Little Black Mountain** [SONOMA].

Black Mountain Conservation Camp: see **Murphy Mill** [SONOMA].

Black Mountain Ridge [SONOMA]: *ridge,* southeast- to south-southeast-trending, 1.25 miles long, 4.25 miles east of Fort Ross (lat. 38°30'30" N, long. 123°09'55" W); Black Mountain (1) is at the south end of the ridge. Named on Fort Ross (1978) 7.5' quadrangle.

Black Oak Ridge [SONOMA]: *ridge,* south-southwest- to west-trending, 1 mile long, 3 miles west-northwest of Big Mountain (lat. 38° 43'20" N, long. 123°11'50" W). Named on Tombs Creek (1978) 7.5' quadrangle.

Black Oaks [SONOMA]: *locality,* 4.5 miles north of Geyser Peak (lat. 38°49'50" N, long. 122°49'55" W; sec. 2, T 11 N, R 9 W). Named on The Geysers (1959) 7.5' quadrangle.

Black Peak [SONOMA]: *peak,* 3 miles east of Healdsburg (lat. 38°36'50" N, long. 122°48'35" W). Named on Healdsburg (1955) 7.5' quadrangle.

Black Point [SONOMA]: *promontory,* 2.5 miles northwest of the village of Stewarts Point along the coast (lat. 38°40'45" N, long. 123°25'50" W). Named on Stewarts Point (1978) 7.5' quadrangle. Called Bihler Pt. on Plantation (1915) 15' quadrangle.

Black Point Landing [SONOMA]: *locality,* 2.5 miles northwest of the village of Stewarts Point along the coast (lat. 38°40'45" N, long. 123°25'45" W); the place is just east of Black Point. Named on Stewarts Point (1978) 7.5' quadrangle. Called Bihler Landing on Plantation (1915) 15' quadrangle. The name "Bihler" was for William "Dutch Bill" Bihler, who came to California in 1848 and became a stock breeder in Sonoma County (Gudde, 1949, p. 31).

Black Rock [SONOMA]: *peak,* 3.5 miles north of Cazadero (lat. 38° 34'50" N, long. 123°04'45" W; sec. 33, T 9 N, R 11 W). Altitude 1332 feet. Named on Cazadero (1978) 7.5' quadrangle.

Black Rock Creek [SONOMA]: *stream,* flows 2.5 miles to East Austin Creek 1.5 miles northeast of Cazadero (lat. 38°33' N, long. 123°04' W; sec. 10, T 8 N, R 11 W); the stream heads west of Black Rock. Named on Cazadero (1978) 7.5' quadrangle.

Black Sulphur Creek [SONOMA]: *stream,* flows less than 1 mile to Little Warm Springs Creek nearly 1 mile south-southwest of Skaggs Springs (lat. 38°40'50" N, long. 123°01'45" W; sec. 25, T 10 N, R 11 W). Named on Warm Springs Dam (1978) 7.5' quadrangle.

Blind Beach [SONOMA]: *beach,* 1 mile south-southwest of Jenner along the coast (lat. 38°26'15" N, long. 123°07'15" W). Named on Duncans Mills (1979) 7.5' quadrangle.

Bloomfield [SONOMA]: *town,* 6 miles south-southwest of Sebastopol (lat. 38°18'50" N, long. 122°51'10" W). Named on Two Rock (1954) 7.5' quadrangle. Postal authorities established Bloomfield post office in 1856 and discontinued it in 1955 (Salley, p. 23). The name may commemorate F.G. Blume, who owned Cañada de Pogolimi grant where the town is situated, or the name may be from Bloomfield, Kentucky, hometown of Larkin Cockrill, one of the purchasers of the site (Hansen and Miller, p. 44, 46).

Blossom Creek [NAPA]: *stream,* flows nearly 3 miles to Napa River 1 mile west-northwest of Calistoga (lat. 38°35'15" N, long. 122°35'45" W). Named on Calistoga (1958) 7.5' quadrangle.

Blucher [SONOMA]: *land grant,* inland from the coast along Estero San Antonio and Americano Creek on Marin-Sonoma county line. Named on Two Rock (1954) and Valley Ford (1954) 7.5' quadrangles. Jean Vioget received 6 leagues in 1844; heirs of Stephen Smith claimed 26,759 acres patented in 1858 (Cowan, p. 19). Vioget had the nickname "Blucher" because of his resemblance to Prussian Field Marshall Gebhard von Blucher, famous for his role at the Battle of Waterloo; from the nickname came the designation of the grant (Gudde, 1949, p. 34).

Blucher Creek [SONOMA]: *stream,* flows 5

miles to Laguna de Santa Rosa 3 miles south-east of Sebastopol (lat. 38°22'40" N, long. 122°46'55" W); the stream is mainly on Blucher grant. Named on Two Rock (1954) 7.5' quadrangle.

Blue Grouse Ridge [SONOMA]: *ridge,* south-to southeast-trending, 0.5 mile long, 2.5 miles north-northeast of Cazadero (lat. 38°33'45" N, long. 123°03'55" W). Named on Cazadero (1978) 7.5' quadrangle.

Bluegum Creek [SONOMA]: *stream,* flows 1.5 miles to McDonnell Creek 6 miles west of Mount Saint Helena (lat. 38°41'10" N, long. 122°44'30" W; near W line sec. 27, T 10 N, R 8 W). Named on Jimtown (1955) and Mount Saint Helena (1959) 7.5' quadrangles.

Blue Jay Creek [SONOMA]: *stream,* flows 2.5 miles to Ward Creek 6 miles east-northeast of Fort Ross (lat. 38°32'05" N, long. 123° 08'05" W; sec. 13, T 8 N, R 12 W); the stream is east of Blue Jay Ridge. Named on Fort Ross (1978) 7.5' quadrangle.

Blue Jay Ridge [SONOMA]: *ridge,* south-trend-ing, 2 miles long, 6 miles east-northeast of Fort Ross (lat. 38°33'10" N, long. 123°08'35" W); the ridge is west of Blue Jay Creek. Named on Fort Ross (1978) 7.5' quadrangle.

Blue Mountain: see **Mount Vaca** [NAPA].

Blue Mountains: see **Vaca Mountains** [NAPA].

Blue Ridge [NAPA]: *ridge,* extends north-north-west for 20 miles from near Berryessa Peak to Cache Creek, mainly on Napa-Yolo county line. Named on Brooks (1959), Guinda (1959), and Knoxville (1958) 7.5' quad-rangles. Called Rumsey Range on Durst's (1916) map.

Blue Ridge [NAPA]: *ridge,* generally south-trending, 15 miles long, extends from Putah Creek along Napa-Solano county line to the southeast corner of Napa County. Named on Capell Valley (1951), Fairfield North (1951), Monticello Dam (1959), and Mount Vaca (1951) 7.5' quadrangles.

Blue Rock [SONOMA]: *relief feature,* 5.25 miles north-northeast of Cazadero (lat. 38°36'05" N, long. 123°02'35" W). Named on Cazadero (1978) 7.5' quadrangle.

Bodega [SONOMA]:
(1) *land grant,* along the coast between Rus-sian River and Estero Americano. Named on Arched Rock (1977), Bodega Head (1972), Camp Meeker (1954), Duncans Mills (1979), and Valley Ford (1954) 7.5' quadrangles. Stephen Smith received the land in 1844; M.T. Curtis and others claimed 35,488 acres pat-ented in 1859 (Cowan, p. 19).
(2) *town,* 3.25 miles northwest of Valley Ford (lat. 38°20'45" N, long. 122°58'20" W); the town is on Bodega grant. Named on Valley Ford (1954) 7.5' quadrangle. Postal authori-ties established Bodega post office by 1852, discontinued it in 1867, reestablished it in 1882, and discontinued it in 1887; they es-tablished Smith's Ranch post office in 1854

and discontinued in 1901, when they moved it 5 miles west and changed the name to Bodega—the name "Smith's Ranch" was from Captain Stephen Smith, who received Bodega grant (Salley, p. 23, 200, 206). Present Bodega was called Bodega Corners in the early days (Hanna, P.T., p. 35). Russians had a settlement called Kuskov that was 1 mile north of present Bodega in the valley of Salmon Creek (1)—the name was for the Russian leader, Ivan Kuskov (Miller, J.T., p. 39).

Bodega Bay [SONOMA]:
(1) *embayment,* north-northwest of the mouth of Tomales Bay and southeast of Bodega Head along the coast on Marin-Sonoma county line (lat. 38°16' N, long. 123° 00' W). Named on Bodega Head (1972), Tomales (1954) and Valley Ford (1954) 7.5' quadrangles. Called Puerto de la Bodega on Ringgold's (1850) map. The name is for Juan Francisco Bodega y Quadra, who entered the embayment in 1775 (Wagner, p. 376-377). Ivan A. Ruskov built the first Russian structure in California at the place, which he called Port Rumyantsev (Schwartz, p. 37).
(2) *village,* 20 miles west-southwest of Santa Rosa on the east side of Bodega Harbor (lat. 38°20' N, long. 123° 02'45" W). Named on Bodega Head (1972) 7.5' quadrangle. Postal authorities established Bay post office in 1895 and changed the name to Bodega Bay in 1941 (Frickstad, p. 194). United States Board on Geographic Names (1950, p. 4) rejected the name "Bay" for the place.

Bodega Bay: see **Bodega Harbor** [SONOMA].

Bodega Corners: see **Bodega** [SONOMA] (2).

Bodega Harbor [SONOMA]: *bay,* opens into the northwest end of Bodega Bay [SONOMA] 2 miles south of the village of Bodega Bay (lat. 38°18'20" N, long. 122°03'05" W). Named on Bodega Head (1972) 7.5' quad-rangle. Called Bodega Bay on Duncans Mills (1921) 15' quadrangle, but United States Board on Geographic Names (1943, p. 10) rejected the names "Bodega Bay" and "Bodega Lagoon" for the feature.

Bodega Head [SONOMA]: *peninsula,* 2 miles south-southwest of the village of Bodega Bay (lat. 38°18'30" N, long. 123°03'40" W); the feature is west of the mouth of Bodega Har-bor. Named on Bodega Head (1972) 7.5' quadrangle. Called C. Romanzoff on Ringgold's (1850) map. The place is known locally as Campbells Point, for Captain John Campbell, a pioneer landowner in the neigh-borhood (Gudde, 1949, p. 53).

Bodaga Island [SONOMA]: *hill,* 1 mile south-east of the village of Bodega Bay in lowlands along Bodega Harbor (lat. 38°19'15" N, long. 123°02'05" W). Named on Bodega Head (1942) 7.5' quadrangle.

Bodega Lagoon [SONOMA]: see **Bodega Har-bor** [SONOMA].

Bodega Point [SONOMA]: *locality,* 1.25 miles

south-southeast of the present village of Bodega Bay in present Bodega Harbor (lat. 38° 19'10" N, long. 123°02' W). Named on Duncans Mills (1921) 15' quadrangle.

Bodega Rock [SONOMA]: *island,* 250 feet long, 2.5 miles south of the village of Bodega Bay and 1700 feet southeast of Bodega Head (lat. 38°17'45" N, long. 123°02'50" W). Named on Bodega Head (1972) 7.5' quadrangle. This probably is the feature that members of Vancouver's expedition called Gibson Island in 1793 (Hoover, Rensch, and Rensch, p. 525).

Boggs Creek [SONOMA]: *stream,* heads in Mendocino County and flows 0.5 mile to Cascade Creek 6 miles north-northeast of Asti (lat. 38°50'35" N, long. 122°56'05" W; near E line sec. 35, T 12 N, R 10 W). Named on Asti (1959) 7.5' quadrangle.

Bohemian Grove [SONOMA]: *area,* 4.25 miles north-northwest of Occidental (lat. 38°28' N, long. 122°58'30" W). Named on Camp Meeker (1954) 7.5' quadrangle. The name was applied to the place in 1891 because the Bohemian Club of San Francisco held summer outings there (Gudde, 1949, p. 36).

Bohn Lake: see **Upper Bohn Lake**, under **Aetna Springs** [NAPA].

Bone Creek [SONOMA]: *stream,* flows 0.5 mile to Austin Creek less than 1 mile north of Cazadero (lat. 38°32'35" N, long. 122°05'15" W; sec. 16, T 8 N, R 11 W). Named on Cazadero (1978) 7.5' quadrangle.

Bonilla [SONOMA]: *locality,* 1.5 miles southeast of Sonoma along Northwestern Pacific Railroad (lat. 38°16'40" N, long. 122°26'10" W). Named on Sonoma (1951) 7.5' quadrangle.

Boulder Creek [SONOMA]: *stream,* flows 2.25 miles to Galloway Creek 11 miles west of Cloverdale (lat. 38°47'10" N, long. 123°12'55" W; sec. 20, T 11 N, R 12 W). Named on Hopland (1960) 15' quadrangle.

Boyd Creek [SONOMA]:
(1) *stream,* flows less than 1 mile to Mill Creek (1) 6.5 miles north of Guerneville (lat. 38°35'50" N, long. 122°59'15" W; sec. 29, T 9 N, R 10 W). Named on Guerneville (1955) 7.5' quadrangle.
(2) *stream,* flows 1.25 miles to Fuller Creek 2.5 miles southeast of Annapolis (lat. 38°41'50" N, long. 123°19'40" W; sec. 20, T 10 N, R 13 W). Named on Annapolis (1977) 7.5' quadrangle.

Boyer Creek [SONOMA]: *stream,* flows 1 mile to Pena Creek 3.25 miles south-southeast of Skaggs Springs (lat. 38°38'55" N, long. 123°00'20" W; near N line sec. 7, T 9 N, R 10 W). Named on Warm Springs Dam (1978) 7.5' quadrangle.

Boyes Hot Springs [SONOMA]: *town,* 2 miles northwest of Sonoma in Valley of the Moon (lat. 38°18'45" N, long. 122°28'40" W). Named on Sonoma (1951) 7.5' quadrangle. Called Boyes Springs on Sonoma (1942) 15' quadrangle. Postal authorities established

Boyes Springs post office in 1911 and changed the name to Boyes Hot Springs in 1938 (Frickstad, p. 194). The name commemorates Captain Henry Boyes and his wife, who came to the place in 1888 and started a popular resort (Hansen and Miller, p. 133). Crawford (1896, p. 521) used the name "Agua Rica Hot Sulphur Springs" for 16 springs located 2 miles north of Sonoma along the railroad. A resort called Ohms Spring was situated about 0.5 mile southeast of Boyes Hot Springs, where in 1909 it had accommodations for 20 guests (Waring, p. 113).

Boyes Springs: see **Boyes Hot Springs** [SONOMA].

Boysen: see **Cherry** [SONOMA].

Bradford Mountain [SONOMA]: *peak,* 4 miles west-southwest of Geyserville (lat. 38°41'05" N, long. 122°58'20" W; sec. 28, T 10 N, R 10 W). Altitude 1229 feet. Named on Geyserville (1955) 7.5' quadrangle.

Brady Ridge [SONOMA]: *ridge,* south-trending, 1 mile long, 2.5 miles east-northeast of Guerneville (lat. 38°30'55" N, long. 122°57'05" W). Named on Guerneville (1955) 7.5' quadrangle.

Brain Ridge [SONOMA]: *ridge,* northwest-trending, 1.25 miles long, 4.5 miles east-northeast of Fort Ross (lat. 38°32'15" N, long. 121° 10' W). Named on Fort Ross (1978) 7.5' quadrangle.

Brazos [NAPA]: *locality,* 3.25 miles west-north-west of Napa Junction along Southern Pacific Railroad (lat. 38°12'30" N, long. 122° 18'10" W; sec. 9, T 4 N, R 4 W). Named on Cuttings Wharf (1949, photorevised 1968) 7.5' quadrangle.

Bridgehaven [SONOMA]: *settlement,* 1.5 miles southeast of Jenner (lat. 38°26'05" N, long. 123°05'55" W); the place is at the south end of a highway bridge across Russian River. Named on Duncans Mills (1979) 7.5' quadrangle. Called Bridge Haven on Duncans Mills (1943) 7.5' quadrangle, but United States Board on Geographic Names (1979, p. 2) rejected this form of the name.

Briggs Creek [SONOMA]: *stream,* flows 5.5 miles to join McDonnell Creek and form Maacama Creek 6 miles west of Mount Saint Helena (lat. 38°40'25" N, long. 122°44'30" W; near W line sec. 34, T 10 N, R 8 W). Named on Mount Saint Helena (1959) 7.5' quadrangle.

Briggs Creek: see **Little Briggs Creek** [SONOMA].

Brink Creek: see **Britain Creek** [SONOMA].

Britain Creek [SONOMA]: *stream,* flows 3.25 miles to House Creek 4.25 miles south-south-west of Big Mountain (lat. 38°39'20" N, long. 123°10'40" W; near W line sec. 3, T 9 N, R 12 W); the stream is north of Britain Ridge. Named on Tombs Creek (1978) 7.5' quadrangle. Called Brink Creek on Tombs Creek (1943) 7.5' quadrangle.

Britain Ridge [SONOMA]: *ridge,* west- to south-trending, about 1.25 miles long, 3.25 miles south-southwest of Big Mountain (lat. 38° 39'50" N, long. 123°09'40" W); the ridge is south of Britain Creek. Named on Tombs Creek (1978) 7.5' quadrangle. Called Shoeheart Ridge on Tombs Creek (1943) 7.5' quadrangle.

Brooks Creek [SONOMA]: *stream,* flows 3.5 miles to Russian River 4.5 miles east of Healdsburg (lat. 38°36'20" N, long. 122°47'05" W). Named on Healdsburg (1955) and Mark West Springs (1958) 7.5' quadrangles.

Brooks Gulch [SONOMA]: *canyon,* drained by a stream that flows 1 mile to marsh along Bodega Harbor 1 mile southeast of the village of Bodega Bay (lat. 38°19'20" N, long. 123°02' W). Named on Bodega Head (1972) 7.5' quadrangle.

Brown: see **Johnny Brown Springs** [SONOMA].

Browns Gulch [SONOMA]: *canyon,* drained by a stream that flows less than 1 mile to Russian River 3.5 miles east-northeast of Jenner (lat. 38°27'55" N, long. 123°03'05" W). Named on Duncans Mills (1979) 7.5' quadrangle.

Browns Hill [NAPA]: *peak,* 3.5 miles north-northeast of Calistoga (lat. 38°37'20" N, long. 122°32'15" W; near SW cor. sec. 16, T 9 N, R 6 W). Altitude 2768 feet. Named on Calistoga (1958) 7.5' quadrangle.

Browns Valley [NAPA]: *valley,* 3 miles west-northwest of downtown Napa (lat. 38°18'30" N, long. 122°20' W). Named on Napa (1951) 7.5' quadrangle.

Browns Valley Creek [NAPA]: *stream,* flows 4 miles to join Redwood Creek and form Napa Creek 1.5 miles west-northwest of downtown Napa (lat. 38°18'15" N, long. 122°18'45" W); the stream goes through Browns Valley. Named on Sonoma (1951) 7.5' quadrangle. On Napa (1902) 30' quadrangle, the stream is called South Branch [Napa Creek].

Brush Creek [SONOMA]: *stream,* flows 2.25 miles to Yorty Creek 5 miles southwest of Cloverdale (lat. 38°45'40" N, long. 123°05'10" W; sec. 33, T 11 N, R 11 W). Named on Cloverdale (1960) 7.5' quadrangle.

Brushy Canyon [NAPA]: *canyon,* drained by a stream that flows 2.5 miles to Gosling Canyon nearly 6 miles south-southeast of Berryessa Peak (lat. 38°35'05" N, long. 122°09'30" W). Named on Lake Berryessa (1959) 7.5' quadrangle.

Brushy Ridge [SONOMA]: *ridge,* west-north-west-trending, 3 miles long, 6 miles north-northeast of the village of Stewarts Point (lat. 38°44'10" N, long. 123°22'30" W). Named on Annapolis (1977) and Stewarts Point (1978) 7.5' quadrangles.

Buchli [NAPA]: *locality,* 5 miles west-northwest of Napa Junction along Southern Pacific Rail-road (lat. 38°12'55" N, long. 122°19'50" W). Named on Cuttings Wharf (1949) 7.5' quadrangle.

Buckeye Creek [SONOMA]:
(1) *stream,* heads in Mendocino County and flows 2.5 miles to Galloway Creek 9.5 miles west of Cloverdale (lat. 38°47'30" N, long. 123°11'15" W; sec. 22, T 11 N, R 12 W). Named on Hopland (1960) 15' quadrangle.
(2) *stream,* flows 18 miles to South Fork Gualala River 7 miles north-northwest of the village of Stewarts Point (lat. 38°44'25" N, long. 123°27'25" W). Named on Ornbaun Valley (1960) 15' quadrangle, and on Annapolis (1977) and Stewarts Point (1978) 7.5' quadrangles. North Fork enters from the north 3 miles north-northeast of Annapolis; it is 5.5 miles long and is named on Ornbaun Valley (1960) 15' quadrangle.

Buckeye Creek: see **Wheatfield Fork**, under **Gualala River** [SONOMA].

Buckeye Spring [SONOMA]: *spring,* 9 miles north-northeast of Healdsburg (lat. 38°44'30" N, long. 122°49'40" W; sec. 2, T 10 N, R 9 W). Named on Jimtown (1955) 7.5' quadrangle.

Buckhorn Ridge [SONOMA]: *ridge,* south-trending, 1 mile long, 3.5 miles south-south-west of Big Mountain (lat. 38°39'50" N, long. 123°10'35" W). Named on Tombs Creek (1978) 7.5' quadrangle.

Buck Knoll [SONOMA]: *peak,* 6 miles north-northeast of Cazadero (lat. 38°36'10" N, long. 123°01'50" W; sec. 25, T 9 N, R 11 W). Named on Cazadero (1978) 7.5' quadrangle.

Buck Knoll Ridge [SONOMA]: *ridge,* east- to southeast-trending, 1.5 miles long, 6 miles northeast of Cazadero (lat. 38°36'15" N, long. 123°01'10" W); Buck Knoll is at the west end of the ridge. Named on Cazadero (1978) 7.5' quadrangle.

Buck Mountain [NAPA]: *peak,* 3.5 miles south of Knoxville (lat. 38°46'25" N, long. 122°19'45" W; sec. 29, T 11 N, R 4 W). Named on Knoxville (1958) 7.5' quadrangle.

Buck Mountain [SONOMA]:
(1) *peak,* 10 miles west of Cloverdale (lat. 38°48'20" N, long. 123° 11'40" W; sec. 16, T 11 N, R 12 W). Altitude 1575 feet. Named on Hopland (1960) 15' quadrangle.
(2) *peak,* 2.5 miles northwest of Big Mountain (lat. 38°44'20" N, long. 123°10'45" W; near SW cor. sec. 3, T 10 N, R 12 W). Named on Tombs Creek (1978) 7.5' quadrangle.

Buck Spring [SONOMA]: *spring,* 7 miles south-east of Annapolis (lat. 38°38'50" N, long. 123°16'45" W; near NW cor. sec. 11, T 9 N, R 13 W). Named on Annapolis (1977) 7.5' quadrangle.

Buena Vista [SONOMA]: *settlement,* about 1.25 miles east of Sonoma (lat. 38°17'20" N, long. 122°26' W). Named on Sonoma (1951) 7.5' quadrangle. Called Buenavista on Sonoma (1942) 15' quadrangle.

Bull Barn Gulch [SONOMA]: *canyon,* drained by a stream that flows less than 1 mile to Austin Creek 4 miles west of Guerneville (lat. 38°29'30" N, long. 123°03'55" W; sec. 34, T 8 N, R 11 W). Named on Duncans Mills (1979) 7.5' quadrangle.

Bull Canyon [NAPA]: *canyon,* drained by a stream that flows 2 miles to Lake Curry 2.5 miles south-southwest of Mount Vaca (lat. 38°21'55" N, long. 122°07' W). Named on Fairfield North (1951) 7.5' quadrangle.

Bull Canyon: see **East Bull Canyon** [NAPA]; **West Bull Canyon** [NAPA].

Bull Flat [SONOMA]: *area,* 4 miles south of Big Mountain (lat. 38° 39'10" N, long. 123°09'20" W; sec. 2, T 9 N, R 12 W). Named on Tombs Creek (1978) 7.5' quadrangle.

Bull Hill [NAPA]: *peak,* nearly 3 miles south of Mount Vaca (lat. 38° 21'30" N, long. 122°07' W); the peak is south of the mouth of Bull Canyon. Altitude 702 feet. Named on Fairfield North (1951) 7.5' quadrangle.

Bull Island [NAPA]: *island,* 3300 feet long, 3.5 miles northwest of Napa Junction along Napa River (lat. 38°13'20" N, long. 122°18'15" W; on E line sec. 4, T 4 N, R 4 W). Named on Cuttings Wharf (1949) 7.5' quadrangle.

Bull Opening [SONOMA]: *area,* 3.5 miles west of Big Mountain (lat. 38°43' N, long. 123°12'25" W; sec. 17, T 10 N, R 12 W). Named on Tombs Creek (1978) 7.5' quadrangle.

Bummer Peak [SONOMA]: *peak,* less than 1 mile north of Skaggs Springs (lat. 38°42'10" N, long. 123°01'30" W; sec. 24, R 10 N, R 11 W). Altitude 1150 feet. Named on Warm Springs Dam (1978) 7.5' quadrangle.

Burke: see **Fulton** [SONOMA].

Burned Mountain [SONOMA]: *ridge,* generally west-trending, 2 miles long, 4.5 miles east-northeast of Geyser Peak (lat. 38°47'50" N, long. 122°46'15" W). Named on The Geysers (1959) 7.5' quadrangle.

Burns Creek [SONOMA]: *stream,* flows 1.5 miles to Sausal Creek 8 miles north-north-east of Healdsburg (lat. 38°43' N, long. 122°47'30" W; sec. 18, T 10 N, R 8 W). Named on Jimtown (1955) 7.5' quadrangle.

Burnt Knoll Ridge [SONOMA]: *ridge,* north-trending, 1 mile long, 3.25 miles southeast of Annapolis (lat. 38°41' N, long. 123°20' W). Named on Annapolis (1977) 7.5' quadrangle.

Burnt Ridge [SONOMA]:
(1) *ridge,* east-northeast-trending, 1 mile long, 10 miles north-northeast of Stewarts Point (2) (lat. 38°47'15" N, long. 123°20'15" W). Named on Ornbaun Valley (1960) 15' quadrangle.
(2) *ridge,* southeast- to south-trending, 3 miles long, 5 miles west-southwest of Big Mountain (lat. 38°41'20" N, long. 123°13'55" W). Named on Tombs Creek (1978) 7.5' quadrangle.

Burnt Ridge Creek [SONOMA]: *stream,* flows

1.25 miles to Rockpile Creek 11 miles north-northeast of the village of Stewarts Point at Sonoma-Mendocino county line (lat. 38°48'20" N, long. 123°20'45" W; at N line sec. 18, T 11 N, R 13 W); the stream is north of Burnt Ridge (1). Named on Ornbaun Valley (1960) 15' quadrangle.

Burrell Canyon [NAPA]: *canyon,* drained by a stream that flows 1 mile to Steel Canyon 8 miles northwest of Mount Vaca (lat. 38°29'15" N, long. 122°11'30" W; near N line sec. 4, T 7 N, R 3 W). Named on Capell Valley (1951) 7.5' quadrangle.

Burton Creek [NAPA]: *stream,* flows 7.25 miles to Maxwell Creek 9 miles northeast of Saint Helena (lat. 38°36'15" N, long. 122°21'55" W). Named on Chiles Valley (1958) and Saint Helena (1960) 7.5' quadrangles.

Bush Slough [SONOMA]: *water feature,* 2 miles north-northeast of Sears Point (lat. 38°10'45" N, long. 122°25'45" W). Named on Sears Point (1951) 7.5' quadrangle.

Butcherknife: see **The Butcherknife** [SONOMA].

Butler Canyon [SONOMA]: *canyon,* drained by a stream that flows 1.5 miles to Valley of the Moon 5 miles north-northwest of Sonoma (lat. 38°21'25" N, long. 122°30' W). Named on Sonoma (1951) 7.5' quadrangle.

Butts Canyon [NAPA]: *canyon,* 4.5 miles long, on Napa-Lake county line along Butts Creek above a point 5 miles northeast of Aetna Springs (lat. 38°42'20" N, long. 122°25'25" W; near SW cor. sec. 16, T 10 N, R 5 W). Named on Aetna Springs (1958) 7.5' quadrangle.

Butts Creek [NAPA]: *stream,* heads in Lake County and flows 8 miles to Putah Creek 6.5 miles northeast of Aetna Springs (lat. 38°42'15" N, long. 122°22'50" W; near N line sec. 23, T 10 N, R 5 W). Named on Aetna Springs (1958) 7.5' quadrangle.

Buzzard Creek [SONOMA]: *stream,* flows 1.25 miles to Spanish Creek 3 miles southwest of Big Mountain (lat. 38°41'05" N, long. 123°11'25" W; sec. 28, T 10 N, R 12 W). Named on Tombs Creek (1978) 7.5' quadrangle.

Buzzard Peak [SONOMA]: *peak,* 4.5 miles northwest of Kenwood (lat. 38°28' N, long. 122°35'55" W; sec. 11, T 7 N, R 7 W). Altitude 1542 feet. Named on Kenwood (1954) 7.5' quadrangle.

Buzzard Rock [NAPA]: *peak,* 8 miles northwest of Mount Vaca (lat. 38°28'45" N, long. 122°12'30" W; sec. 5, T 7 N, R 3 W). Altitude 1701 feet. Named on Capell Valley (1951) 7.5' quadrangle.

Buzzard Rock [SONOMA]: *relief feature,* 1.5 miles west-northwest of Skaggs Springs (lat. 38°42' N, long. 123°03'15" W; at E line sec. 22, T 10 N, R 11 W). Named on Warm Springs Dam (1978) 7.5' quadrangle.

Buzzard Spring [SONOMA]: *spring,* 6 miles

north-northeast of Guerneville (lat. 38°34'40" N, long. 122°56'15" W). Named on Guerneville (1955) 7.5' quadrangle.

— C —

Cabeza de Santa Rosa [SONOMA]: *land grant,* around Santa Rosa. Named on Santa Rosa (1954) 7.5' quadrangle. The name is from Santa Rosa Creek (Hanna, P.T., p. 292). Maria Ignacia Lopez received the land in 1841; Julio Carrillo claimed 4500 acres patented in 1866; F. Carrillo de Castro claimed 336 acres patented in 1881; James Eldridge claimed 1668 acres patented in 1880; John Hendley claimed 640 acres patented in 1879; Juana de J. Mallagh claimed 256 acres patented in 1879; J.R. Meyer and others claimed 1485 acres patented in 1879 (Cowan, p. 95).

Cadwell [SONOMA]: *locality,* 5 miles northeast of Bloomfield along Petaluma and Santa Rosa Railroad (lat. 38°21'25" N, long. 122°46'35" W; near NW cor. sec. 20, T 6 N, R 8 W). Named on Two Rock (1954) 7.5' quadrangle.

Calabazas Creek [SONOMA]: *stream,* flows 5.25 miles to Sonoma Creek in Glen Ellen (lat. 38°21'45" N, long. 122°31'25" W). Named on Glen Ellen (1954), Kenwood (1954), and Rutherford (1951) 7.5' quadrangles. Called Arroyo de los Guilicos on a diseño of Agua Caliente grant (Becker, 1964). United States Board on Geographic Names (1933, p. 183) rejected the forms "Calabazas" and "Calebezas" for the name.

Calebezas Creek: see **Calabazas Creek** [SONOMA].

Calistoga [NAPA]: *town,* 8 miles northwest of Saint Helena (lat. 38° 34'45" N, long. 122°34'40" W). Named on Calistoga (1958) 7.5' quadrangle. Postal authorities established Calistoga post office in 1865 (Frickstad, p. 111), and the town incorporated in 1886. Samuel Brannan purchased land at the site in 1859 and built a resort based on hot springs there (Hoover, Rensch, and Rensch, p. 245). The place first was called Agua Caliente (Gudde, 1949, p. 51). It also was known as Little Geysers and as Hot Sulphur Springs before Brannan gave the name "Calistoga" to his resort to suggest a comparison with the famous spa at Saratoga, New York (Hanna, P.T., p. 51). The springs have been called Calistoga Hot Sulphur Springs (Goodyear, 1890a, p. 349), Calistoga Springs (Crawford, 1894, p. 341), and Calistoga Hot Springs (Waring, p. 108). A small bath establishment called Lathrop Hot Sulphur and Mud Spring was situated 1 mile south of Calistoga (Bradley, p. 278). Calistoga (1959) 15' quadrangle shows Silverado mine located 5.25 miles north-northwest of Calistoga (lat. 38°39'05" N, long. 122°36'15" W; sec. 2, T 9 N, R 7 W). Brannan's nephew, Alexander Badlam, built a stamp mill to process ore mined 7 miles north of Calistoga; the community that grew around the mill was called Silverado City, but the place was abandoned by 1877 (Archuleta, p. 61, 63).

Calistoga Hot Springs: see **Calistoga** [NAPA].

Calistoga Hot Sulphur Springs: see **Calistoga** [NAPA].

Calistoga Springs: see **Calistoga** [NAPA].

Camille: see **Lake Camille** [NAPA].

Campbell Canyon: see **Dry Creek** [NAPA].

Campbell Cove [SONOMA]: *embayment,* 2 miles south-southwest of the village of Bodega Bay (lat. 38°18'20" N, long. 123°03'20" W); the feature is on the east side of Bodega Head, which is known locally as Campbells Point (Gudde, 1949, p. 53). Named on Bodega Head (1972) 7.5' quadrangle.

Campbell Flat [NAPA]: *area,* 2.5 miles south-southwest of Rutherford (lat. 38°25'30" N, long. 122°26'05" W; sec. 29, T 7 N, R 5 W). Named on Rutherford (1951) 7.5' quadrangle.

Campbells Point: see **Bodega Head** [SONOMA].

Camp C.C. Moore: see **Camp Royaneh** [SONOMA].

Camp Five [SONOMA]: *locality,* 6.25 miles northeast of Sears Point (lat. 38°12'50" N, long. 122°22'10" W). Named on Cuttings Wharf (1949) 7.5' quadrangle.

Camp Four [SONOMA]: *locality,* 5 miles north-northeast of Sears Point (lat. 38°12'45" N, long. 122°24'10" W). Named on Sears Point (1951) 7.5' quadrangle.

Camp Maacama [SONOMA]: *locality,* 6.5 miles east-northeast of Healdsburg (lat. 38°38'30" N, long. 122°45'05" W; sec. 9, T 9 N, R 8 W); the place is along Maacama Creek. Named on Jimtown (1955) 7.5' quadrangle.

Camp Meeker [SONOMA]: *settlement,* 1.5 miles north-northwest of Occidental (lat. 38°25'35" N, long. 122°57'30" W; in and near sec. 27, T 7 N, R 10 W). Named on Camp Meeker (1954) 7.5' quadrangle. Postal authorities established Camp Meeker post office in 1900; the name commemorates Melvin C. Meeker, an early lumberman (Salley, p. 35).

Campmeeting Ridge [SONOMA]: *ridge,* north-northwest-trending, 1.25 miles long, nearly 3 miles north of Fort Ross (lat. 38°33'15" N, long. 123°14'05" W). Named on Fort Ross (1978) 7.5' quadrangle.

Camp One [SONOMA]: *locality,* 3 miles north of Sears Point (lat. 38°11'40" N, long. 122°26' W). Named on Sears Point (1951) 7.5' quadrangle.

Camp Rose [SONOMA]: *settlement,* 2 miles east of Healdsburg along Russian River (lat. 38°36'55" N, long. 122°50' W). Named on Healdsburg (1955) 7.5' quadrangle.

Camp Rosenberg [SONOMA]: *locality,* 7 miles north of Guerneville along Mill Creek (1) (lat. 38°36'10" N, long. 122°58'15" W; sec. 28, T 9 N, R 10 W). Named on Guerneville (1955) 7.5' quadrangle.

Camp Royaneh [SONOMA]: *locality,* 1.25 miles east-southeast of Cazadero (lat. 38°31'10" N, long. 123°03'55" W; sec. 22, T 8 N, R 11 W). Named on Cazadero (1978) 7.5' quadrangle. Called Camp C.C. Moore on Cazadero (1943) 7.5' quadrangle.

Camp Six [SONOMA]: *locality,* 2.5 miles northeast of Sears Point (lat. 38°10'35" N, long. 122°24'50" W). Named on Sears Point (1951) 7.5' quadrangle.

Camp Thayer [SONOMA]: *locality,* 4 miles northeast of Jenner along Austin Creek (lat. 38°29'30" N, long. 122°03'45" W). Named on Duncans Mills (1943) 7.5' quadrangle. California Division of Highways' (1934) map shows a place called Fraser just southeast of Camp Thayer.

Camp Three [SONOMA]: *locality,* 3.5 miles north-northeast of Sears Point (lat. 38°12'05" N, long. 122°25'20" W). Named on Sears Point (1951) 7.5' quadrangle.

Camp Two [SONOMA]: *locality,* 5 miles north of Sears Point (lat. 38°13'20" N, long. 122°26'10" W). Named on Sears Point (1951) 7.5' quadrangle.

Cañada de Jonive [SONOMA]: *land grant,* mainly west of Sebastopol. Named on Camp Meeker (1954) and Sebastopol (1954) 7.5' quadrangles. James Black received 2 leagues in 1845, and Jasper O'Farrell claimed 10,787 acres patented in 1858 (Cowan, p. 42).

Cañada de Pogolimi [SONOMA]: *land grant,* at Bloomfield and Valley Ford. Named on Two Rock (1954) and Valley Ford (1954) 7.5' quadrangles. Antonio Caceres (or Cazares) received 2 leagues in 1844 and claimed 8781 acres patented in 1858 (Cowan, p. 62; Cowan listed the grant under the name "Cañada de Pogolomi," and gave the name "Cañada de Pogolimi" as an alternate).

Candlestick Ridge [NAPA]: *ridge,* north-trending, nearly 1 mile long, 8 miles north of Saint Helena (lat. 38°37'05" N, long. 122°29'15" W). Named on Saint Helena (1960) 7.5' quadrangle.

Cannon Gulch [SONOMA]: *canyon,* drained by a stream that flows 1 mile to the sea 2.25 miles west-northwest of Plantation at Fisk Mill Cove (lat. 38°35'50" N, long. 123°21' W). Named on Plantation (1977) 7.5' quadrangle.

Canshea Creek: see **Conshea Creek** [SONOMA]; **Tiny Creek** [SONOMA].

Capell [NAPA]: *locality,* nearly 6 miles westnorthwest of Mount Vaca in Capell Valley (lat. 38°26'50" N, long. 122°11'45" W; near S line sec. 16, T 7 N, R 3 W). Named on Napa (1902) 30' quadrangle. Postal authorities established Capell post office in 1873, discontinued it for a time in 1901, and discontinued it finally in 1914 (Frickstad, p. 111).

Capell Creek [NAPA]: *stream,* flows 10.5 miles to Lake Berryessa 11 miles south of Berryessa Peak (lat. 38°30'25" N, long. 122°14'05" W; sec. 30, T 8 N, R 3 W). Named on Capell Val-

ley (1951) and Lake Berryessa (1959) 7.5' quadrangles.

Capell Valley [NAPA]: *valley,* 6.5 miles northwest of Mount Vaca (lat. 38°27'15" N, long. 122°12'15" W); Capell Creek drains the valley. Named on Capell Valley (1951) 7.5' quadrangle.

Cape Romanzoff: see **Bodega Head** [SONOMA].

Carillo: see **Sebastopol** [SONOMA].

Carmet [SONOMA]: *village,* 3.25 miles northwest of the village of Bodega Bay (lat. 38°22'25" N, long. 123°04'30" W). Named on Bodega Head (1972) and Duncans Mills (1979) 7.5' quadrangles.

Carmet Beach [SONOMA]: *beach,* 3.25 miles north-northwest of the village of Bodega Bay along the coast (lat. 38°22'25" N, long. 123° 04'35" W); the beach is at Carmet. Named on Bodega Head (1972) 7.5' quadrangle. Bodega Head (1942) 7.5' quadrangle shows the place as part of Arched Rock Beach.

Carne Humana [NAPA]: *land grant,* near Calistoga and Saint Helena in Napa Valley. Named on Calistoga (1958), Mark West Springs (1958), Rutherford (1951), and Saint Helena (1960) 7.5' quadrangles. Edward T. Bale received 4 leagues in 1841, and his heirs claimed 17,962 acres patented in 1879 (Cowan, p. 24; Cowan gave the name "Colijolmanoc" as an alternate). Bale twisted the Indian name of the place into the designation for his grant—*carne humana* means "human flesh" in Spanish (Gudde, 1949, p. 21).

Carnero Mountain: see **Bismark Knob** [NAPA-SONOMA].

Carneros [NAPA]: *locality,* 4.5 miles northwest of Napa along Southern Pacific Railroad (lat. 38°13'45" N, long. 122°18'30" W); the place is on Rincon de los Carneros grant. Named on Mare Island (1916) 15' quadrangle. Postal authorities established Carneros post office in 1867 and discontinued it in 1868 (Frickstad, p. 111).

Carneros Creek [NAPA]: *stream,* flows 10.5 miles to Napa River 4 miles northwest of Napa Junction (lat. 38°13'20" N, long. 122°18'35" W; sec. 4, T 4 N, R 4 W); the stream is on Rincon de los Carneros grant. Named on Cuttings Wharf (1949), Napa (1951), and Sonoma (1951) 7.5' quadrangles. Called Corneros Creek on Sonoma (1942) 15' quadrangle.

Carneros Valley [NAPA]: *valley,* 4.5 miles westsouthwest of downtown Napa (lat. 38°16'50" N, long. 122°21'45" W); the valley is along Carneros Creek. Named on Napa (1951) and Sonoma (1951) 7.5' quadrangles.

Carriger Creek [SONOMA]: *stream,* flows 8 miles to join Felder Creek and form Fowler Creek 2 miles south-southwest of Sonoma (lat. 38°16'05" N, long. 122°28'30" W). Named on Glen Ellen (1954) and Sonoma (1951) 7.5' quadrangles. The name commemorates Nicholas Carriger, a farmer in the neighborhood after 1850 (Gudde, 1949, p. 58).

Carson Creek [SONOMA]: *stream,* flows 2.25 miles to join McKenzie Creek and form Marshall Creek 4 miles north-northeast of Fort Ross (lat. 38°33'50" N, long. 123°12'20" W; sec. 5, T 8 N, R 12 W). Named on Fort Ross (1978) 7.5' quadrangle.

Cascade [SONOMA]: *locality,* 2.5 miles southsouthwest of Guerneville along Northwestern Pacific Railroad near Russian River (lat. 38°28' N, long. 123°01' W). Named on Duncans Mills (1921) 15' quadrangle.

Cascade Creek [SONOMA]: *stream,* flows 0.5 mile to Frasier Creek 6 miles north-northeast of Asti (lat. 38°50'35" N, long. 122°56' W; near E line sec. 35, T 12 N, R 10 W). Named on Asti (1959) 7.5' quadrangle.

Caslamayomi [SONOMA]: *land grant,* northeast of Asti and Geyserville. Named on Asti (1959), Geyserville (1955), Jimtown (1955), and The Geysers (1959) 7.5' quadrangles. Eugenio Montenegro received 8 leagues in 1844; William Forbes claimed 26,788 acres patented in 1874 (Cowan, p. 25; Cowan gave the name "Laguna de los Gentiles" as an alternate). Kroeber (p. 37) noted that the name "Caslamayomi" seems to be of Indian origin.

Castle Peak [NAPA]: *peak,* nearly 5 miles east of Yountville (lat. 38°23'50" N, long. 122°16'35" W; sec. 2, T 6 N, R 4 W). Altitude 1318 feet. Named on Yountville (1951) 7.5' quadrangle.

Castle Rock [NAPA]: *relief feature,* 8 miles west-northwest of downtown Napa (lat. 38°20'35" N, long. 122°24'45" W; near W line sec. 28, T 6 N, R 5 W). Named on Sonoma (1951) 7.5' quadrangle.

Castle Rock [SONOMA]:
(1) *peak,* 10.5 miles northeast of Healdsburg (lat. 38°44'35" N, long. 122°45'10" W; sec. 4, T 10 N, R 8 W). Altitude 2662 feet. Named on Jimtown (1955) 7.5' quadrangle.
(2) *relief feature,* 6 miles north-northwest of Kenwood (lat. 38°29'45" N, long. 122°35'45" W; near E line sec. 35, T 8 N, R 7 W). Named on Kenwood (1954) 7.5' quadrangle.

Catacula [NAPA]: *land grant,* at and near Chiles Valley. Named on Chiles Valley (1958), Saint Helena (1960), and Yountville (1951) 7.5' quadrangles. Joseph B. Chiles received 2 leagues in 1844 and claimed 8546 acres patented in 1865 (Cowan, p. 25).

Cave Dale: see **Agua Caliente** [SONOMA] (2).

Cayetano Creek: see **Spencer Creek** [NAPA].

Caymus [NAPA]:
(1) *land grant,* near Rutherford and Yountville in Napa Valley. Named on Rutherford (1951) and Yountville (1951) 7.5' quadrangles. George C. Yount received 2 leagues in 1836 and claimed 11,887 acres patented in 1863 (Cowan, p. 25). Perez (p. 61) gave the size of the grant as 11,814.52 acres. The grant has

the name of an Indian village that was at the site of present Yountville (Kroeber, p. 38).
(2) *locality,* 1.5 miles southeast of Rutherford along Southern Pacific Railroad (lat. 38°26'30" N, long. 122°24'20" W); the place is on Caymus grant. Named on Sonoma (1942) 15' quadrangle.

Cazadero [SONOMA]: *village,* 13 miles westsouthwest of Healdsburg (lat. 38°31'50" N, long. 123°05'10" W; sec. 16, 21, T 8 N, R 11 W); the village is along Austin Creek. Named on Cazadero (1978) 7.5' quadrangle. Postal authorities established Austin post office in 1881, changed the name to Ingrams in 1886, and changed it to Cazadero in 1889; the name "Austin" was for Henry Austin, a pioneer settler, and the name "Ingrams" was for Silas D. Ingrams, first postmaster of Ingrams post office (Salley, p. 12, 40, 104). The place also was called Elim Grove in the early days (Mullen). California Mining Bureau's (1917) map shows a place called Magnesite located north of Cazadero at the end of a rail line—this probably was at the property of Sonoma Magnesite Company described by Bradley (p. 328) as located along East Austin Creek at the end of a 24-inch gauge railroad (in and north of sec. 20, T 9 N, R 11 W).

C.C. Moore: see **Camp C.C. Moore**, under **Camp Royaneh** [SONOMA].

Cedar Canyon [NAPA]: *canyon,* drained by a stream that flows 2.25 miles to James Creek 7 miles north-northeast of Calistoga (lat. 38°40'10" N, long. 122°31'20" W; near E line sec. 33, T 10 N, R 6 W). Named on Detert Reservoir (1958) 7.5' quadrangle.

Cedar Creek [NAPA]: *stream,* flows 4.25 miles to Hunting Creek 4.25 miles west-southwest of Knoxville (lat. 38°47'40" N, long. 122°24'20" W; sec. 22, T 11 N, R 5 W); the stream flows through Cedar Valley (1). Named on Jericho Valley (1958) and Knoxville (1958) 7.5' quadrangles.

Cedar Creek [SONOMA]: *stream,* flows 3 miles to House Creek 4.25 miles south-southwest of Big Mountain (lat. 38°39'10" N, long. 123°10'05" W; sec. 3, T 9 N, R 12 W); the stream is south of Cedar Ridge. Named on Tombs Creek (1978) 7.5' quadrangle.

Cedar Opening [SONOMA]: *area,* 8 miles north of Guerneville (lat. 38°37'10" N, long. 122°59'25" W; near N line sec. 20, T 9 N, R 10 W). Named on Guerneville (1955) 7.5' quadrangle.

Cedar Ridge [SONOMA]: *ridge,* northwest- to west-trending, 1.5 miles long, nearly 4 miles south of Big Mountain (lat. 38°39'15" N, long. 123°09'05" W); the ridge is north of Cedar Creek. Named on Tombs Creek (1978) 7.5' quadrangle.

Cedar Roughs [NAPA]: *area,* 11 miles eastnortheast of Saint Helena (lat. 38°34'30" N, long. 122°18' W). Named on Chiles Valley (1958) 7.5' quadrangle.

Cedars: see **The Cedars** [SONOMA].

Cedar Valley [NAPA]:
(1) *valley,* 4 miles south-southwest of Knoxville along Cedar Creek (lat. 38°46'15" N, long. 122°21'30" W; sec. 25, T 11 N, R 5 W). Named on Knoxville (1958) 7.5' quadrangle.
(2) *area,* 4.5 miles north-northeast of Walter Springs (lat. 38°43'10" N, long. 122°19'55" W). Named on Walter Springs (1959) 7.5' quadrangle.

Cement Creek [NAPA]: *stream,* flows 3 miles to Putah Creek 3.5 miles north-northwest of Walter Springs (lat. 38°42'15" N, long. 122°22'15" W; near NE cor. sec. 23, T 10 N, R 5 W). Named on Walter Springs (1959) 7.5' quadrangle.

Centennial Mountain [SONOMA]: *peak,* 1 mile southeast of Big Mountain (lat. 38°42'05" N, long. 123°08' W; sec. 24, T 10 N, R 12 W). Altitude 2443 feet. Named on Tombs Creek (1978) 7.5' quadrangle.

Chalk Hill [SONOMA]: *peak,* 5 miles east of Healdsburg (lat. 38°36'15" N, long. 122°46'35" W). Named on Healdsburg (1955) 7.5' quadrangle.

Chalk Mountain [SONOMA]: *ridge,* east-southeast-trending, less than 1 mile long, 2.5 miles east-northeast of Mark West Springs (lat. 38°33'35" N, long. 122°40'20" W). Named on Mark West Springs (1958) 7.5' quadrangle.

Chalk Point [SONOMA]: *peak,* 2 miles west of Mount Saint Helena (lat. 38°39'55" N, long. 122°40'15" W; near SE cor. sec. 31, T 10 N, R 7 W). Named on Mount Saint Helena (1959) 7.5' quadrangle.

Champlin Creek [SONOMA]: *stream,* flows 3 miles to Rodgers Creek 3 miles south-southwest of Sonoma (lat. 38°15'20" N, long. 122°28'50" W). Named on Petaluma River (1954), Sears Point (1951), and Sonoma (1951) 7.5' quadrangles.

Chapman Branch: see **Pena Creek** [SONOMA].

Chapman Canyon: see **East Chapman Canyon** [NAPA]; **West Chapman Canyon** [NAPA].

Charley Haupt Creek: see **Haupt Creek** [SONOMA].

Cheney Gulch [SONOMA]: *canyon,* drained by a stream that flows nearly 4 miles to Bodega Harbor 1.25 miles south-southeast of the village of Bodega Bay (lat. 38°19' N, long. 123°02'10" W). Named on Bodega Head (1972) and Valley Ford (1954) 7.5' quadrangles.

Cherry [SONOMA]: *locality,* 3.5 miles southwest of Cotati along Petaluma and Santa Rosa Railroad (lat. 38°17'10" N, long. 122°44'50" W). Named on Santa Rosa (1944) 15' quadrangle. California Division of Highways' (1934) map shows a place called Garden and a place called Robinson located along the railroad between Cherry and Liberty, and a place

called Houx and a place called Boysen located along the railroad between Cherry and Two Rock.

Cherry Creek [SONOMA]: *stream,* heads in Mendocino County and flows 7.25 miles to Dry Creek 5 miles southwest of Cloverdale (lat. 38°45'55" N, long. 123°05'45" W; at S line sec. 28, T 11 N, R 11 W). Named on Cloverdale (1960) 7.5' quadrangle.

Cherry Valley [NAPA]: *area,* 5.5 miles north-northwest of Mount Vaca in Wragg Canyon (lat. 38°28'15" N, long. 122°09'20" W). Named on Capell Valley (1951) 7.5' quadrangle.

Chianti [SONOMA]: *locality,* 3 miles northwest of Geyserville along Northwestern Pacific Railroad (lat. 38°44'15" N, long. 123°56'30" W). Named on Geyserville (1955) 7.5' quadrangle.

Childs: see **Chiles Valley** [NAPA].

Chileno Valley [SONOMA]: *valley,* on Marin-Sonoma county line, mainly in Marin County, along Chileno Creek above a point 5 miles east-southeast of Tomales (lat. 38°12'50" N, long. 122°49'30" W). Named on Petaluma (1953) and Point Reyes NE (1954) 7.5' quadrangles. The name is from natives of Chili that Adrian Godoy, a Chilean immigrant himself, brought to the place after 1868 (Mason, 1976, p. 163).

Chiles: see **Chiles Valley** [NAPA].

Chiles Creek [NAPA]: *stream,* flows 4.5 miles to Lake Hennessey 6.25 miles east of Saint Helena (lat. 38°30'15" N, long. 122°21'15" W; sec. 31, T 8 N, R 4 W); the stream heads in Chiles Valley. Named on Chiles Valley (1958) and Yountville (1951) 7.5' quadrangles.

Chiles Valley [NAPA]: *valley,* 8 miles east-north-east of Saint Helena (lat. 38°32' N, long. 122°19'30" W); the valley is on upper reaches of Chiles Creek on Catacula grant. Named on Chiles Valley (1958) 7.5' quadrangle. The name commemorates Joseph B. Chiles, who came to California in 1841 and received Catacula grant in 1844 (Gudde, 1949, p. 65). California Division of Highways' (1934) map shows a place called Chiles located near the southeast end of present Chiles Valley, near where Saint Helena (1942) 15' quadrangle shows Chiles Valley Sch. Postal authorities established Childs post office in 1888, changed the name to Chiles the same year, moved it 0.75 mile east in 1894, moved it 1 mile northwest in 1908, and discontinued it in 1924 (Salley, p. 43).

Chimiles [NAPA]: *land grant,* southwest of Mount Vaca. Named on Capell Valley (1951), Fairfield North (1951), Mount George (1951), and Mount Vaca (1951) 7.5' quadrangles. Jose Ignacio Berryessa received 4 leagues in 1846; William Gordon and Nathan Coombs claimed 17,762 acres patented in 1860 (Cowan, p. 27).

Chimney Canyon [NAPA]: *canyon,* drained by a stream that flows 2 miles to Gordon Valley

3 miles south of Mount Vaca (lat. 38°21'20" N, long. 122°06'45" W). Named on Fairfield North (1951) 7.5' quadrangle.

Chimney Rock [SONOMA]: *peak,* 2.5 miles southeast of Cazadero (lat. 38°30'10" N, long. 123°03' W; near NW cor. sec. 35, T 8 N, R 11 W). Altitude 1283 feet. Named on Cazadero (1978) 7.5' quadrangle. Water from Chimney Rock Spring, located near the peak, was bottled by hand for many years (Bradley, p. 336).

Chimney Rock Spring: see **Chimney Rock** [SONOMA].

China Slough [NAPA-SONOMA]: *water feature,* on Napa-Sonoma county line, joins South Slough nearly 6 miles west-southwest of Napa Junction (lat. 38°09'50" N, long. 122°21'05" W; near W line sec. 30, T 4 N, R 4 W). Named on Cuttings Wharf (1949) 7.5' quadrangle.

Chinese Gulch [SONOMA]: *canyon,* drained by a stream that flows 1 mile to the sea 2 miles west of Plantation (lat. 38°35'20" N, long. 123°20'35" W). Named on Plantation (1977) 7.5' quadrangle.

Chino Flat [NAPA]: *area,* 3.5 miles northwest of Calistoga (lat. 38° 37'15" N, long. 122°37'15" W). Named on Calistoga (1958) 7.5' quadrangle.

Chiquita [SONOMA]: *locality,* 1.25 miles north of Healdsburg along Northwestern Pacific Railroad (lat. 38°38'05" N, long. 122°52'25" W). Named on Jimtown (1955) 7.5' quadrangle.

Cinnabar: see **Petaluma** [SONOMA] (2).

Clairville: see **Geyserville** [SONOMA].

Clam Beach [SONOMA]: *beach,* 0.5 mile west of Fort Ross along the coast (lat. 38°30'55" N, long. 123°15'10" W). Named on Plantation (1977) 7.5' quadrangle.

Clark: see **Patty Clark Springs**, under **Bald Hills** [SONOMA].

Clark Creek [SONOMA]: *stream,* flows 1 mile to Laguna de Santa Rosa less than 1 mile north-northwest of Cotati (lat. 38°20'10" N, long. 122°42'40" W). Named on Santa Rosa (1954) 15' quadrangle.

Clarks Crossing [SONOMA]: *locality,* 5 miles southeast of Annapolis along Wheatfield Fork Gualala River (lat. 38°39'55" N, long. 123°18'45" W; sec. 33, T 10 N, R 13 W). Named on Annapolis (1977) 7.5' quadrangle.

Clear Creek [NAPA]: *stream,* flows 3 miles to Sage Canyon 6.25 miles north-northeast of Yountville (lat. 38°29'15" N, long. 122°18'30" W; sec. 4, T 7 N, R 4 W). Named on Chiles Valley (1958) and Yountville (1951) 7.5' quadrangles.

Cloudy Bend [SONOMA]: *bend,* 5 miles east-southeast of downtown Petaluma along Petaluma River (lat. 38°12' N, long. 122°33'45" W). Named on Petaluma River (1954) 7.5' quadrangle.

Cloverdale [SONOMA]: *town,* 15 miles north-

northwest of Healdsburg near Russian River (lat. 38°48'20" N, long. 123°00'55" W). Named on Cloverdale (1960) 7.5' quadrangle. Postal authorities established Cloverdale post office in 1857 (Frickstad, p. 195), and the town incorporated in 1872. The site first was known as Markle's Place and Markleville, for R.B. Markle, who owned land there; the name "Cloverdale" was given for wild fodder growing in the vicinity (Gudde, 1949, p. 71; Salley, p. 46). California Mining Bureau's (1909) map shows a place called Throop situated west of Cloverdale about halfway to the coast. Postal authorities established Throop post office 18 miles west of Cloverdale in 1906, discontinued it in 1911, reestablished it in 1916, and discontinued it in 1918; the name was for Charles W. Throop, first postmaster (Salley, p. 221). California Division of Highways' (1934) map shows a place called McCrays located just north of Cloverdale.

Cloverdale Creek [SONOMA]: *stream,* flows 3 miles to Russian River at Cloverdale (lat. 38°48'25" N, long. 123°00'25" W). Named on Cloverdale (1960) 7.5' quadrangle.

Cobb Creek [SONOMA]: *stream,* flows 3 miles to Big Sulphur Creek 3.25 miles northeast of Geyser Peak (lat. 38°47'35" N, long. 122°47'40" W; sec. 19, T 11 N, R 8 W). Named on The Geysers (1959) 7.5' quadrangle.

Cobb Mountain Range: see **Mayacmas Mountains** [NAPA-SONOMA].

Cold Spring [NAPA]: *spring,* 5 miles northeast of Calistoga (lat. 38° 37'10" N, long. 122°30'05" W; near NW cor. sec. 23, T 9 N, R 6 W). Named on Calistoga (1958) 7.5' quadrangle.

Cold Springs [SONOMA]: *springs,* 1.25 miles southeast of Geyser Peak (lat. 38°45'10" N, long. 122°49'25" W; sec. 2, T 10 N, R 9 W). Named on The Geysers (1959) 7.5' quadrangle.

Coldwater Canyon [SONOMA]: *canyon,* drained by a stream that flows 1 mile to Squaw Creek 4.5 miles north of Geyser Peak (lat. 38°49'50" N, long. 122°49'35" W; sec. 2, T 11 N, R 9 W). Named on The Geysers (1959) 7.5' quadrangle.

Coldwater Gulch [SONOMA]: *canyon,* drained by a stream that flows 0.5 mile to Mill Creek (1) 6.5 miles north-northeast of Guerneville (lat. 38°35'35" N, long. 122°57'45" W). Named on Guerneville (1955) 7.5' quadrangle.

Cole Flat [NAPA]: *area,* 2.25 miles south-southwest of Rutherford (lat. 38°28'25" N, long. 122°29'20" W; near N line sec. 11, T 7 N, R 6 W). Named on Rutherford (1951) 7.5' quadrangle.

Coleman Beach [SONOMA]: *beach,* 2.5 miles north-northwest of the village of Bodega Bay along the coast (lat. 38°21'55" N, long. 123° 04'15" W). Named on Bodega Head (1972) 7.5' quadrangle.

Coleman Canyon [NAPA]: *canyon,* drained by a stream that flows 1 mile to Wragg Canyon 6.25 miles north-northwest of Mount Vaca (lat. 38°28'55" N, long. 122°09'30" W; sec. 2, T 7 N, R 3 W). Named on Capell Valley (1951) 7.5' quadrangle.

Coleman Field [SONOMA]: *area,* nearly 7 miles south-southwest of Big Mountain (lat. 38°37'35" N, long. 123°12'50" W; near NW cor. sec. 17, T 9 N, R 12 W). Named on Tombs Creek (1978) 7.5' quadrangle.

Coleman Hill [SONOMA]: *ridge,* west-north-west-trending, 1 mile long, 1.5 miles north of the village of Bodega Bay (lat. 38°21'15" N, long. 123°02'45" W). Named on Bodega Head (1972) 7.5' quadrangle.

Coleman Valley [SONOMA]: *valley,* 2.25 miles west of Occidental (lat. 38°24'25" N, long. 122°59'20" W). Named on Camp Meeker (1954) 7.5' quadrangle. The place first was called Kolmer Valley for Michael Kolmer, who settled there in 1848 (Gudde, 1949, p. 74).

Coleman Valley Creek [SONOMA]: *stream,* flows 5.5 miles to Salmon Creek (1) 2.5 miles northeast of the village of Bodega Bay (lat. 38°21'40" N, long. 123°00'55" W); the stream goes through Coleman Valley. Named on Bodega Head (1972), Camp Meeker (1954), and Duncans Mills (1979) 7.5' quadrangles.

Colijolmanoc: see **Carne Humana** [NAPA].

Collins [NAPA]: *locality,* 1.5 miles south of Napa Junction along Southern Pacific Railroad (lat. 38°09'55" N, long. 122°15'05" W; sec. 25, T 4 N, R 4 W). Named on Cuttings Wharf (1949) 7.5' quadrangle.

Congress Spring: see **Congress Valley** [NAPA].

Congress Valley [NAPA]: *valley,* 2.5 miles west-southwest of downtown Napa (lat. 38°17'15" N, long. 122°19'45" W). Named on Napa (1951) 7.5' quadrangle. Waring (p. 156) listed Congress Spring, a spring of carbonated saline water located 3.5 miles southwest of Napa.

Conn Creek [NAPA]: *stream,* flows 20 miles to Napa River 1 mile northeast of Yountville (lat. 38°25'10" N, long. 122°21'10" W). Named on Rutherford (1951), Saint Helena (1960), and Yountville (1951) 7.5' quadrangles. Called Sage Creek on Pope Valley (1921) 15' quadrangle.

Conn Valley [NAPA]: *valley,* 4.5 miles east of Saint Helena (lat. 38° 30'30" N, long. 122°24'10" W); the valley is along Conn Creek. Named on Saint Helena (1960) 7.5' quadrangle. The name commemorates John Conn, who came to California in 1843 (Gudde, 1949, p. 77). Water of Lake Hennessey now covers part of the valley.

Conn Valley Reservoir: see **Lake Hennessey** [NAPA].

Conshea Creek [SONOMA]: *stream,* flows 1 mile to East Austin Creek 4.5 miles north of Cazadero (lat. 38°35'40" N, long. 123°05'05" W; near W line sec. 28, T 9 N, R 11 W).

Named on Cazadero (1978) 7.5' quadrangle. Called Canshea Creek on Cazadero (1943) 7.5' quadrangle, which also has this name for present Tiny Creek, a tributary of present Conshea Creek.

Consolli Gulch [SONOMA]: *canyon,* drained by a stream that flows 0.5 mile to Austin Creek 4 miles northeast of Jenner (lat. 38°29'05" N, long. 123°03'30" W). Named on Duncans Mills (1979) 7.5' quadrangle.

Cooksley Lake [NAPA]: *lake,* 750 feet long, 6.5 miles north of Saint Helena (lat. 38°36' N, long. 122°28'25" W; sec. 25, T 9 N, R 6 W). Named on Saint Helena (1960) 7.5' quadrangle.

Cooks Peak [SONOMA]: *peak,* 4 miles south-southeast of downtown Santa Rosa (lat. 38°23'30" N, long. 122°40'35" W). Named on Santa Rosa (1954) 7.5' quadrangle.

Coon Creek [SONOMA]: *stream,* flows nearly 3 miles to Briggs Creek 4.5 miles west of Mount Saint Helena (lat. 38°40'35" N, long. 122°42'45" W; near N line sec. 35, T 10 N, R 8 W). Named on Mount Saint Helena (1959) 7.5' quadrangle.

Coon Island [NAPA]: *marsh,* 4 miles west of Napa Junction between Napa Slough and Mud Slough (lat. 38°11'30" N, long. 122°19'15" W; sec. 17, T 4 N, R 4 W). Named on Cuttings Wharf (1949) 7.5' quadrangle.

Copeland Creek [SONOMA]: *stream,* flows 6 miles to lowlands 2.5 miles east-northeast of Cotati (lat. 38°20'35" N, long. 122°40' W). Named on Cotati (1954) and Glen Ellen (1954) 7.5' quadrangles.

Corneros Creek: see **Carneros Creek** [NAPA].

Corona [SONOMA]: *locality,* 5 miles south-southeast of Cotati along Petaluma and Santa Rosa Railroad (lat. 38°15'50" N, long. 122°39'30" W). Named on Santa Rosa (1944) 15' quadrangle.

Corral Valley: see **Wooden Valley** [NAPA].

Cotate [SONOMA]: *land grant,* at and near Cotati. Named on Cotati (1954) and Santa Rosa (1954) 7.5' quadrangles. Juan Castañeda received 4 leagues in 1844; T.S. Page claimed 17,239 acres patented in 1858 (Cowan, p. 30). The name is from the chief of an Indian village on the grant (Mullen).

Cotati [SONOMA]: *town,* 7.5 miles south of Santa Rosa (lat. 38°19'35" N, long. 122°42'20" W); the town is on Cotate grant. Named on Cotati (1954) 7.5' quadrangle, which shows Cotati siding situated nearly 1 mile east-northeast of the center of the town along Northwestern Pacific Railroad. The railroad stop at Cotati originally was called Page's Station, for Dr. Thomas Stokes Page, owner of Cotate grant (Mullen). Postal authorities established Cotati post office in 1894 (Frickstad, p. 195), and the town incorporated in 1963.

Cotati Plain: see **Cotati Valley** [SONOMA].

Cotati Valley [SONOMA]: *valley,* between

Cotati and Sonoma Mountains (lat. 38°19'30" N, long. 122°41'30" W). Named on Santa Rosa (1944) 15' quadrangle. Cardwell's (1958) map has the name "Cotati Plain" for the feature.

Cove: see The Cove [NAPA].

Cow Creek [SONOMA]: stream, flows nearly 1 mile to Danfield Creek 6 miles south-southwest of Big Mountain (lat. 38°38'05" N, long. 123°11'25" W; sec. 9, T 9 N, R 12 W). Named on Tombs Creek (1978) 7.5' quadrangle.

Coyote Knoll [SONOMA]: peak, 5.5 miles northeast of Guerneville (lat. 38°33' N, long. 122°55' W). Named on Guerneville (1955) 7.5' quadrangle.

Cozzens: see Cozzens Corner [SONOMA].

Cozzens Corner [SONOMA]: locality, 3 miles west of Geyserville (lat. 38°42'10" N, long. 122°57'20" W). Named on Healdsburg (1940) 15' quadrangle. Postal authorities established Cozzens post office 5 miles northwest of Clairville (present Geyserville) in 1881 and discontinued it in 1910; the name was for Davenport Cozzens, Jr., first postmaster (Salley, p. 52).

Crab Island [SONOMA]: island, 200 feet long, less than 0.5 mile west-southwest of Jenner in Russian River (lat. 38°26'50" N, long. 123°07'20" W). Named on Duncans Mills (1943) 7.5' quadrangle.

Crane [NAPA]: locality, nearly 3 miles northwest of Rutherford along Southern Pacific Railroad (lat. 38°29'30" N, long. 122°27'10" W). Named on Napa (1902) 30' quadrangle.

Crane Canyon [SONOMA]: canyon, 1 mile long, 4.25 miles northeast of Cotati (lat. 38°22'05" N, long. 122°38'45" W); the canyon is north of Crane Creek (2). Named on Cotati (1954) 7.5' quadrangle.

Crane Creek [SONOMA]:
 (1) stream, flows 3 miles to Dry Creek 4 miles south-southwest of Geyserville (lat. 38°39' N, long. 122°55'25" W). Named on Geyserville (1955) 7.5' quadrangle.
 (2) stream, flows 4 miles to lowlands 3 miles northeast of Cotati (lat. 38°21'20" N, long. 122°40' W). Named on Cotati (1954) and Glen Ellen (1954) 7.5' quadrangles.

Crane Peak [SONOMA]: peak, 2.25 miles northwest of Big Mountain (lat. 38°44'10" N, long. 123°10'15" W; on S line sec. 3, T 10 N, R 12 W). Named on Tombs Creek (1978) 7.5' quadrangle.

Crawford Gulch [SONOMA]: canyon, less than 1 mile long, 4 miles south of Guerneville (lat. 38°26'45" N, long. 123°00'20" W). Named on Duncans Mills (1979) 7.5' quadrangle.

Creighton Ridge [SONOMA]: ridge, generally west-trending, 1.5 miles long, nearly 4 miles northeast of Fort Ross (lat. 38°33'15" N, long. 123°11'35" W). Named on Fort Ross (1978) 7.5' quadrangle.

Crinkley Gulch: see Kohute Gulch [SONOMA].

Crocker Creek [SONOMA]: stream, flows nearly 3 miles to Russian River 0.5 mile north of Asti (lat. 38°46'10" N, long. 122°58'20" W). Named on Asti (1959) 7.5' quadrangle.

Crown [SONOMA]: locality, 5 miles southeast of Cotati along Northwestern Pacific Railroad (lat. 38°16'05" N, long. 122°39'20" W). Named on Cotati (1954) 7.5' quadrangle.

Crystal Lake [NAPA]: intermittent lake, 550 feet long, 9 miles northwest of Mount Vaca (lat. 38°28'35" N, long. 122°14'45" W; on S line sec. 1, T 7 N, R 4 W). Named on Capell Valley (1951) 7.5' quadrangle. Mount Vaca (1951) 15' quadrangle shows a perennial lake.

Crystal Springs: see Sanitarium [NAPA].

Cunningham [SONOMA]: locality, 5.25 miles northeast of Bloomfield (lat. 38°21'50" N, long. 122°46'35" W; near E line sec. 18, T 6 N, R 8 W). Named on Two Rock (1954) 7.5' quadrangle. The name was given in 1904 for the Cunningham family, landholders in the neighborhood (Gudde, 1949, p. 86). California Division of Highways' (1934) map shows a place called Stones located along Petaluma and Santa Rosa Railroad just northwest of Cunningham.

Cup and Saucer [NAPA]: ridge, south-southeast- to southeast-trending, less than 1 mile long, 1 mile northeast of downtown Napa (lat. 38°18'25" N, long. 122°15'55" W). Named on Napa (1951) 7.5' quadrangle.

Curry: see Lake Curry [NAPA].

Cut B [SONOMA]: water feature, artificial waterway 4 miles east-southeast of downtown Petaluma across the neck of a meander in Petaluma River (lat. 38°12'20" N, long. 122°34'25" W). Named on Petaluma River (1954) 7.5' quadrangle.

Cuttings Wharf [NAPA]: locality, 4 miles northwest of Napa Junction along Napa River (lat. 38°13'30" N, long. 122°18'30" W). Named on Cuttings Wharf (1949) 7.5' quadrangle.

Cypress Dunes Campground [SONOMA]: locality, 0.5 mile north of the village of Bodega Bay (lat. 38°20'25" N, long. 123°02'50" W). Named on Bodega Head (1972) 7.5' quadrangle.

Cyrus Creek [NAPA]: stream, flows 2.25 miles to Napa River 0.5 mile west-northwest of Calistoga (lat. 38°34'50" N, long. 122°35'10" W). Named on Calistoga (1958) 7.5' quadrangle.

– D –

Daglia Canyon [NAPA]: canyon, drained by a stream that flows 1.5 miles to Middle Creek 8 miles west-northwest of Mount Vaca (lat. 38°28' N, long. 122°14'40" W; sec. 12, T 7 N, R 4 W). Named on Capell Valley (1951) and Yountville (1951) 7.5' quadrangles.

Dago Valley [NAPA]: valley, 3.5 miles north-northwest of Saint Helena (lat. 38°33'10" N, long. 122°29'15" W). Named on Saint Helena (1960) 7.5' quadrangle.

Danfield Creek [SONOMA]: *stream,* flows 4.25 miles to Pepperwood Creek 6.25 miles south-southwest of Big Mountain (lat. 38° 37'45" N, long. 123°11'50" W; near SW cor. sec. 9, T 9 N, R 12 W); the stream is south of Danfield Ridge. Named on Tombs Creek (1978) 7.5' quadrangle.

Danfield Ridge [SONOMA]: *ridge,* east-northeast to east-southeast-trending, 1.5 miles long, 4.5 miles south-southwest of Big Mountain (lat. 38°39' N, long. 123°11' W); the ridge is north of Danfield Creek. Named on Tombs Creek (1978) 7.5' quadrangle.

Dangers: see **Liberty** [SONOMA].

Dardon Canyon [NAPA]: *canyon,* drained by a stream that flows nearly 1 mile to Gosling Canyon 7 miles south of Berryessa Peak (lat. 38°34' N, long. 122°10'25" W). Named on Lake Berryessa (1959) 7.5' quadrangle.

Deadhorse Creek [SONOMA]: *stream,* flows 0.5 mile to Humbug Creek 4.5 miles east of Mark West Springs (lat. 38°32'25" N, long. 122°38'05" W; sec. 16, T 8 N, R 7 W). Named on Mark West Springs (1958) 7.5' quadrangle. Calistoga (1959) 15' quadrangle has the form "Dead Horse Creek" for the name.

Deadman Cliff [SONOMA]: *relief feature,* 2 miles north of Big Mountain on the north side of Rancheria Creek (lat. 38°44'25" N, long. 123°08'45" W; on E line sec. 2, T 10 N, R 12 W). Named on Tombs Creek (1978) 7.5' quadrangle.

Deadman Gulch [SONOMA]: *canyon,* drained by a stream that flows 1 mile to the sea 3 miles west-northwest of Plantation (lat. 38°36'05" N, long. 123°21'40" W). Named on Plantation (1977) 7.5' quadrangle.

Death Rock [SONOMA]: *promontory,* 4 miles south-southeast of Jenner along the coast (lat. 38°23'40" N, long. 123°05'45" W). Named on Duncans Mills (1979) 7.5' quadrangle.

Decker Canyon [NAPA]: *canyon,* drained by a stream that flows 1 mile to Lake Berryessa 7.25 miles north-northwest of Mount Vaca (lat. 38°29'45" N, long. 122°09'15" W). Named on Capell Valley (1951, photorevised 1968) 7.5' quadrangle.

Deer Creek [SONOMA]: *stream,* flows 1 mile to Sausal Creek 6 miles northeast of Healdsburg (lat. 38°40'55" N, long. 122°48' W; sec. 25, T 10 N, R 9 W). Named on Jimtown (1955) 7.5' quadrangle.

Deer Knoll [SONOMA]: *peak,* 8 miles north-northeast of Healdsburg (lat. 38°42'55" N, long. 122°47'25" W; sec. 18, T 10 N, R 8 W). Named on Jimtown (1955) 7.5' quadrangle.

Deer Lake [NAPA]: *lake,* 950 feet long, 6.25 miles north of Saint Helena (lat. 38°35'50" N, long. 122°28'20" W; sec. 25, T 9 N, R 6 W); the lake is north of Doe Lake. Named on Saint Helena (1960) 7.5' quadrangle.

Deer Park: see **Sanitarium** [NAPA].

Del Mar Landing [SONOMA]: *locality,* 8.5 miles northwest of the village of Stewarts Point along the coast (lat. 38°44'30" N, long. 123°30'25" W); the place is just east of Del Mar Point. Named on Stewarts Point (1978) 7.5' quadrangle.

Del Mar Point [SONOMA]: *promontory,* 8.5 miles northwest of the village of Stewarts Point along the coast (lat. 38°44'25" N, long. 123°30'30" W). Named on Stewarts Point (1978) 7.5' quadrangle.

Del Rio Woods [SONOMA]: *settlement,* 2 miles east-northeast of Healdsburg along Russian River (lat. 38°37'20" N, long. 122°50'15" W). Named on Healdsburg (1955) 7.5' quadrangle.

Denman [SONOMA]: *locality,* 4 miles south-southeast of Cotati along Petaluma and Santa Rosa Railroad (lat. 38°16'25" N, long. 122°40'30" W); the place is at present Denman Flat. Named on Santa Rosa (1944) 15' quadrangle.

Denman Flat [SONOMA]: *area,* 4.25 miles south-southeast of Cotati (lat. 38°16'25" N, long. 122°40' W). Named on Cotati (1954) 7.5' quadrangle.

Denner Ridge [SONOMA]: *ridge,* east-south-east-trending, 1 mile long, 5.25 miles east-northeast of Guerneville (lat. 38°32'05" N, long. 122°54'30" W). Named on Guerneville (1955) 7.5' quadrangle.

Devil Creek [SONOMA]: *stream,* flows 4 miles to East Austin Creek 4.5 miles north of Cazadero (lat. 38°35'40" N, long. 123°04'40" W; sec. 28, T 9 N, R 11 W). Named on Cazadero (1978) 7.5' quadrangle. Called Devils Creek on California Division of Forestry's (1945) map, which names a North Fork of the stream.

Devils Backbone [SONOMA]: *ridge,* generally northeast-trending, 0.5 mile long, 2.25 miles northeast of Cazadero (lat. 38°32'50" N, long. 123°03' W). Named on Cazadero (1978) 7.5' quadrangle.

Devil's Cañon: see **Geyser Canyon** [SONOMA].

Devils Canyon [NAPA]: *canyon,* drained by a stream that flows 2.5 miles to Redwood Canyon 8.5 miles west-northwest of downtown Napa (lat. 38°21'15" N, long. 122°25'15" W; sec. 21, T 6 N, R 5 W). Named on Sonoma (1951) 7.5' quadrangle.

Devils Creek: see **Devil Creek** [SONOMA].

Devils Den Canyon [SONOMA]: *canyon,* 5.25 miles long, along North Branch Little Sulphur Creek, which joins Little Sulphur Creek 4 miles east-northeast of Asti (lat. 38°47'25" N, long. 122° 54'40" W). Named on Asti (1959) and The Geysers (1959) 7.5' quadrangles.

Devils Elbow [NAPA]: *ridge,* east-southeast-trending, 0.5 mile long, 1 mile southeast of Berryessa Peak at the southeast end of Blue Ridge (1) (lat. 38°39'20" N, long. 122°10'30" W). Named on Brooks (1959) 7.5' quadrangle.

Devils Head: see **Devils Head Peak** [NAPA].

Devils Head Peak [NAPA]: *peak,* 8 miles northeast of Aetna Springs (lat. 38°44'55" N, long. 122°23'40" W). Altitude 1112 feet. Named on Aetna Springs (1958) 7.5' quadrangle. Called Devils Head on Pope Valley (1921) 15' quadrangle.

Devils Kitchen [SONOMA]: *area,* 3 miles northeast of Mark West Springs (lat. 38°34'45" N, long. 122°40'45" W; near SW cor. sec. 31, T 9 N, R 7 W). Named on Mark West Springs (1958) 7.5' quadrangle.

Devil's Mount: see **Mount Saint Helena** [SONOMA].

Devils Ribs [SONOMA]: *ridge,* north-trending, 0.5 mile long, 6.5 miles northeast of Fort Ross (lat. 38°35'20" N, long. 123°09'50" W). Named on Fort Ross (1978) 7.5' quadrangle.

Devils Slough [NAPA]: *water feature,* extends from Napa Slough to China Slough 5 miles west-southwest of Napa Junction (lat. 38°10'10" N, long. 122°20'20" W; sec. 30, T 4 N, R 4 W). Named on Cuttings Wharf (1949) 7.5' quadrangle.

Diamond Mountain [SONOMA]: *ridge,* extends west from Sonoma-Napa county line, 1.25 miles long, 7.25 miles east of Mark West Springs (lat. 38°32'20" N, long. 122°35'10" W). Named on Calistoga (1958) 7.5' quadrangle.

Dianna Rock [SONOMA]: *relief feature,* 4.25 miles east-northeast of Geyser Peak (lat. 38°47'05" N, long. 122°47'20" W; on S line sec. 19, T 11 N, R 8 W). Named on The Geysers (1959) 7.5' quadrangle.

Digger Bend [SONOMA]: *bend,* 2 miles east-northeast of Healdsburg along Russian River (lat. 38°37'45" N, long. 122°50'10" W). Named on Jimtown (1955) 7.5' quadrangle.

Divide [SONOMA]: *locality,* 4.25 miles south of Cotati along Petaluma and Santa Rosa Railroad (lat. 38°17'35" N, long. 122°42'30" W). Named on Santa Rosa (1944) 15' quadrangle. California Division of Highways' (1934) map shows a place called Live Oaks located along the railroad north-northwest of Divide.

Dodgeville: see **Healdsburg** [SONOMA].

Doe Lake [NAPA]: *lake,* 500 feet long, 6 miles north of Saint Helena (lat. 38°35'40" N, long. 122°28'20" W; near S line sec. 25, T 9 N, R 6 W); the lake is between Deer Lake and Fawn Lake. Named on Saint Helena (1960) 7.5' quadrangle.

Doe Ridge [SONOMA]: *ridge,* west-northwest-trending, less than 1 mile long, 6 miles southwest of Big Mountain (lat. 38°39'30" N, long. 123°14'05" W). Named on Tombs Creek (1978) 7.5' quadrangle.

Donahue [SONOMA]: *locality,* 6.25 miles east-southeast of downtown Petaluma on the east side of Petaluma River at the end of a spur of Northwestern Pacific Railroad (lat. 38°11'20" N, long. 122° 32'30" W). Named on Petaluma (1914) 15' quadrangle. Postal authorities established Donahue post office in 1874 and

discontinued it in 1875; the place also was known as Donahue Landing (Salley, p. 60). Peter Donahue built a landing at the place as the terminus of the railroad that he began constructing in 1870 (Miller, J.T., p. 19).

Donahue Landing: see **Donahue** [SONOMA].

Donahue Slough [SONOMA]: *water feature,* waterway that parallels Petaluma River in marsh west of the river—the midpoint of the feature is 7 miles southeast of downtown Petaluma (lat. 38°10'25" N, long. 122°32'10" W). Named on Petaluma River (1954) 7.5' quadrangle.

Doran Beach [SONOMA]: *beach,* 2 miles long, center 1.5 miles south-southeast of the village of Bodega Bay (lat. 38°18'50" N, long. 123°02'20" W); the beach is at the northwest end of Bodega Bay (1). Named on Bodega Head (1972) 7.5' quadrangle.

Dorman Canyon [SONOMA]: *canyon,* drained by a stream that flows 1 mile to Crane Creek (1) 5 miles south-southwest of Geyserville (lat. 38°38'35" N, long. 122°56'55" W; sec. 10, T 9 N, R 10 W). Named on Geyserville (1955) 7.5' quadrangle.

Dos Piedras [SONOMA]: *relief feature,* 4.5 miles southeast of Bloomfield near the village of Two Rock (lat. 38°16'10" N, long. 122°47'30" W). Named on Two Rock (1954) 7.5' quadrangle.

Dowdall Creek [SONOMA]: *stream,* flows 4 miles to Sonoma Creek 1.25 miles southwest of Sonoma (lat. 38°16'55" N, long. 122°28'30" W). Named on Glen Ellen (1954) and Sonoma (1951) 7.5' quadrangles.

Dry Creek [NAPA]: *stream,* flows 15 miles to Napa River 5.25 miles north-northwest of downtown Napa (lat. 38°22'20" N, long. 122° 18'20" W). Named on Napa (1951), Rutherford (1951), Sonoma (1951), and Yountville (1951) 7.5' quadrangles. The canyon of Dry Creek is called Wing Canyon on Sonoma (1942) 15' quadrangle. United States Board on Geographic Names (1986, p. 3) approved the name "Campbell Canyon" for a canyon, 1.5 miles long, that opens into the canyon of Dry Creek 3.5 miles south of Rutherford (lat. 34°24'27" N, long. 122°25'57" W; sec. 32, T 7 N, R 5 W); the name commemorates Duncan Campbell, who homesteaded at the place in 1875.

Dry Creek [SONOMA]: *stream,* heads in Mendocino County and flows 27 miles in Sonoma County to Russian River 2 miles south-southeast of Healdsburg (lat. 38°35'10" N, long. 122°51'25" W). Named on Hopland (1960) 15' quadrangle, and on Geyserville (1955), Guerneville (1955), Healdsburg (1955), and Warm Springs Dam (1978) 7.5' quadrangles. Hoods Hot Springs are in the canyon of Dry Creek near the north line of Sonoma County; they probably are the springs sometimes referred to as Fairmont Hot Springs (Waring, p. 82).

Ducker Creek [SONOMA]: *stream*, flows 3 miles to Rincon Creek 2.5 miles northeast of downtown Santa Rosa (lat. 38°27'50" N, long. 122°40'30" W). Named on Santa Rosa (1954) 7.5' quadrangle.

Dugans Pond [SONOMA]: *lake*, 300 feet long, 2.25 miles northwest of Cazadero (lat. 38°33'20" N, long. 123°06'45" W; sec. 7, T 8 N, R 11 W). Named on Cazadero (1978) 7.5' quadrangle.

Duncan Point: see **Duncans Point** [SONOMA].

Duncans Cove [SONOMA]: *embayment*, 4 miles south-southeast of Jenner along the coast (lat. 38°23'40" N, long. 123°05'30" W). Named on Duncans Mills (1979) 7.5' quadrangle. The cove is the site of Duncan's Landing, which was at the end of a horse-drawn railway that brought lumber from the mill of Alexander Duncan and Samuel Duncan for shipment in the 1860's and 1870's (Miller, J.T., p. 42).

Duncan's Landing: see **Duncans Cove** [SONOMA].

Duncans Mills [SONOMA]: *settlement*, 3.5 miles east of Jenner along Russian River (lat. 38°27'10" N, long. 123°03'10" W). Named on Duncans Mills (1979) 7.5' quadrangle. Postal authorities established Duncans Mills post office in 1862 (Frickstad, p. 195). Duncans Mills (1921) 15' quadrangle shows Duncans Mill situated south of Russian River near present Bridgehaven, where Alexander Duncan and Samuel Duncan operated a lumber mill, and where by 1860 a village called Duncansville had 300 inhabitants; Alexander Duncan moved the mill in 1876 to the site of present Duncans Mills (Hansen and Miller, p. 47-48).

Duncans Point [SONOMA]: *promontory*, 4.25 miles south-southeast of Jenner along the sea coast (lat. 38°23'35" N, long. 123°05'40" W). Named on Duncans Mills (1979) 7.5' quadrangle. Called Duncan Pt. on Duncans Mills (1943) 7.5' quadrangle.

Duncansville: see **Duncans Mills** [SONOMA].

Dunn: see **Petaluma** [SONOMA] (2).

Dutch Bill Creek [SONOMA]: *stream*, flows 6.25 miles to Russian River 2.5 miles south-southwest of Guerneville at Monte Rio (lat. 38°27'55" N, long. 123°00'35" W; sec. 7, T 7 N, R 10 W). Named on Camp Meeker (1954) and Duncans Mills (1979) 7.5' quadrangles. The name is for William Howard, who came to the region in the 1840's (Hansen and Miller, p. 48).

Dutcher Creek [SONOMA]: *stream*, flows 3.5 miles to Dry Creek 4 miles west of Geyserville (lat. 38°42'25" N, long. 123°58'25" W). Named on Geyserville (1955) 7.5' quadrangle.

Dutch Henry Canyon [NAPA]: *canyon*, drained by a stream that flows 3 miles to Napa Valley 3.25 miles east of Calistoga (lat. 38° 34'40" N, long. 122°31'05" W). Named on Calistoga (1958) 7.5' quadrangle.

Dutton Landing [NAPA]: *locality*, 3.5 miles west-northwest of Napa Junction along Napa River (lat. 38°12'40" N, long. 122°18'20" W; sec. 9, T 4 N, R 4 W). Named on Cuttings Wharf (1949, photorevised 1968) 7.5' quadrangle.

Dutton Ridge: see **Thompson Ridge** [SONOMA] (2).

Duvall Lake [NAPA]: *lake*, 1100 feet long, 1 mile southeast of Aetna Springs (lat. 38°38'35" N, long. 122°28'20" W; sec. 12, T 9 N, R 6 W). Named on Aetna Springs (1958) 7.5' quadrangle.

Duvoul Creek [SONOMA]: *stream*, flows 2 miles to Dutch Bill Creek nearly 3 miles north-northwest of Occidental (lat. 38°26'35" N, long. 122°58'30" W; near N line sec. 21, T 7 N, R 10 W). Named on Camp Meeker (1954) 7.5' quadrangle.

Dyer Creek [NAPA]: *stream*, flows 3.5 miles to Lake Berryessa 3 miles east of Walter Springs (lat. 38°39'20" N, long. 122°18'20" W; sec. 4, T 9 N, R 4 W). Named on Walter Springs (1959) 7.5' quadrangle.

— E —

Eaglenest: see **Rio Nido** [SONOMA].

Eagle Rock [SONOMA]:
(1) *relief feature*, nearly 3 miles north of Geyser Peak (lat. 38°48'20" N, long. 122°50'20" W; near NW cor. sec. 14, T 11 N, R 9 W). Named on The Geysers (1959) 7.5' quadrangle.
(2) *relief feature*, 4 miles southeast of Jenner (lat. 38°24'15" N, long. 123°04'45" W). Named on Duncans Mills (1979) 7.5' quadrangle.
(3) *peak*, 5.5 miles west-northwest of Skaggs Springs (lat. 38°43' N, long. 123°07'15" W; sec. 18, T 10 N, R 11 W). Named on Warm Springs Dam (1978) 7.5' quadrangle.

East Austin Creek [SONOMA]: *stream*, flows 13 miles to Austin Creek less than 2 miles southeast of Cazadero (lat. 38°30'35" N, long. 123°04' W). Named on Cazadero (1978) and Warm Springs Dam (1978) 7.5' quadrangles.

East Bull Canyon [NAPA]: *canyon*, nearly 2 miles long, opens into Wragg Canyon 4.5 miles northwest of Mount Vaca (lat. 38°27'15" N, long. 122°09'05" W; near W line sec. 13, T 7 N, R 3 W); the mouth of the canyon is opposite the mouth of West Bull Canyon. Named on Capell Valley (1951) 7.5' quadrangle.

East Chapman Canyon [NAPA]: *canyon*, 0.5 mile long, opens into Wragg Canyon nearly 5 miles north-northwest of Mount Vaca (lat. 38°27'35" N, long. 122°09'55" W; near NE cor. sec. 14, T 7 N, R 3 W); the mouth of the canyon is opposite the mouth of West Chapman Canyon. Named on Capell Valley (1951) 7.5' quadrangle.

East Guernewood [SONOMA]: *settlement,* less than 0.5 mile southwest of Guerneville along Russian River (lat. 38°29'50" N, long. 123°00'10" W; sec. 31, T 8 N, R 10 W). Named on Duncans Mills (1979) 7.5' quadrangle.

East Mitchell Canyon [NAPA]: *canyon,* 1 mile long, opens into Wragg Canyon 5.5 miles north-northwest of Mount Vaca (lat. 38°28'15" N, long. 122°09'15" W; sec. 11, T 7 N, R 3 W); the mouth of the canyon is opposite the mouth of West Mitchell Canyon. Named on Capell Valley (1951) 7.5' quadrangle.

East Napa Reservoir [NAPA]: *lake,* 600 feet long, 1 mile east-northeast of downtown Napa (lat. 38°18'10" N, long. 122°16' W). Named on Napa (1951) 7.5' quadrangle.

East Side Reservoir [NAPA]: *lake,* 250 feet long, 1.5 miles north-northeast of downtown Napa (lat. 38°19'10" N, long. 122°16'05" W). Named on Napa (1951) 7.5' quadrangle.

East Windsor [SONOMA]: *settlement,* 6 miles southeast of Healdsburg (lat. 38°32'45" N, long. 122°48'15" W; sec. 13, T 8 N, R 9 W); the place is 0.5 mile east of Windsor. Named on Healdsburg (1955) 7.5' quadrangle.

Eaton H. Magoon Lake: see **Upper Bohn Lake**, under **Aetna Springs** [NAPA].

Ebabais Creek: see **Ebabias Creek** [SONOMA].

Ebabaza Creek: see **Ebabias Creek** [SONOMA].

Ebabias Creek [SONOMA]: *stream,* flows 5.25 miles to Estero Americano 0.5 mile west-southwest of Valley Ford (lat. 38°18'50" N, long. 122°56'05" W). Named on Valley Ford (1954) 7.5' quadrangle. United States Board on Geographic Names (1943, p. 11) rejected the forms "Ababais," "Ebabais," "Ebabaza," "Ebebais," and "Erabais" for the name.

Ebabias Creek: see **Americano Creek** [SONOMA].

Ebebais Creek: see **Ebabias Creek** [SONOMA].

Eddicut Flat [SONOMA]: *area,* nearly 5 miles west of Big Mountain along Wheatfield Fork Gualala River (lat. 38°41'55" N, long. 123°13'45" W; sec. 19, T 10 N, R 12 W). Named on Tombs Creek (1978) 7.5' quadrangle.

Edendale [SONOMA]: *settlement,* 1 mile south-southwest of Guerneville along Russian River (lat. 38°29'10" N, long. 123°00'10" W; sec. 6, T 7 N, R 10 W). Named on Duncans Mills (1979) 7.5' quadrangle.

Edgerley Island [NAPA]: *island,* nearly 4 miles west-northwest of Napa Junction along Napa River (lat. 38°12' N, long. 122°19' W). Named on Cuttings Wharf (1949) 7.5' quadrangle.

El Bonita [SONOMA]: *settlement,* 1 mile north-east of Guerneville along Russian River (lat. 38°30'45" N, long. 122°59' W; sec. 29, T 8 N, R 10 W). Named on Guerneville (1955) 7.5' quadrangle.

Elder Valley [NAPA]: *valley,* 10 miles east of Saint Helena (lat. 38° 31'15" N, long. 122°17' W). Named on Chiles Valley (1958) 7.5' quadrangle.

Eldridge [SONOMA]: *locality,* 1.25 miles south-southeast of Glen Ellen (lat. 38°21' N, long. 122°30'40" W). Named on Santa Rosa (1944) 15' quadrangle. Santa Rosa (1916) 15' quadrangle shows the place along Southern Pacific Railroad. Glen Ellen (1954) 7.5' quadrangle has the designation "Sonoma State Home (Eldridge P.O.)" near the site. Postal authorities established Eldridge post office in 1894 and named it for a pioneer rancher (Salley, p. 67).

Eleda Hot Springs: see **Fetters Hot Springs** [SONOMA].

Elim Grove: see **Cazadero** [SONOMA].

Elk Creek [SONOMA]: *stream,* flows 2 miles to Wheatfield Fork Gualala River 7 miles east-southeast of Annapolis (lat. 38°40'35" N, long. 123°15'15" W; sec. 25, T 10 N, R 13 W). Named on Annapolis (1977) and Tombs Creek (1978) 7.5' quadrangles.

Elkhead Creek [SONOMA]: *stream,* flows 1.5 miles to Tombs Creek 4 miles west of Big Mountain (lat. 38°43' N, long. 123°12'50" W; near W line sec. 17, T 10 N, R 12 W). Named on Tombs Creek (1978) 7.5' quadrangle.

Elkhorn Peak [NAPA]: *peak,* 3.5 miles west-northwest of Cordelia on Napa-Solano county line (lat. 38°13'50" N, long. 122° 11'40" W; near S line sec. 33, T 5 N, R 3 W). Altitude 1330 feet. Named on Cordelia (1951) 7.5' quadrangle.

El Verano [SONOMA]: *town,* 1.5 miles west-northwest of Sonoma (lat. 38°18' N, long. 122°29'15" W). Named on Sonoma (1951) 7.5' quadrangle. Napa (1902) 30' quadrangle has the form "Elverano" for the name. Postal authorities established El Verano post office in 1889 (Frickstad, p. 195). George H. Maxwell named the place for its climate—*el verano* means "the summer" in Spanish (Gudde, 1949, p. 107).

Ely [SONOMA]: *locality,* 4 miles southeast of Cotati along Northwestern Pacific Railroad (lat. 38°16'45" N, long. 122°39'50" W). Named on Santa Rosa (1944) 15' quadrangle.

Embarcadero [SONOMA]: *locality,* 6.25 miles north of Sears Point along Sonoma Creek (lat. 38°14'30" N, long. 122°26'55" W). Named on Mare Island (1916) 15' quadrangle.

Enchanted Hills [NAPA]: *settlement,* 5.25 miles south of Rutherford (lat. 38°23' N, long. 122°25'30" W; sec. 8, 9, T 6 N, R 5 W). Named on Rutherford (1951) 7.5' quadrangle.

English Hill [SONOMA]: *ridge,* south-south-east- to east-trending, 1.5 miles long, 2.5 miles north-northwest of Bloomfield (lat. 38°20'50" N, long. 122°51'55" W). Named on Two Rock (1954) 7.5' quadrangle.

Entre Napa [NAPA]: *land grant,* south of down-town Napa. Named on Napa (1951) 7.5' quadrangle. Nicolas Higuera received the land in

1836; between 1858 and 1897, eight people received patents for parcels ranging form 307 to 2558 acres (Perez, p. 65-66).

Ephlin Hill [NAPA]: *peak,* 3.25 miles south of Mount Vaca (lat. 38° 21'10" N, long. 122°06'05" W). Altitude 984 feet. Named on Fairfield North (1951) 7.5' quadrangle.

Erabais Creek: see **Ebabias Creek** [SONOMA].

Estero Americano [SONOMA]: *water feature,* estuary that forms part of Marin-Sonoma county line; heads at the mouth of Americano Creek and extends to Bodega Bay [SONOMA] (1) 6.25 miles west-northwest of Tomales (lat. 38°17'45" N, long. 123°00'05" W). Named on Valley Ford (1954) 7.5' quadrangle. United States Board on Geographic Names (1943, p. 9) rejected the name "Estero de San Antonio" for the feature.

Estero Americano [SONOMA]: *land grant,* around Bodega and north of Estero Americano. Named on Camp Meeker (1954) and Valley Ford (1954) 7.5' quadrangles. Edward M. McIntosh received 2 leagues in 1839; Jasper O'Farrell claimed 8849 acres patented in 1858 (Cowan, p. 35).

Estero Americano: see **Americano Creek** [SONOMA]

Estero Americano Creek: see **Americano Creek** [SONOMA].

Estero de las Mercedes: see **Petaluma River** [SONOMA].

Estero de Nuestra Señora de la Merced: see **Petaluma River** [SONOMA].

Estero de Petaluma: see **Petaluma River** [SONOMA].

Estero de San Antonio: see **Estero Americano** [SONOMA]

Eticuera Creek [NAPA]: *stream,* formed by the confluence of Knoxville Creek and Foley Creek, flows 12.5 miles to Lake Berryessa 4.5 miles northeast of Walter Springs (lat. 38°41'40" N, long. 122°17'15" W; sec. 22, T 10 N, R 4 W). Named on Knoxville (1958) and Walter Springs (1959) 7.5' quadrangles. United States Board on Geographic Names (1962a, p. 11) rejected the forms "Eticura Creek" and "Eticurea Creek" for the name.

Eticura Creek: see **Eticuera Creek** [NAPA].

Eticurea Creek: see **Eticuera Creek** [NAPA].

Etna Springs: see **Aetna Springs** [NAPA].

Evans Ridge [SONOMA]: *ridge,* west-north-west-trending, 1.25 miles long, 2.5 miles east-northeast of Annapolis (lat. 38°44'05" N, long. 123°19'40" W). Named on Annapolis (1977) 7.5' quadrangle.

Excelsior: see **Healdsburg** [SONOMA].

— F —

Fagan Creek [NAPA]: *stream,* flows 4.5 miles to lowlands 2 miles north-northwest of Napa Junction (lat. 38°12'50" N, long. 122° 16' W;

sec. 11, T 4 N, R 4 W). Named on Cordelia (1951) and Cuttings Wharf (1949) 7.5' quadrangles.

Fagan Slough [NAPA]: *water feature,* joins Napa River 3.5 miles west-northwest of Napa Junction (lat. 38°12'45" N, long. 122°18'20" W). Named on Cuttings Wharf (1949) 7.5' quadrangle.

Fairmont Hot Springs: see **Hoods Hot Springs**, under **Dry Creek** [SONOMA].

Fairville [SONOMA]: *locality,* 2 miles north of Sears Point along Northwestern Pacific Railroad (lat. 38°10'40" N, long. 122°26'40" W). Named on Sears Point (1951) 7.5' quadrangle.

Fall Creek [SONOMA]:
(1) *stream,* flows 2.5 miles to Dry Creek 4 miles west of Geyserville (lat. 38°42'25" N, long. 123°58'45" W). Named on Geyserville (1955) and Warm Springs Dam (1978) 7.5' quadrangles.
(2) *stream,* flows 1.5 miles to Warm Springs Creek nearly 4 miles southwest of Skaggs Springs (lat. 38°39'20" N, long. 123°04'35" W; at E line sec. 4, T 9 N, R 11 W). Named on Warm Springs Dam (1978) 7.5' quadrangle.

False Bay [SONOMA]: *water feature,* wide place in Petaluma River 8 miles southeast of downtown Petaluma (lat. 38°09'40" N, long. 122°31'35" W). Named on Petaluma (1914) 15' quadrangle. Water no longer covers the place.

Fawn Lake [NAPA]: *lake,* 500 feet long, 6 miles north of Saint Helena (lat. 38°35'35" N, long. 122°28'20" W; near N line sec. 36, T 9 N, R 6 W); the lake is south of Doe Lake. Named on Saint Helena (1960) 7.5' quadrangle.

Fay Creek [SONOMA]: *stream,* flows 4 miles to Salmon Creek (1) 3 miles northeast of the village of Bodega Bay (lat. 38°21'25" N, long. 123°00' W). Named on Bodega Head (1972), Camp Meeker (1954), and Valley Ford (1954) 7.5' quadrangles.

Felder Creek [SONOMA]: *stream,* flows nearly 4 miles to join Carriger Creek and form Fowler Creek 2 miles south-southwest of Sonoma (lat. 38°16'05" N, long. 122°28'30" W). Named on Glen Ellen (1954) and Sonoma (1951) 7.5' quadrangles.

Felice [SONOMA]: *locality,* 2 miles south-southeast of Kenwood along Southern Pacific Railroad (lat. 38°23'30" N, long. 122°31'55" W). Named on Santa Rosa (1916) 15' quadrangle.

Felta Creek [SONOMA]: *stream,* flows 3.5 miles to Mill Creek (1) 2.5 miles south-south-west of Healdsburg (lat. 38°34'50" N, long. 122°52'55" W). Named on Guerneville (1955) 7.5' quadrangle.

Fern Lake [SONOMA]: *lake,* 1650 feet long, 1.25 miles south-southwest of Glen Ellen (lat. 38°20'40" N, long. 122°31'55" W). Named on Glen Ellen (1954) 7.5' quadrangle.

Fern Spring [NAPA]: *spring,* 6 miles north-

northwest of Berryessa Peak (lat. 38°44'15" N, long. 122°14'40" W; sec. 1, T 10 N, R 4 W). Named on Brooks (1959) 7.5' quadrangle.

Fern Spring [SONOMA]: *spring,* 5 miles south of Guerneville (lat. 38°25'50" N, long. 123°00'45" W). Named on Duncans Mills (1979) 7.5' quadrangle.

Fetters Hot Springs [SONOMA]: *town,* 2.25 miles northwest of Sonoma in Valley of the Moon (lat. 38°19'05" N, long. 122°29'05" W). Named on Sonoma (1951) 7.5' quadrangle. Postal authorities established Fetters Springs post office in 1913, changed the name to Fetters Hot Springs in 1939, and discontinued it in 1955; the name is for George Fetters, who discovered hot water at the site (Salley, p. 74). The first resort at the place was started in 1909 and was known as Eleda Hot Springs (Waring, p. 114).

Fetters Springs: see **Fetters Hot Springs** [SONOMA].

Fiege Reservoir [NAPA]: *intermittent lake,* 150 feet long, 1.25 miles west of Calistoga (lat. 38°34'30" N, long. 122°36'10" W; sec. 2, T 8 N, R 7 W). Named on Calistoga (1958) 7.5' quadrangle.

Fife Creek [SONOMA]: *stream,* flows 5 miles to Russian River at Guerneville (lat. 38°30' N, long. 123°00' W). Named on Cazadero (1978) and Guerneville (1955) 7.5' quadrangles.

Finley Creek [SONOMA]: *stream,* flows 3.25 miles to Salmon Creek (1) 2.5 miles northeast of the village of Bodega Bay (lat. 38°21'35" N, long. 123°01'05" W). Named on Bodega Head (1972) and Duncans Mills (1979) 7.5' quadrangles.

Fir Canyon [NAPA]: *canyon,* drained by a stream that flows 2.5 miles to Sage Canyon 6.5 miles north-northeast of Yountville (lat. 38°29'10" N, long. 122°17'45" W; sec. 3, T 7 N, R 4 W). Named on Yountville (1951) 7.5' quadrangle. Called Fur Canyon on Sonoma (1942) 15' quadrangle.

Fisherman Bay [SONOMA]: *embayment,* 0.25 mile south-southwest of the village of Stewarts Point along the coast (lat. 38°38'50" N, long. 123°24' W). Named on Stewarts Point (1978) 7.5' quadrangle. Postal authorities established Fisherman's Bay post office in 1863, moved it 3 miles north in 1888, and discontinued it in 1902 (Salley, p. 75). They established Monti post office 9 miles northeast of Fisherman's Bay post office in 1884 and discontinued it in 1888 (Salley, p. 145).

Fisherman's Bay: see **Fisherman Bay** [SONOMA].

Fisher Point [SONOMA]: *ridge,* northwest-trending, less than 0.5 mile long, 1.5 miles northwest of Mount Saint Helena (lat. 38°40'50" N, long. 122°39'05" W). Named on Mount Saint Helena (1959) 7.5' quadrangle.

Fisk: see **Plantation** [SONOMA].

Fisk Mill Cove [SONOMA]: *embayment,* 2.25 miles west of Plantation along the coast (lat. 38°35'50" N, long. 123°20'55" W). Named on Plantation (1977) 7.5' quadrangle.

Fisk's Mill: see **Plantation** [SONOMA].

Fitch Mountain [SONOMA]: *peak,* 1.5 miles east of Healdsburg (lat. 38°37'05" N, long. 122°50'25" W). Altitude 991 feet. Named on Healdsburg (1955) 7.5' quadrangle. The name commemorates Captain Henry D. Fitch, owner of Sotoyome grant (Davis, W.H., p. 24).

Five Creek [SONOMA]: *water feature,* artificial watercourse in lowlands 2.5 miles north of Cotati (lat. 38°21'50" N, long. 122°41'45" W). Named on Cotati (1954) 7.5' quadrangle.

Flat Ridge [SONOMA]: *ridge,* east-southeast-trending, 1.25 miles long, 10 miles northeast of the village of Stewarts Point (lat. 38°46'15" N, long. 123°18' W). Named on Ornbaun Valley (1960) 15' quadrangle.

Flat Ridge Creek [SONOMA]: *stream,* flows 4.5 miles to Buckeye Creek (2) 8.5 miles northeast of the village of Stewarts Point (lat. 38°15'15" N, long. 123°18'25" W; sec. 33, T 11 N, R 13 W); the stream is south of Flat Ridge. Named on Ornbaun Valley (1960) 15' quadrangle. On Ornbaun (1944) 15' quadrangle, the name has the form "Flatridge Creek."

Flat Top [NAPA]: *peak,* 4.5 miles east-northeast of Calistoga on Rattlesnake Ridge (lat. 38°36'20" N, long. 122°30'05" W; at NW cor. sec. 26, T 9 N, R 6 W). Named on Calistoga (1958) 7.5' quadrangle.

Florence Creek: see **Anna Belcher Creek** [SONOMA].

Fly Bay [NAPA]: *marsh,* 4.25 miles west-northwest of Napa Junction (lat. 38°12'25" N, long. 122°19'20" W; sec. 8, T 4 N, R 4 W). Named on Cuttings Wharf (1949) 7.5' quadrangle.

Foley Creek [NAPA]: *stream,* flows 3.5 miles to join Knoxville Creek and form Eticuera Creek 2.25 miles southeast of Knoxville (lat. 38°47'55" N, long. 122°18'45" W; sec. 16, T 11 N, R 4 W). Named on Knoxville (1958) 7.5' quadrangle.

Foote Creek [SONOMA]: *stream,* flows 3 miles to Redwood Creek (1) 4.25 miles west-southwest of Mount Saint Helena in Knights Valley (lat. 38°38'20" N, long. 122°42' W). Named on Mount Saint Helena (1959) 7.5' quadrangle.

Forest Hills [SONOMA]: *settlement,* 4 miles east of Guerneville along Russian River (lat. 38°30'30" N, long. 122°55'30" W; sec. 25, T 8 N, R 10 W). Named on Guerneville (1955) 7.5' quadrangle.

Forestville [SONOMA]: *town,* 5.5 miles north-northeast of Occidental (lat. 38°28'25" N, long. 122°53'20" W). Named on Camp Meeker (1954) 7.5' quadrangle. Postal authorities established Forestville post office in 1872 (Frickstad, p. 195). The name commemorates A.J. Forrest, an early settler (Hansen and Miller, p. 48).

Forgotten Valley [SONOMA]: *canyon,* 0.5 mile long, 1.5 miles northwest of Guerneville (lat. 38°31'10" N, long. 123°00'45" W). Named on Cazadero (1978) 7.5' quadrangle. The name was given about 1925 (Clar, p. 14-15).

Fort Ross [SONOMA]: *locality,* 29 miles west of Santa Rosa near the coast (lat. 38°30'50" N, long. 123°14'35" W). Named on Fort Ross (1978) 7.5' quadrangle. Ivan A. Kuskov began construction of the principal Russian establishment in California at the site in 1812; he called the place Slavyansk or Ross—the name "Ross" is from an old form of the word *Rossiia,* which means "Russia" (Schwartz, p. 37).

Fort Ross Cove [SONOMA]: *embayment,* 0.25 mile southwest of Fort Ross along the coast (lat. 38°30'40" N, long. 123°14'45" W). Named on Fort Ross (1978) 7.5' quadrangle.

Fort Ross Creek [SONOMA]: *stream,* flows 2.25 miles to the sea 700 feet south of Fort Ross (lat. 38°30'40" N, long. 123°14'35" W). Named on Fort Ross (1978) 7.5' quadrangle.

Fort Ross Reef [SONOMA]: *shoal* and *rocks,* 1 mile south-southeast of Fort Ross (lat. 38°30'05" N, long. 123°14' W). Named on Fort Ross (1978) 7.5' quadrangle.

Four Corners [NAPA]: *locality,* 3.5 miles north of Saint Helena (lat. 38°33'10" N, long. 122°27'20" W; near S line sec. 7, T 8 N, R 5 W). Named on Saint Helena (1960) 7.5' quadrangle.

Four Corners [SONOMA]: *locality,* 1 mile south of Sonoma (lat. 38° 16'35" N, long. 122°27'35" W). Named on Sonoma (1951) 7.5' quadrangle.

Fowler Creek [SONOMA]: *stream,* formed by the confluence of Carriger Creek and Felder Creek, flows 2.5 miles to Sonoma Creek 6.25 miles north of Sears Point (lat. 38°14'30" N, long. 122° 27' W). Named on Sears Point (1951) and Sonoma (1951) 7.5' quadrangles.

Fox Canyon [SONOMA]: *canyon,* drained by a stream that flows 1 mile to Felta Creek 3.5 miles southwest of Healdsburg (lat. 38°34'30" N, long. 122°53'55" W). Named on Guerneville (1955) 7.5' quadrangle.

Fox Mountain [SONOMA]: *peak,* 3 miles north-northeast of Cazadero (lat. 38°34'15" N, long. 123°03'50" W; sec. 3, T 8 N, R 11 W). Named on Cazadero (1978) 7.5' quadrangle.

Franchini Creek [SONOMA]: *stream,* flows 2 miles to Buckeye Creek (2) 1.5 miles north of Annapolis (lat. 38°44'30" N, long. 123°22'05" W; sec. 1, T 10 N, R 14 W). Named on Ornbaun Valley (1960) 15' quadrangle, and on Annapolis (1977) 7.5' quadrangle.

Franklin Town: see **Santa Rosa** [SONOMA].

Franz Creek [SONOMA]: *stream,* flows about 10 miles to Maacama Creek 5.25 miles east of Healdsburg (lat. 38°36'45" N, long. 122° 46'15" W); the stream goes through Franz Valley. Named on Healdsburg (1955) and Mark West Springs (1958) 7.5' quadrangles.

Franz Valley [SONOMA]: *valley,* 3.5 miles northeast of Mark West Springs (lat. 38°35' N, long. 122°40'15" W); the valley is along Franz Creek. Named on Mark West Springs (1958) 7.5' quadrangle. The name commemorates Captain Frederick W. Franz, who acquired land in the valley in 1875 (Archuleta, p. 33).

Fraser: see **Camp Thayer** [SONOMA].

Frasier Creek [SONOMA]: *stream,* heads just inside Mendocino County and flows nearly 3 miles to Big Sulphur Creek 5.5 miles northeast of Asti (lat. 38°49'40" N, long. 122°54'40" W; sec. 6, T 11 N, R 9 W). Named on Asti (1959) 7.5' quadrangle.

Frazier Gulch [SONOMA]: *canyon,* drained by a stream that flows 0.5 mile to Austin Creek 4 miles east-northeast of Jenner (lat. 38° 28'55" N, long. 123°03'20" W). Named on Duncans Mills (1979) 7.5' quadrangle.

Fredericks [SONOMA]: *locality,* 2.5 miles southeast of Sebastopol along Petaluma and Santa Rosa Railroad (lat. 38°22'25" N, long. 122°47'45" W). Named on Sebastopol (1942) 15' quadrangle.

Freestone [SONOMA]: *village,* nearly 4 miles north of Valley Ford (lat. 38°22'20" N, long. 122°54'55" W; near S line sec. 12, T 6 N, R 10 W). Named on Valley Ford (1954) 7.5' quadrangle. Postal authorities established Analy post office in 1860, discontinued it in 1861, reestablished it in 1866, changed the name to Freestone in 1870, and discontinued it in 1951 (Frickstad, p. 194, 195). Jasper O'Farrell, owner of Estero Americano grant, gave the name "Analy Valley" to the place that the village is situated—the misspelled name is from Annaly, Ireland, the O'Farrell family home (Gudde, 1949, p. 11). The name "Freestone" is from volcanic rock used to build fireplaces and chimneys (Goodyear, 1890b, p. 678).

Freezeout Creek [SONOMA]: *stream,* flows 2.5 miles to Russian River 3.5 miles east of Jenner (lat. 38°27' N, long. 123°03' W). Named on Duncans Mills (1979) 7.5' quadrangle.

Freezeout Flat [SONOMA]: *area,* nearly 4 miles east of Jenner (lat. 38°27' N, long. 123°02'50" W); place is near the mouth of Freezeout Creek. Named on Duncans Mills (1979) 7.5' quadrangle.

Frog Lake [SONOMA]: *lake,* 300 feet long, 5 miles east-northeast of Mark West Springs (lat. 38°34'20" N, long. 122°38' W; sec. 4, T 8 N, R 7 W). Named on Mark West Springs (1958) 7.5' quadrangle.

Fuller Creek [SONOMA]: *stream,* formed by the confluence of North Fork and South Fork, flows 3.25 miles to Wheatfield Fork Gualala River 4 miles south-southeast of Annapolis (lat. 38°40'15" N, long. 123°20'05" W; sec. 32, T 10 N, R 13 W). Named on Annapolis (1977) 7.5' quadrangle. North Fork is 2.5

miles long and South Fork is 4.25 miles long; both forks are named on Annapolis (1977) 7.5' quadrangle.

Fuller Mountain [SONOMA]: *ridge,* west-northwest-trending, 1.25 miles long, 3.5 miles east-southeast of Annapolis (lat. 38°42' N, long. 123°18'15" W). Named on Annapolis (1977) 7.5' quadrangle.

Fulton [SONOMA]: *village,* 7 miles north-northeast of Sebastopol (lat. 38°29'45" N, long. 122°46'10" W). Named on Sebastopol (1954) 7.5' quadrangle. Postal authorities established Fulton post office in 1871, discontinued it in 1872, reestablished it in 1873, and discontinued it briefly in 1874; the name commemorates Thomas Fulton and James Fulton, who founded the community (Salley, p. 81-82). California Mining Bureau's (1909) map shows a place called Mt. Olivet located 3 miles west of Fulton along the railroad. Postal authorities established Mount Olivet post office in 1890 and discontinued it in 1909 (Frickstad, p. 197). The same map shows a place called Burke located 3 miles east of Fulton along a stage line. Postal authorities established Altruria post office in 1895, changed the name to Burke in 1903; and discontinued it in 1925—founders of the place, who were altruists, coined the name "Altruria"; the name "Burke" was for William P. Burke, first postmaster (Salley, p. 6, 29).

Fur Canyon: see **Fir Canyon** [NAPA].

Furlong Gulch [SONOMA]: *canyon,* drained by stream that flows 2 miles to the sea nearly 3 miles south-southeast of Jenner (lat. 38°24'50" N, long. 123°06'05" W). Named on Duncans Mills (1979) 7.5' quadrangle.

— G —

Gabes Rock [SONOMA]: *peak,* 1 mile west of Guerneville (lat. 38° 30'20" N, long. 123°01' W; near SW cor. sec. 30, T 8 N, R 10 W). Altitude 942 feet. Named on Cazadero (1978) 7.5' quadrangle. The name of this isolated mass of rock commemorates George Gabriel (Clar, p. 48).

Gaffney Point [SONOMA]: *promontory,* 1.5 miles south-southwest of the village of Bodega Bay on the west side of Bodega Harbor (lat. 38°18'50" N, long. 123°03'20" W). Named on Bodega Head (1972) 7.5' quadrangle.

Galloway Creek [SONOMA]: *stream,* heads in Mendocino County and flows 8.5 miles to Dry Creek 8 miles west of Cloverdale (lat. 38°47'50" N, long. 123°09'50" W; sec. 14, T 11 N, R 12 W). Named on Hopland (1960) and Ornbaun Valley (1960) 15' quadrangles.

Garden: see **Cherry** [SONOMA].

Garnett Creek [NAPA]: *stream,* flows 5 miles to Napa River less than 1 mile west-north-west of Calistoga (lat. 38°35'05" N, long.

122°35'30" W). Named on Calistoga (1958) and Detert Reservoir (1958) 7.5' quadrangles.

Gates Canyon [SONOMA]: *canyon,* 1 mile long, along Humbug Creek 4.5 miles east of Mark West Springs (lat. 38°32'30" N, long. 122°38' W). Named on Mark West Springs (1958) 7.5' quadrangle. California Division of Forestry's (1945) map shows a settlement called Sunbeam Acres situated along Humbug Creek near the mouth of Gates Canyon.

George Mountain: see **Mount George** [NAPA].

George Young Creek [SONOMA]: *stream,* flows 2.5 miles to Sausal Creek 7.25 miles northeast of Healdsburg (lat. 38°41'55" N, long. 122°47'20" W; sec. 19, T 10 N, R 8 W). Named on Jimtown (1955) 7.5' quadrangle.

German [SONOMA]: *land grant,* along the coast between the mouth of Gualala River and Salt Point. Named on Ornbaun Valley (1960) 15' quadrangle, and on Annapolis (1977), Gualala (1960), Plantation (1977), and Stewarts Point (1978) 7.5' quadrangles. Ernest Rufus received 5 leagues in 1846; Charles Meyer and others claimed 17,580 acres patented in 1872 (Cowan, p. 37). Developers purchased the grant in 1962 and started the community called Sea Ranch (Miller, J.T., p. 50).

Gerstle Cove [SONOMA]: *embayment,* 2 miles south-southwest of Plantation along the coast (lat. 38°33'50" N, long. 123°19'35" W). Named on Plantation (1977) 7.5' quadrangle.

Geyser Canyon [SONOMA]: *canyon,* drained by a stream that flows 1 mile to Big Sulphur Creek 3 miles northeast of Geyser Peak (lat. 38°48' N, long. 122°48'25" W; sec. 13, T 11 N, R 9 W); the canyon is near The Geysers. Named on The Geysers (1959) 7.5' quadrangle. Anderson (p. 152) called the feature Devil's Cañon.

Geyser Hotel: see **Geysers Resort** [SONOMA].

Geyser Peak [SONOMA]: *peak,* 7 miles east of Asti (lat. 38°45'50" N, long. 122°50'40" W). Altitude 3457 feet. Named on The Geysers (1959) 7.5' quadrangle. Called Sulphur Peak on Kelseyville (1944) 15' quadrangle, but United States Board on Geographic Names (1962b, p. 17) rejected this name for the feature.

Geyser Rock [SONOMA]: *relief feature,* 5.5 miles northeast of Geyser Peak on Sonoma-Lake county line (lat. 38°48'50" N, long. 122°45'55" W; at S line sec. 8, T 11 N, R 8 W). Named on The Geysers (1959) 7.5' quadrangle.

Geysers: see **The Geysers** [SONOMA]; **The Geysers**, under **Geysers Resort** [SONOMA].

Geyser Springs: see **Geyserville** [SONOMA].

Geysers Resort [SONOMA]: *locality,* 3 miles northeast of Geyser Peak (lat. 38°47'55" N, long. 122°48'25" W; sec. 13, T 11 N, R 9 W); the place is near The Geysers. Named on The Geysers (1959) 7.5' quadrangle. Called Geyser Hotel on Kelseyville (1921) 15' quadrangle. The resort began as early as 1852 (Allen and Day, p. 11). Postal authorities established The Geysers post office in 1893, discontinued it for a time in 1905, and discontinued it finally in 1935 (Frickstad, p. 198).

Geysers Spa: see **Lytton Springs**, under **Lytton** [SONOMA].

Geyserville [SONOMA]: *town,* nearly 7 miles north-northwest of Healdsburg near Russian River (lat. 38°42'25" N, long. 122°54'10" W). Named on Geyserville (1955) 7.5' quadrangle. Postal authorities established Clairville post office in 1858, changed the name to Guyserville in 1887, and to Geyserville in 1888 (Salley, p. 44, 84). Elisha Ely founded the community in 1851; the name "Clairville" was for John Clar, and the name "Geyserville" is from nearby thermal features (Gudde, 1949, p. 126). Postal authorities established Geyser Springs post office at a resort near present Geyserville in 1874 and discontinued it in 1887 (Salley, p. 84).

Gibson Flat [NAPA]: *area,* 3.5 miles northeast of Walter Springs (lat. 38°41'10" N, long. 122°18'35" W; sec. 28, T 10 N, R 4 W). Named on Walter Springs (1959) 7.5' quadrangle.

Gibson Island: see **Bodega Rock** [SONOMA].

Gibson Ridge [SONOMA]: *ridge,* southwest- to west-trending, 1.5 miles long, 4.25 miles west-northwest of Big Mountain (lat. 38°43'45" N, long. 123°13'15" W). Named on Tombs Creek (1978) 7.5' quadrangle.

Gilder Ridge [SONOMA]: *ridge,* east- to southeast-trending, 2.25 miles long, 4.5 miles northeast of Guerneville (lat. 38°32'10" N, long. 122°55'30" W). Named on Guerneville (1955) 7.5' quadrangle.

Gill Creek [SONOMA]: *stream,* flows 3 miles to Russian River 1.5 miles north-northwest of Geyserville (lat. 38°43'35" N, long. 122°55'05" W). Named on Asti (1959) and Geyserville (1955) 7.5' quadrangles.

Gilliam Creek [SONOMA]: *stream,* flows 4 miles to East Austin Creek 2.5 miles northeast of Cazadero (lat. 38°33'35" N, long. 123°03'10" W; sec. 2, T 8 N, R 11 W); the stream is north of Gilliam Ridge. Named on Cazadero (1978) 7.5' quadrangle. Called East Br. Austin Cr. on Healdsburg (1940) 15' quadrangle, and called Gilman Creek on Cazadero (1943) 7.5' quadrangle.

Gilliam Ridge [SONOMA]: *ridge,* west-trending, 1 mile long, 4.5 miles east-northeast of Cazadero (lat. 38°33'45" N, long. 123°00'35" W); the ridge is south of Gilliam Creek. Named on Cazadero (1978) 7.5' quadrangle. Called Gilman Ridge on Cazadero (1943) 7.5' quadrangle.

Gilman Creek: see **Gilliam Creek** [SONOMA].

Gilman Ridge: see **Gilliam Ridge** [SONOMA].

Gird Creek [SONOMA]: *stream,* flows 3.5 miles to Russian River 4.5 miles north-northeast of Healdsburg (lat. 38°40'35" N, long.

122°50'45" W). Named on Jimtown (1955) 7.5' quadrangle.

Girdle: see **The Girdle** [SONOMA].

Glass Mountain [NAPA]: *ridge,* west-northwest-trending, less than 1 mile long, 2 miles north-northwest of Saint Helena (lat. 38°32' N, long. 122°29' W). Named on Saint Helena (1960) 7.5' quadrangle.

Gleason Beach [SONOMA]: *beach,* 4.5 miles south-southeast of Jenner along the coast (lat. 38°23'20" N, long. 123°05' W). Named on Duncans Mills (1979) 7.5' quadrangle.

Gleason Gulch: see **Scotty Creek** [SONOMA].

Glen Ellen [SONOMA]: *town,* 11.5 miles east-southeast of Santa Rosa in Valley of the Moon (lat. 38°21'50" N, long. 122°31'25" W). Named on Glen Ellen (1954) 7.5' quadrangle. Postal authorities established Glen Ellen post office in 1871; Colonel J.B. Armstrong named the place for his wife (Salley, p. 86). California Mining Bureau's (1917) map shows a place called Triniti located about 5 miles east-northeast of Glen Ellen near Sonoma-Napa county line. Postal authorities established Triniti post office in 1907 and discontinued it in 1935 (Frickstad, p. 198).

Goat Rock [SONOMA]:

(1) *peak,* 4 miles north-northwest of Cazadero (lat. 38°34'55" N, long. 123°07'15" W; sec. 31, T 9 N, R 11 W). Altitude 874 feet. Named on Cazadero (1978) 7.5' quadrangle.

(2) *peak,* 8 miles north-northeast of Healdsburg (lat. 38°42'55" N, long. 123°47'35" W; sec. 18, T 10 N, R 8 W). Altitude 870 feet. Named on Jimtown (1955) 7.5' quadrangle.

(3) *promontory,* less than 1 mile southwest of Jenner along the coast (lat. 38°26'25" N, long. 123°07'35" W). Named on Arched Rock (1977) 7.5' quadrangle.

Goat Rock Beach [SONOMA]: *beach,* 0.5 mile west-southwest of Jenner along the coast south of the mouth of Russian River (lat. 38°26'50" N, long. 123°07'35" W); the beach is north of Goat Rock (3). Named on Arched Rock (1977) 7.5' quadrangle.

Goat Roost Rock [SONOMA]: *peak,* 1.25 miles north-northwest of Mount Saint Helena (lat. 38°41' N, long. 122°38'35" W; sec. 28, T 10 N, R 7 W). Altitude 3263 feet. Named on Mount Saint Helena (1959) 7.5' quadrangle.

Good Luck Point [NAPA]: *promontory,* 3 miles west of Napa Junction along Napa River (lat. 38°11' N, long. 122°18'20" W; sec. 21, T 4 N, R 4 W). Named on Cuttings Wharf (1949) 7.5' quadrangle.

Goose Lake [SONOMA]: *intermittent lake,* 300 feet long, 4.25 miles north-northwest of Sears Point (lat. 38°12'20" N, long. 122°28'50" W). Named on Sears Point (1951) 7.5' quadrangle.

Gordon: see **John Gordon Creek** [SONOMA].

Gordon Valley [NAPA]: *valley,* along Suisun Creek above a point nearly 5 miles south-southwest of Mount Vaca (lat. 38°20'05" N, long. 122°07'35" W). Named on Capell Valley (1951), Fairfield North (1951), and Mount George (1951) 7.5' quadrangles.

Gordon Valley Creek [NAPA]: *stream,* heads in Napa County and flows 6.5 miles to Ledgewood Creek 4.5 miles west-northwest of Fairfield in Solano County (lat. 38°17'05" N, long. 122°06'50" W). Named on Fairfield North (1951) 7.5' quadrangle.

Gosling Canyon [NAPA]: *canyon,* drained by a stream that flows 6 miles to Lake Berryessa 7 miles south of Berryessa Peak (lat. 38° 33'50" N, long. 122°10'55" W). Named on Lake Berryessa (1959) 7.5' quadrangle.

Gossage Creek [SONOMA]: *stream,* flows 3.5 miles to lowlands 2 miles northwest of Cotati (lat. 38°20'30" N, long. 122°44' W). Named on Cotati (1954) and Two Rock (1954) 7.5' quadrangles.

Government Spring [SONOMA]: *spring,* 2.25 miles northwest of Cazadero (lat. 38°33'05" N, long. 123°07' W; sec. 7, T 8 N, R 11 W). Named on Cazadero (1978) 7.5' quadrangle.

Government Trail Canyon [NAPA]: *canyon,* 1.25 miles long, 3 miles south-southeast of Mount Vaca (lat. 38°21'35" N, long. 122° 05'30" W). Named on Fairfield North (1951) 7.5' quadrangle.

Graham Creek [SONOMA]: *stream,* flows 2.5 miles to Sonoma Creek 1 mile northwest of Glen Ellen (lat. 38°22'10" N, long. 122° 32'20" W). Named on Glen Ellen (1954) 7.5' quadrangle.

Grandville: see **Mesa Grande** [SONOMA].

Granite Lake [NAPA]: *lake,* 400 feet long, 6 miles north of Saint Helena (lat. 38°35'40" N, long. 122°28'10" W; near SE cor. sec. 25, T 9 N, R 6 W). Named on Saint Helena (1960) 7.5' quadrangle.

Grant [SONOMA]: *locality,* 2 miles southeast of Healdsburg along Northwestern Pacific Railroad (lat. 38°35'25" N, long. 122°50'50" W). Named on Healdsburg (1955) 7.5' quadrangle.

Grape Creek [SONOMA]: *stream,* flows nearly 3 miles to Dry Creek 3.5 miles south-southwest of Geyserville (lat. 38°39'35" N, long. 122°56'05" W). Named on Geyserville (1955) 7.5' quadrangle.

Grapevine Creek [SONOMA]: *stream,* flows 1.25 miles to Sausal Creek 8 miles northnortheast of Healdsburg (lat. 38°43'15" N, long. 122°47'45" W; at NW cor. sec. 18, T 10 N, R 8 W). Named on Jimtown (1955) 7.5' quadrangle.

Grasshopper Creek [SONOMA]:

(1) *stream,* flows 5 miles to Buckeye Creek (2) 1.5 miles north of Annapolis (lat. 38°44'30" N, long. 123°22'05" W; sec. 1, T 10 N, R 14 W). Named on Annapolis (1977) 7.5' quadrangle.

(2) *stream,* flows nearly 2 miles to Pepperwood Creek 8.5 miles north-northeast of Fort Ross (lat. 38°37'20" N, long. 123°09'45" W; near E line sec. 15, T 9 N, R 12 W). Named on Tombs Creek (1978) 7.5' quadrangle.

Grass Valley [SONOMA]: *area,* 5 miles west of Geyserville (lat. 38° 41'35" N, long. 122°59'45" W; sec. 20, 29, T 10 N, R 10 W). Named on Geyserville (1955) 7.5' quadrangle.

Grassy Hill [NAPA]: *peak,* nearly 4 miles northeast of Calistoga (lat. 38°37' N, long. 122°31'40" W; sec. 21, T 9 N, R 6 W). Named on Calistoga (1958) 7.5' quadrangle.

Graton [SONOMA]: *town,* 3.25 miles northwest of Sebastopol (lat. 38°26'05" N, long. 122°52' W). Named on Sebastopol (1954) 7.5' quadrangle. Postal authorities established Graton post office in 1906 (Frickstad, p. 195). James H. Gray and J.H. Brush founded the town in 1904 and coined the name from letters in the word "Graytown" (Gudde, 1949, p. 134).

Gravelly Lake [SONOMA]: *lake,* 300 feet long, 5 miles north-northwest of Sears Point (lat. 38°12'50" N, long. 122°29'30" W). Named on Sears Point (1951) 7.5' quadrangle.

Gravelly Spring [SONOMA]: *spring,* 5.25 miles north-northwest of Cazadero (lat. 38°36'10" N, long. 123°07'30" W; near NW cor. sec. 30, T 9 N, R 11 W). Named on Cazadero (1978) 7.5' quadrangle.

Gravelly Springs Creek [SONOMA]: *stream,* flows less than 0.5 mile to Austin Creek 8.5 miles northeast of Fort Ross (lat. 38° 36' N, long. 123°07'45" W; near N line sec. 25, T 9 N, R 12 W); the stream heads at Gravelly Spring. Named on Fort Ross (1978) 7.5' quadrangle.

Gravenstein [SONOMA]: *locality,* 1 mile east of Sebastopol along Petaluma and Santa Rosa Railroad (lat. 38°24'20" N, long. 122°48'25" W). Named on Sebastopol (1954) 7.5' quadrangle.

Gray Creek [SONOMA]: *stream,* flows 5.5 miles to East Austin Creek 4.25 miles northnortheast of Cazadero (lat. 38°35'20" N, long. 123°03'40" W; at N line sec. 34, T 9 N, R 11 W). Named on Cazadero (1978) 7.5' quadrangle. Called Little Austin Creek on Guerneville (1955) 7.5' quadrangle, but United States Board on Geographic Names (1978, p. 3) rejected this name, and noted that the name "Gray Creek" is for Isaac Gray, an early settler.

Graystone [SONOMA]: *locality,* 1.25 miles southwest of Guerneville along Northwestern Pacific Railroad near Russian River (lat. 38° 29'20" N, long. 123°01'05" W). Named on Duncans Mills (1921) 15' quadrangle.

Greeg Mountain [NAPA]: *ridge,* northwesttrending, 2.5 miles long, 8 miles east of Saint Helena (lat. 38°31' N, long. 122°19'40" W). Named on Chiles Valley (1958) 7.5' quadrangle.

Green Canyon [NAPA]: *canyon,* drained by a stream that flows 3.5 miles to Lake Berryessa 5.5 miles east-northeast of Walter Springs (lat. 38°40'20" N, long. 122°15'20" W). Named on Brooks (1959) and Walter Springs (1959) 7.5' quadrangles.

Green Creek [SONOMA]: *stream,* flows 0.5

mile to Coleman Valley Creek 3.25 miles north-northeast of the village of Bodega Bay (lat. 38°22'20" N, long. 123°00'50" W). Named on Duncans Mills (1979) 7.5' quadrangle.

Green Island [NAPA]: *hill,* 3 miles west-northwest of Napa Junction (lat. 38°12'10" N, long. 122°18'10" W; on S line sec. 9, T 4 N, R 4 W). Named on Cuttings Wharf (1949, photorevised 1968) 7.5' quadrangle, which shows the hill surrounded by salt evaporators. Mare Island (1916) 15' quadrangle shows the hill surrounded by marsh.

Green Valley Creek [SONOMA]: *stream,* flows 10.5 miles to Russian River 4.5 miles east of Guerneville (lat. 38°30'15" N, long. 122°54'30" W; near SE cor. sec. 25, T 8 N, R 10 W). Named on Camp Meeker (1954) 7.5' quadrangle.

Greenwood [SONOMA]: *locality,* 1.5 miles southwest of Sears Point along Northwestern Pacific Railroad (lat. 38°08' N, long. 122°27'40" W). Named on Mare Island (1916) 15' quadrangle.

Grouse Spring [NAPA]: *spring,* 4.25 miles east-northeast of Calistoga (lat. 38°36'20" N, long. 122°30'20" W; near N line sec. 27, T 9 N, R 6 W). Named on Calistoga (1958) 7.5' quadrangle.

Groves: see **Skaggs Springs** [SONOMA].

Grub Creek [SONOMA]: *stream,* flows 1.25 miles to Dutch Bill Creek 2.5 miles northwest of Occidental (lat. 38°26'20" N, long. 122°58'25" W; sec. 21, T 7 N, R 10 W). Named on Camp Meeker (1954) 7.5' quadrangle.

Gualala Point [SONOMA]: *promontory,* 1.25 miles south-southeast of the mouth of Gualala River along the coast (lat. 38°45'10" N, long. 123°31'35" W). Named on Gualala (1960) 7.5' quadrangle.

Gualala Point Island [SONOMA]: *island,* 500 feet long, 1.25 miles south-southeast of the mouth of Gualala River (lat. 38°45'05" N, long. 123°31'40" W); the island is 550 feet off Gualala Point. Named on Gualala (1960) 7.5' quadrangle.

Gualala River [SONOMA]: *stream,* formed by the confluence of North Fork (which is in Mendocino County) and South Fork at Sonoma-Mendocino county line, flows 3.5 miles along the county line to the sea 10.5 miles northwest of the village of Stewarts Point (lat. 38°46'10" N, long. 123°31'55" W). Named on Gualala (1960) 7.5' quadrangle. The stream also was called Walalla River (Gudde, 1949, p. 138). South Fork is 35 miles long and is named on Ornbaun Valley (1960) 15' quadrangle, and on Annapolis (1977), Fort Ross (1978), Plantation (1977), and Stewarts Point (1978) 7.5' quadrangles. South Fork is called Gualala River on Ornbaun (1944) 15' quadrangle. Wheatfield Fork joins South Fork 3.5 miles north-northwest of the village of

Stewarts Point; it is 33 miles long and is named on Hopland (1960) 15' quadrangle, and on Annapolis (1977), Stewarts Point (1978), and Tombs Creek (1978) 7.5' quadrangles. Present Wheatfield Fork is called Buckeye Creek on Hopland (1944) 15' quadrangle.

Guerne Park: see **Guernewood Park** [SONOMA].

Guerneville [SONOMA]: *town,* 10 miles southwest of Healdsburg along Russian River (lat. 38°30'05" N, long. 122°59'45" W). Named on Camp Meeker (1954), Cazadero (1978), and Guerneville (1955) 7.5' quadrangles. Postal authorities established Guerneville post office in 1870; the name commemorates George E. Guerne, who settled at the place in 1864 and built a sawmill there (Salley, p. 91). California Mining Bureau's (1909) map shows a place called Mercury located 4 miles by stage line north of Guerneville. Postal authorities established Mercuryville post office in 1874, discontinued it in 1876, reestablished it in 1878, discontinued it in 1879, reestablished it with the name "Mercury" in 1899, and discontinued it in 1909 (Salley, p. 138).

Guernewood: see **East Guernewood** [SONOMA]; **Guernewood Park** [SONOMA]; **West Guernewood** [SONOMA].

Guernewood Park [SONOMA]: *settlement,* less than 1 mile southwest of Guerneville along Russian River (lat. 38°29'40" N, long. 122°00'35" W; sec. 31, T 8 N, R 10 W). Named on Duncans Mills (1979) 7.5' quadrangle. Called Guerne Park on Duncans Mills (1921) 15' quadrangle, and called Guernewood on California Division of Forestry's (1945) map. Postal authorities established Guernewood Park post office in 1925; the name is for Bert Guerne, who build a summer resort at the place (Salley, p. 91).

Gull Rock [SONOMA]: *island,* 300 feet long, nearly 2 miles south of Jenner, and 1350 feet offshore (lat. 38°25'30" N, long. 123°07'15" W). Named on Duncans Mills (1979) 7.5' quadrangle.

Guthrie: see **Napa Junction** [NAPA].

Guyserville: see **Geyserville** [SONOMA].

– H –

Hacienda [SONOMA]: *settlement,* 3.5 miles east of Guerneville (lat. 38°30'45" N, long. 122°55'40" W; near E line sec. 26, T 8 N, R 10 W). Named on Guerneville (1955) 7.5' quadrangle.

Haggin Creek: see **Willow Brook** [SONOMA].

Halfmile Rock [SONOMA]: *rock,* 1 mile west-southwest of Jenner, and nearly 0.5 mile off the coast (lat. 38°26'35" N, long. 123° 08' W). Named on Arched Rock (1977) 7.5' quadrangle.

Haraszthy Creek [SONOMA]: *stream,* flows 2.25 miles to Arroyo Seco 2 miles east-southeast of Sonoma (lat. 38°16'35" N, long. 122°25'30" W). Named on Sonoma (1951) 7.5' quadrangle.

Haraszthy Falls [SONOMA]: *waterfall,* 2 miles east of Sonoma (lat. 38°17'35" N, long. 122°25'05" W); the feature is along Haraszthy Creek. Named on Sonoma (1951) 7.5' quadrangle.

Harbine [SONOMA]: *locality,* nearly 6 miles northwest of Sebastopol along Petaluma and Santa Rosa Railroad (lat. 38°27'50" N, long. 122°53'05" W). Named on Sebastopol (1942) 15' quadrangle.

Hardin Creek [NAPA]: *stream,* flows 6.5 miles to Maxwell Creek 9.5 miles northeast of Saint Helena (lat. 38°36'35" N, long. 122°21'20" W). Named on Chiles Valley (1958) 7.5' quadrangle.

Harness Camp [SONOMA]: *locality,* 2.25 miles north of Geyser Peak (lat. 38°47'50" N, long. 122°50'30" W; sec. 15, T 11 N, R 9 W). Named on The Geysers (1959) 7.5' quadrangle.

Harris Canyon [NAPA]: *canyon,* drained by a stream that flows 2.5 miles to lowlands along Lake Berryessa 3 miles west of Berryessa Peak (lat. 38°39'45" N, long. 122°14'45" W). Named on Brooks (1959) 7.5' quadrangle. Capay (1945) 15' quadrangle shows Harris ranch located near the mouth of the canyon.

Harrison Gulch [SONOMA]: *canyon,* drained by a stream that flows 0.5 mile to Russian River 2.5 miles south-southwest of Guerneville (lat. 38°28'05" N, long. 123°00'45" W; sec. 7, T 7 N, R 10 W). Named on Duncans Mills (1979) 7.5' quadrangle.

Haupt Creek [SONOMA]: *stream,* flows 5.5 miles to Wheatfield Fork Gualala River 4.5 miles southeast of Annapolis (lat. 38°39'45" N, long. 123°19'15" W; near SW cor. sec. 33, T 10 N, R 13 W). Named on Annapolis (1977) and Plantation (1977) 7.5' quadrangles. United States Board on Geographic Names (1977b, p. 3) noted that the name commemorates Charles Haupt, who settled in the neighborhood in the 1860's. The stream is called Charley Haupt Creek on a map of 1879 (Gudde, 1949, p. 143).

Hayfield Hill: see **Bald Hill** [SONOMA].

Haystack [SONOMA]: *locality,* 2 miles east-southeast of downtown Petaluma along Northwestern Pacific Railroad (lat. 38°13'25" N, long. 122°36'30" W; near NE cor. sec. 3, T 4 N, R 7 W). Named on Petaluma River (1954) 7.5' quadrangle. Petaluma (1914) 15' quadrangle shows a place called Haystack Landing located along Petaluma River near the site. Steamers docked at Haystack Landing, which was named for some haystacks left there in the 1840's; the place also was known as Rudesill's Landing (Heig, p. 72).

Haystack [NAPA]: *peak,* 3.5 miles northeast of Yountville (lat. 38° 26'30" N, long. 122°18'55" W; near W line sec. 21, T 7 N, R 4 W). Alti-

tude 1672 feet. Named on Yountville (1951) 7.5' quadrangle.

Haystack Landing: see **Haystack** [SONOMA].

Healdsburg [SONOMA]: *town,* 14 miles northwest of Santa Rosa near Russian River (lat. 38°36'40" N, long. 122°52'10" W). Named on Healdsburg (1955) 7.5' quadrangle. Postal authorities established Russian River post office in 1854 and changed the name to Healdsburgh (with the final "h") in 1857 (Frickstad, p. 198)—the name had the form "Healdsburg" by 1880 (Hansen and Miller, p. 47). The town incorporated in 1867. The name commemorates H.G. Heald, who opened a store at the site in 1852 (Bancroft, 1888, p. 508). Postal authorities established Dodgeville post office 13 miles northeast of Healdsburg in 1874, changed the name to Pine Flat the same year, discontinued it in 1876, reestablished it in 1878, discontinued it in 1880, reestablished it with the name "Pineflat" in 1900, moved it 4 miles northeast in 1906, and discontinued it in 1932 (Salley, p. 60, 172). They established Pacific Home post office 7 miles northeast of Healdsburg (sec. 36, T 10 N, R 9 W) in 1858 and discontinued it in 1860 (Salley, p. 164). They established Excelsior post office 8 miles northeast of Healdsburg at Excelsior mine (sec. 35, T 9 N, R 8 W) in 1875 and discontinued it in 1877 (Salley, p. 71) They established Lambert post office 4.5 miles north of Healdsburg in 1897 and discontinued it in 1903; the name was for Charles L. Lambert, a pioneer settler (Salley, p. 116).

Heath Canyon [NAPA]: *canyon,* drained by a stream that flows 2.5 miles to Sulphur Creek 1.25 miles south-southwest of Saint Helena (lat. 38°29'15" N, long. 122°28'40" W). Named on Rutherford (1951) 7.5' quadrangle.

Hedgpeth Lake [SONOMA]: *lake,* 2800 feet long, 6 miles south-southwest of Big Mountain (lat. 38°37'45" N, long. 123°11' W). Named on Tombs Creek (1978) 7.5' quadrangle.

Helen: see **Mount Helen**, under **Mount Saint Helena** [SONOMA].

Heller: see **Mount Heller** [SONOMA].

Hell Hole [SONOMA]: *canyon,* 5.5 miles east-northeast of Fort Ross along Ward Creek (lat. 38°33' N, long. 123°09'10" W). Named on Fort Ross (1978) 7.5' quadrangle.

Helm's Creek: see **Hulbert Creek** [SONOMA].

Henne: see **Lake Henne** [NAPA].

Hennessey: see **Lake Hennessey** [NAPA].

Henry: see **Mount Henry**, under **Mount Saint John** [NAPA].

Hessel [SONOMA]: *locality,* 4.5 miles east-northeast of Bloomfield along Petaluma and Santa Rosa Railroad (lat. 38°20'50" N, long. 122°46'35" W). Named on Two Rock (1954) 7.5' quadrangle.

Hidden Valley [SONOMA]: *canyon,* drained by a stream that flows 1 mile to Hulbert Creek

1.25 miles west of Guerneville (lat. 38°29'55" N, long. 123°01'10" W; sec. 36, T 8 N, R 11 W). Named on Duncans Mills (1979) 7.5' quadrangle.

Highcroft [SONOMA]: *locality,* 3 miles east of Guerneville along Russian River (lat. 38°30'05" N, long. 122°56'35" W; near NW cor. sec. 35, T 8 N, R 10 W). Named on Sebastopol (1942) 15' quadrangle and Guerneville (1955) 7.5' quadrangle.

High Point [NAPA]: *peak,* 4 miles northeast of Calistoga (lat. 38°37'05" N, long. 122°31'20" W; near NE cor. sec. 21, T 9 N, R 6 W). Altitude 2758 feet. Named on Calistoga (1958) 7.5' quadrangle.

High Rock [SONOMA]: *peak,* 8 miles northeast of Fort Ross (lat. 38° 36'25" N, long. 123°09'30" W; sec. 23, T 9 N, R 12 W). Altitude 2003 feet. Named on Fort Ross (1978) 7.5' quadrangle.

Hilton [SONOMA]: *locality,* 3 miles east of Guerneville along Russian River (lat. 38°30'15" N, long. 122°58'20" W; sec. 26, T 8 N, R 10 W). Named on Guerneville (1955) 7.5' quadrangle. Postal authorities established Hilton post office in 1894 and discontinued it in 1953; the name is for Hilton Ridenhour, son of the founder of the community (Salley, p. 98).

Hinebaugh Creek [SONOMA]: *stream,* flows 1.5 miles to lowlands 2.5 miles northeast of Cotati (lat. 38°21'05" N, long. 122°40'10" W). Named on Cotati (1954) 7.5' quadrangle.

Hinman: see **Lake Hinman** [NAPA].

Hirsch Creek [NAPA]: *stream,* flows 0.5 mile to Napa Valley 5.25 miles southeast of Calistoga (lat. 38°31'50" N, long. 122°30'20" W; sec. 22, T 8 N, R 6 W). Named on Calistoga (1958) 7.5' quadrangle.

Hobson Creek [SONOMA]: *stream,* flows 2.5 miles to Russian River 4 miles east of Guerneville (lat. 38°30'25" N, long. 122°55'40" W; sec. 26, T 8 N, R 10 W). Named on Guerneville (1955) 7.5' quadrangle.

Hogback [SONOMA]: *promontory,* 4 miles south-southeast of Jenner along the sea coast (lat. 38°23'45" N, long. 123°05'45" W). Named on Duncans Mills (1979) 7.5' quadrangle. Duncans Mills (1943) 7.5' quadrangle shows the feature as an island.

Hogback Mountain [SONOMA]: *peak,* 4 miles north-northeast of Sonoma (lat. 38°20'40" N, long. 122°25'35" W; at SW cor. sec. 21, T 6 N, R 5 W). Altitude 1753 feet. Named on Sonoma (1951) 7.5' quadrangle.

Hog Island [SONOMA]: *area,* 7.5 miles southeast of downtown Petaluma near Petaluma River (lat. 38°09'30" N, long. 122°32'10" W). Named on Petaluma River (1954) 7.5' quadrangle. Petaluma (1914) 15' quadrangle shows the area as marsh situated between Petaluma River and False Bay.

Hole in Rock [SONOMA]: *relief feature,* 2 miles

north of the village of Bodega Bay (lat. 38°21'50" N, long. 123°02'30" W). Named on Bodega Head (1942) 7.5' quadrangle.

Hole in the Head [SONOMA]: *locality;* water-filled excavation 2 miles south-southwest of the village of Bodega Bay (lat. 38°18'20" N, long. 123°03'30" W); the feature is on Bodega Head. Named on Bodega Head (1972) 7.5' quadrangle. The excavation was for a nuclear generating plant before construction stopped because the site is on the San Andreas fault.

Hollydale [SONOMA]: *settlement,* 4 miles east of Guerneville along Russian River (lat. 38°30'20" N, long. 122°55'10" W; sec. 25, T 8 N, R 10 W). Named on Guerneville (1955) 7.5' quadrangle.

Holmes Canyon [SONOMA]: *canyon,* drained by a stream that flows 1.25 miles to Austin Creek 2.5 miles north-northwest of Cazadero (lat. 38°33'50" N, long. 123°06'15" W; sec. 5, T 8 N, R 11 W). Named on Cazadero (1978) 7.5' quadrangle. California Division of Forestry's (1945) map shows Arroyo Cr. in the canyon.

Holt Hill [SONOMA]: *ridge,* southeast-trending, less than 1 mile long, 6 miles southwest of Big Mountain (lat. 38°38'40" N, long. 123°13'20" W). Named on Tombs Creek (1978) 7.5' quadrangle.

Home Hill [NAPA]: *peak,* 4.5 miles northwest of Napa Junction (lat. 38°14'25" N, long. 122°17'45" W). Named on Cuttings Wharf (1949) 7.5' quadrangle.

Hood: see **Mount Hood** [SONOMA].

Hoods Hot Springs: see **Dry Creek** [SONOMA].

Hooker Canyon [SONOMA]: *canyon,* 4 miles long, along Hooker Creek above a point 3.5 miles north-northwest of Sonoma (lat. 38°20'20" N, long. 122°29'25" W). Named on Rutherford (1951) and Sonoma (1951) 7.5' quadrangles. The name commemorates Joseph Hooker, who purchased part of Agua Caliente grant in 1851, and lived there for several years (Gudde, 1949, p. 152-153).

Hooker Canyon: see **Stuart Canyon** [SONOMA].

Hooker Creek [SONOMA]: *stream,* flows 5 miles to Wilson Creek 2.25 miles southeast of Glen Ellen (lat. 38°20'10" N, long. 122°30'05" W); the stream goes through Hooker Canyon. Named on Sonoma (1951) 7.5' quadrangle.

Hoot Owl Creek [SONOMA]: *stream,* flows 2.25 miles to Russian River 4.5 miles east-northeast of Healdsburg (lat. 38°38'50" N, long. 122°47'45" W). Named on Jimtown (1955) 7.5' quadrangle.

Hoover Ridge [SONOMA]: *ridge,* generally northwest-trending, 3.25 miles long, 3.25 miles east-northeast of Annapolis (lat. 38°44'30" N, long. 122°19' W). Named on Ornbaun Valley (1960) 15' quadrangle, and on Annapolis (1977) 7.5' quadrangle.

Hopyard [SONOMA]: *locality,* 3 miles northwest of Sebastopol along Petaluma and Santa Rosa Railroad (lat. 38°25'50" N, long. 122°52' W). Named on Sebastopol (1942) 15' quadrangle.

Horn: see **The Horn** [SONOMA].

Horse Hill [SONOMA]: *ridge,* west- to south-southwest-trending, 1.5 miles long, 1.5 miles north of Mark West Springs (lat. 38°34'15" N, long. 122°43'05" W). Named on Mark West Springs (1958) 7.5' quadrangle.

Horse Opening [SONOMA]: *area,* 7 miles southwest of Big Mountain (lat. 38°38'25" N, long. 123°14' W; sec. 7, T 9 N, R 12 W). Named on Tombs Creek (1978) 7.5' quadrangle.

Horse Pond [NAPA]: *lake,* 400 feet long, 3 miles east-northeast of Calistoga (lat. 38°35'55" N, long. 122°31'35" W; sec. 28, T 9 N, R 6 W). Named on Calistoga (1958) 7.5' quadrangle.

Horseshoe Bend [NAPA]: *bend,* 3.25 miles south of downtown Napa along Napa River (lat. 38°15'05" N, long. 122°17'35" W). Named on Cuttings Wharf (1949) and Napa (1951) 7.5' quadrangles.

Horseshoe Cove [SONOMA]:

(1) *embayment,* 3.5 miles west-northwest of Plantation along the coast (lat. 38°36'45" N, long. 123°22' W). Named on Plantation (1977) 7.5' quadrangle.

(2) *embayment,* nearly 2 miles southwest of the village of Bodega Bay along the coast (lat. 38°18'55" N, long. 123°04'10" W). Named on Bodega Head (1972) 7.5' quadrangle.

Horseshoe Point [SONOMA]: *promontory,* 3.5 miles west-northwest of Plantation along the coast (lat. 38°36'25" N, long. 123°22'15" W); the feature is on the south side of Horseshoe Cove (1). Named on Plantation (1977) 7.5' quadrangle.

Horsethief Canyon [SONOMA]: *canyon,* 1.5 miles long, 9 miles north of the village of Stewarts Point on Sonoma-Mendocino county line (lat. 38°47'05" N, long. 123°22' W). Named on Ornbaun Valley (1960) 15' quadrangle.

Hot Springs: see **The Geysers** [SONOMA].

Hot Springs Creek [SONOMA]: *stream,* flows 1 mile to Big Sulphur Creek 3.5 miles east-northeast of Geyser Peak (lat. 38°47'15" N, long. 122°47' W; sec. 19, T 11 N, R 8 W). Named on Kelseyville (1959) 15' quadrangle.

Hot Sulphur Springs: see **Calistoga** [NAPA].

House Creek [SONOMA]: *stream,* flows 13 miles to Wheatfield Fork Gualala River 6 miles southwest of Big Mountain (lat. 38°39'45" N, long. 123°14' W; sec. 6, T 9 N, R 12 W). Named on Tombs Creek (1978) and Warm Springs Dam (1978) 7.5' quadrangles.

Houx: see **Cherry** [SONOMA].

Howard's Station: see **Occidental** [SONOMA].

Howell Mountain [NAPA]:

(1) *ridge,* south-southeast-trending, 2 miles long, 5.5 miles north-northeast of Saint Helena (lat. 38°34'45" N, long. 122°26' W). Named on Saint Helena (1960) 7.5' quadrangle. Goodyear (1890a, p. 349) noted that the range northeast of the upper part of Napa Valley is known as Howell Mountains, and F.F. Davis (p. 161) stated that the northeast half of Napa County is separated from Napa Valley by Howell Range, which is the southeast extension of Mayacmas Mountains.

(2) *settlement,* 5.5 miles north-northeast of Saint Helena (lat. 38°34'50" N, long. 122°27' W); the place is west of present Howell Mountain (1). Named on Saint Helena (1942) 15' quadrangle. Pope Valley (1921) 15' quadrangle has the name "White Cottage" at the site. The place now is part of Angwin.

Howell Mountains: see **Howell Mountain** [NAPA] (1).

Howell Range: see **Howell Mountain** [NAPA] (1).

Hudeman Slough [NAPA-SONOMA]: *water feature,* mainly in Sonoma County, but forms a small part of Napa-Sonoma county line; joins Napa Slough 5.5 miles west of Napa Junction (lat. 38° 11'35" N, long. 122°21' W; sec. 18, T 4 N, R 4 W). Named on Cuttings Wharf (1949) and Sears Point (1951) 7.5' quadrangles.

Huichica [NAPA-SONOMA]: *land grant,* southwest of the city of Napa on Napa-Sonoma county line. Named on Cuttings Wharf (1949), Napa (1951), Sears Point (1951), and Sonoma (1951) 7.5' quadrangles. Jacob P. Leese received 2 leagues in 1841 and claimed 18,704 acres patented in 1859 (Cowan, p. 41; Cowan used the form "Huichicha" for the name). The name of the grant is from an Indian village at the site of the present town of Sonoma (Kroeber, p. 43).

Huichica Creek [NAPA]: *stream,* flows 8 miles to marsh 6 miles west-northwest of Napa Junction (lat. 38°12'50" N, long. 122°21'20" W); the stream is on Huichica grant. Named on Cuttings Wharf (1949), Napa (1951), and Sonoma (1951) 7.5' quadrangles.

Hulbert Creek [SONOMA]: *stream,* flows 5.5 miles to Russian River less than 1 mile southwest of Guerneville (lat. 38°29'40" N, long. 123°00'20" W). Named on Cazadero (1978) and Duncans Mills (1979) 7.5' quadrangles. Called Hulbert Creek on Cazadero (1943) and Duncans Mills (1943) 7.5' quadrangles. The stream was called Helm's Creek in the 1860's (Clar, p. 15).

Humbug Creek [SONOMA]: *stream,* flows 3 miles to Mark West Creek 4 miles east-southeast of Mark West Springs (lat. 38°31'10" N, long. 122°39'30" W; near S line sec. 20, T 8 N, R 7 W). Named on Mark West Springs (1958) 7.5' quadrangle.

Hummingbird Creek [SONOMA]: *stream,* heads in Mendocino County and flows 2 miles to Squaw Creek 5.25 miles north of Geyser Peak (lat. 38°50'20" N, long. 122°51'30" W;

at E line sec. 33, T 12 N, R 9 W). Named on The Geysers (1959) 7.5' quadrangle.

Hunting Creek [NAPA]: *stream,* heads in Lake County and flows 9.5 miles along Napa-Lake county line to Putah Creek nearly 6 miles southwest of Knoxville (lat. 38°46'05" N, long. 122°24'55" W; near S line sec. 28, T 11 N, R 5 W). Named on Jericho Valley (1958) and Knoxville (1958) 7.5' quadrangles.

Hurlbut [SONOMA]: *locality,* 1 mile northwest of Sebastopol along Petaluma and Santa Rosa Railroad (lat. 38°24'45" N, long. 122°50'10" W). Named on Sebastopol (1942) 15' quadrangle.

Hurley Creek [SONOMA]: *stream,* flows 1 mile to Little Sulphur Creek 10 miles northeast of Healdsburg at Pine Flat (lat. 38°44'20" N, long. 122°46' W; sec. 5, T 10 N, R 8 W). Named on Jimtown (1955) 7.5' quadrangle.

Husman Canyon [NAPA]: *canyon,* drained by a stream that flows nearly 1 mile to Chiles Valley 7.5 miles east-northeast of Saint Helena (lat. 38°33'05" N, long. 122°20'40" W). Named on Chiles Valley (1958) 7.5' quadrangle.

– I –

Icaria Creek [SONOMA]: *stream,* flows 4 miles to Russian River flood plain 1.5 miles northwest of Asti (lat. 38°46'35" N, long. 122°59'35" W). Named on Asti (1959) and Cloverdale (1960) 7.5' quadrangles. The name recalls the colony established in 1881 by Armand Dehay and Jules Leroux, two Frenchmen who bought land 3 miles south of Cloverdale for a community based upon the ideals of Icaria, the French utopia (Hine, p. 58-59).

Idell: see **Lake Idell** [SONOMA].

Imola [NAPA]: *locality,* 1.25 miles south of downtown Napa along Southern Pacific Railroad (lat. 38°16'45" N, long. 122°16'45" W). Named on Napa (1951) 7.5' quadrangle, which has the designation "Napa State Hospital (Imola P.O.)" at a site less than 1 mile east-southeast of Imola. Postal authorities established Imola post office in 1920 and discontinued it in 1953 (Frickstad, p. 111). The railroad station and post office for the state hospital were named for Imola, Italy, apparently because the Italian city has a hospital for the insane (Gudde, 1949, p. 159).

Indian Mineral Spring [SONOMA]: *spring,* 3 miles northeast of Guerneville (lat. 38°31'50" N, long. 122°57'30" W; near N line sec. 22, T 8 N, R 10 W). Named on Healdsburg (1940) 15' quadrangle.

Indian Spring: see **Pope Mineral Spring**, under **Samuel Springs** [NAPA].

Ingalls Bluff [SONOMA]: *relief feature,* 6.5 miles west-northwest of Mount Saint Helena (lat. 38°43'10" N, long. 122°44' W; near N line sec. 15, T 10 N, R 8 W); the feature is northwest of Ingalls Creek. Named on Mount Saint Helena (1959) 7.5' quadrangle. Called Ingalls Bluffs on Calistoga (1945) 15' quadrangle.

Ingalls Creek [SONOMA]: *stream,* flows 3 miles to McDonnell Creek 6.5 miles westnorthwest of Mount Saint Helena (lat. 38°42'10" N, long. 122°44'35" W; at W line sec. 22, T 10 N, R 8 W). Named on Mount Saint Helena (1959) 7.5' quadrangle.

Ingrams: see **Cazadero** [SONOMA].

Inspiration Point [NAPA]: *peak,* 6.25 miles north of Saint Helena (lat. 38°35'45" N, long. 122°28' W; near SE cor. sec. 25, T 9 N, R 6 W). Named on Saint Helena (1960) 7.5' quadrangle.

Irish Hill [SONOMA]:

(1) *ridge,* west-southwest-trending, 1 mile long, 2.5 miles north of the village of Bodega Bay (lat. 38°22'20" N, long. 123°02'50" W). Named on Bodega Head (1972) 7.5' quadrangle. On Bodega Head (1942) 7.5' quadrangle, the name applies to the peak at the west end of the ridge. Duncans Mills (1921) 15' quadrangle shows a place called Oceanview situated on present Irish Hill (1). Postal authorities established Ocean View post office 8 miles south of Duncans Mills (sec. 22, T 6 N, R 11 W) in 1870 and discontinued it in 1874 (Salley, p. 159).

(2) *peak,* 5.5 miles southeast of present Jenner (lat. 38°24'15" N, long. 123°02'30" W). Named on Duncans Mills (1921) 15' quadrangle.

Iron Mountain [NAPA]: *peak,* 11.5 miles east-northeast of Saint Helena (lat. 38°33' N, long. 121°16'05" W). Altitude 2287 feet. Named on Chiles Valley (1958) 7.5' quadrangle.

Island: see **The Island** [SONOMA].

Island Number 1 [NAPA]: *island,* center 5 miles west-northwest of downtown Vallejo between by Napa Slough, South Slough, Dutchman Slough, and San Pablo Bay on Napa-Solano county line, mainly in Solano County (lat. 38°08'45" N, long. 122° 21' W). Named on Cuttings Wharf (1949), Mare Island (1959), and Sears Point (1951) 7.5' quadrangles.

Island Number 2 [NAPA]: *island,* 4.5 miles west-southwest of Napa Junction between China Slough and South Slough on Napa-Solano county line (lat. 38°09'20" N, long. 122°19'25" W). Named on Cuttings Wharf (1949) 7.5' quadrangle.

– J –

Jack Rabbit Flat [NAPA]: *area,* 8 miles northwest of Mount Vaca along Capell Creek (lat. 38°28'10" N, long. 122°13'40" W; sec. 7, T 7 N, R 3 W). Named on Capell Valley (1951) 7.5' quadrangle.

Jackson: see **Mount Jackson** [SONOMA].

Jackson Canyon [NAPA]: *canyon,* drained by a stream that flows less than 1 mile to Clear Creek 8.5 miles east of Saint Helena (lat. 38°30'10" N, long. 122°19' W; near W line sec. 33, T 8 N, R 4 W). Named on Chiles Valley (1958) 7.5' quadrangle.

Jackson Creek [NAPA]: *stream,* flows 2.5 miles to lowlands along Lake Berryessa 4 miles south-southwest of Berryessa Peak (lat. 38° 36'40" N, long. 122°12'50" W); the stream is south of Jackson Peak. Named on Lake Berryessa (1959) 7.5' quadrangle.

Jackson Peak [NAPA]: *peak,* 3 miles south of Berryessa Peak (lat. 38°37'15" N, long. 122°11'45" W); the peak is north of Jackson Creek. Altitude 1814 feet. Named on Lake Berryessa (1959) 7.5' quadrangle.

Jacksons Napa Soda Springs: see **Napa Soda Springs** [NAPA].

James Creek [NAPA]: *stream,* flows nearly 5 miles to Pope Creek 1.5 miles north-northeast of Aetna Springs (lat. 38°40'20" N, long. 122°28'35" W; sec. 36, T 10 N, R 6 W). Named on Aetna Springs (1958) and Detert Reservoir (1958) 7.5' quadrangles.

Jameson Canyon [NAPA]: *canyons,* two canyons in Napa County and Solano County that head opposite one another, and that together are 4 miles long; one of the canyons opens into lowlands 1 mile west-southwest of Cordelia (lat. 38°12'25" N, long. 122° 09' W; near W line sec. 12, T 4 N, R 3 W). Named on Cordelia (1951) 7.5' quadrangle.

Jauiyomi: see **Russian River** [SONOMA].

Jenkins Rock [NAPA]: *relief feature,* 6.25 miles southwest of Mount Vaca (lat. 38°21'10" N, long. 122°12' W; sec. 21, T 6 N, R 3 W). Named on Mount George (1951) 7.5' quadrangle.

Jenner [SONOMA]: *village,* 7.5 miles west-southwest of Guerneville near the mouth of Russian River (lat. 38°27' N, long. 123°06'55" W). Named on Duncans Mills (1979) 7.5' quadrangle. Duncans Mills (1921) 15' quadrangle shows a place called Jenner-by-the-Sea situated nearly 1 mile southeast of present Jenner. Postal authorities established Jenner post office in 1904 (Frickstad, p. 196). The name is for Charles Jenner, a writer who built a cabin near the mouth of present Jenner Gulch in 1868; officials of A.B. Davis Lumber Company applied the name "Jenner" to the site in 1905, when they started a lumber mill there (Hanna, P.T., p. 154).

Jenner-by-the-Sea: see **Jenner** [SONOMA].

Jenner Gulch [SONOMA]: *canyon,* drained by a stream that flows 3.25 miles to Russian River at Jenner (lat. 38°26'55" N, long. 123° 06'50" W). Named on Duncans Mills (1979) 7.5' quadrangle.

Jerd Creek [NAPA]: *stream,* flows 1.25 miles to Lake Berryessa 2 miles east of Walter Springs (lat. 38°39'05" N, long. 122°19'15" W; sec. 8, T 9 N, R 4 W). Named on Walter Springs (1959) 7.5' quadrangle.

Jericho Canyon [NAPA]: *canyon,* drained by a stream that flows 2.5 miles to Garnett Creek 2 miles north-northwest of Calistoga (lat. 38°36'20" N, long. 122°35'20" W). Named on Calistoga (1958) and Detert Reservoir (1958) 7.5' quadrangles.

Jewell Gulch [SONOMA]: *canyon,* drained by a stream that flows 1 mile to the sea 5 miles northwest of Jenner (lat. 38°29'30" N, long. 123°11'40" W). Named on Arched Rock (1977) 7.5' quadrangle.

Jim Creek [SONOMA]: *stream,* flows 2.5 miles to Pepperwood Creek 8 miles north-northeast of Fort Ross (lat. 38°37'15" N, long. 123°11'20" W; sec. 16, T 9 N, R 12 W). Named on Fort Ross (1978) 7.5' quadrangle.

Jimtown [SONOMA]: *village,* 4.5 miles northeast of Healdsburg (lat. 38°40' N, long. 122°49'05" W). Named on Jimtown (1955) 7.5' quadrangle.

John Gordon Creek [SONOMA]: *stream,* flows 1.25 miles to Porter Creek (1) 4.5 miles northeast of Guerneville (lat. 38°32'35" N, long. 122°55'55" W; sec. 14, T 8 N, R 10 W). Named on Guerneville (1955) 7.5' quadrangle.

Johnny Brown Springs [SONOMA]: *springs,* 1.5 miles north-northwest of Big Mountain (lat. 38°43'55" N, long. 123°09'15" W; sec. 11, T 10 N, R 12 W). Named on Tombs Creek (1978) 7.5' quadrangle.

Johnson Canyon [NAPA]: *canyon,* drained by a stream that flows 1 mile to Lake Berryessa 7 miles north-northwest of Mount Vaca (lat. 38°29'25" N, long. 122°09'35" W; sec. 35, T 8 N, R 3 W). Named on Capell Valley (1951, photorevised 1968) 7.5' quadrangle.

Johnson Gulch [SONOMA]: *canyon,* drained by a stream that flows nearly 2 miles to Bodega Harbor at the village of Bodega Bay (lat. 38°20'05" N, long. 123°02'55" W). Named on Bodega Head (1972) 7.5' quadrangle.

Johnson Spring [NAPA]: *spring,* 6.5 miles east-northeast of Saint Helena (lat. 38°32'10" N, long. 122°21'25" W; near NE cor. sec. 24, T 8 N, R 5 W). Named on Chiles Valley (1958) 7.5' quadrangle.

John West Ridge [SONOMA]: *ridge,* west-trending, 0.5 mile long, 2.5 miles northeast of Annapolis (lat. 38°44'45" N, long. 123°19'55" W). Named on Annapolis (1977) 7.5' quadrangle.

Josephine: see **Lake Josephine** [SONOMA].

– K –

Kawana Springs [SONOMA]: *spring,* 2.25 miles southeast of downtown Santa Rosa (lat. 38°24'55" N, long. 122°41'10" W; near NE cor. sec. 36, T 7 N, R 8 W). Named on Santa Rosa (1954) 7.5' quadrangle. The spring was the basis for a resort built in 1870 and known as Taylor's Springs, Taylor Sulphur Spring, and Taylor's White Sulphur Springs for J.S. Taylor, who owned the place (Bradley, p. 337; Goodyear, 1890b, p. 676; Waring, p. 256). Taylor asked Luther Burbank to rename the resort, and Burbank chose the name "Kawana Springs" (Hansen and Miller, p. 133).

Kelley Creek [SONOMA]: *stream,* flows nearly 3 miles to Dry Creek 5 miles south of Geyserville (lat. 38°37'55" N, long. 123°54' W). Named on Geyserville (1955) 7.5' quadrangle.

Kellogg [SONOMA]: *locality,* 3.25 miles southwest of Mount Saint Helena in Knights Valley (lat. 38°37'55" N, long. 122°40'25" W); the place is near Kellogg Creek. Named on Mount Saint Helena (1959) 7.5' quadrangle. Postal authorities established Kellogg post office in 1875, discontinued it in 1876, re-established it in 1889, and discontinued it in 1935; the name is for a pioneer settler (Salley, p. 110).

Kellogg Creek [SONOMA]: *stream,* flows 4.5 miles to join Yellow Jacket Creek and form Redwood Creek (1) 3 miles southwest of Mount Saint Helena (lat. 38°38'05" N, long. 122°40'15" W). Named on Mount Saint Helena (1959) 7.5' quadrangle.

Kelly: see **Napa Junction** [NAPA].

Kenilworth: see **Sebastopol** [SONOMA].

Kenwood [SONOMA]: *town,* 9 miles east of Santa Rosa on Los Guilicos grant (lat. 38°24'55" N, long. 122°32'50" W). Named on Kenwood (1954) 7.5' quadrangle. Postal authorities established Los Guilicos post office in 1888, changed the name to South Los Guilicos in 1889, and changed it to Kenwood in 1893 (Frickstad, p. 196, 198). The name "Kenwood" is from a town in Illinois (Gudde, 1949, p. 173). Cardwell's (1958) map has the name "Kenwood Valley" for the place where the town lies. Laizure (p. 341) noted that Kenwood Springs, located 1.5 miles northwest of Kenwood along Sonoma Creek, were the basis of a resort with a hotel, cottages, and campground that accommodated about 100 people.

Kenwood Springs: see **Kenwood** [SONOMA].

Kenwood Valley: see **Kenwood** [SONOMA].

Kid Creek: see **Kidd Creek** [SONOMA].

Kidd Canyon [NAPA]: *canyon,* 1.5 miles long, along James Creek above a point 7 miles north-northeast of Calistoga (lat. 38°40'10" N, long. 122°31'40" W; sec. 33, T 10 N, R 6 W). Named on Detert Reservoir (1958) 7.5' quadrangle.

Kidd Creek [SONOMA]: *stream,* flows 2.5 miles to Austin Creek 4 miles west of Guerneville (lat. 38°29'45" N, long. 123°04'05" W; sec. 34, T 8 N, R 11 W). Named on Cazadero (1978) and Duncans Mills (1979) 7.5' quadrangles. Called Kid Creek on Skaggs (1921) 15' quadrangle. California Mining Bureau's (1917) map shows a

place called Kid Creek located about halfway from Duncans Mills to Cazadero along a railroad near the mouth of present Kidd Creek—California Division of Highways' (1934) map has the name "Kidd Creek" at the place.

Kimball Canyon [NAPA]: *canyon,* 1.5 miles long, along Napa River above a point 3.5 miles north-northwest of Calistoga (lat. 38°37'15" N, long. 122°36'40" W). Named on Detert Reservoir (1958) 7.5' quadrangle.

Kings Ridge [SONOMA]: *ridge,* west-north-west-trending, 1.25 miles long, 8 miles north-east of Fort Ross (lat. 38°35'35" N, long. 123° 08'25" W). Named on Fort Ross (1978) 7.5' quadrangle.

Kitty Ridge [SONOMA]: *ridge,* east-trending, about 0.5 mile long, 3.5 miles west-southwest of Big Mountain (lat. 38°41'25" N, long. 123°12'25" W). Named on Tombs Creek (1978) 7.5' quadrangle.

Knight's Creek: see **Redwood Creek** [SONOMA] (1).

Knights Valley [SONOMA]: *valley,* 4 miles southwest of Mount Saint Helena (lat. 38°38' N, long. 122°41'30" W). Named on Mark West Springs (1958) and Mount Saint Helena (1959) 7.5' quadrangles. Postal authorities established Knights Valley post office in Napa County 7 miles northwest of Calistoga in 1860 and discontinued it in 1862, when they moved the post office to Sonoma County and changed the name to Albany; they discontinued Albany post office in 1864—the name "Albany" was from Albany, New York (Salley, p. 3, 113). Thomas Knight, was the first permanent settler in the valley in the 1850's (Archuleta, p. 14). A hotel and houses in Knights Valley had the name "Knightsville" (Menefee, p. 264).

Knightsville: see **Knights Valley** [SONOMA].

Knowles Corner [SONOMA]: *locality,* 3.5 miles northeast of Bloomfield (lat. 38°21'10" N, long. 122°48'55" W). Named on Two Rock (1954) 7.5' quadrangle.

Knoxville [NAPA]: *village,* 23 miles north-northeast of Saint Helena (lat. 38°49'25" N, long. 122°20'10" W; near NE cor. sec. 7, T 11 N, R 4 W). Named on Knoxville (1958) 7.5' quadrangle. Postal authorities established Knoxville post office in 1863, moved it 2 miles northwest in 1904, moved it 1.5 miles southeast in 1907, and discontinued it in 1912; the name is for Ranar B. Knox, first postmaster and an owner of Reddington Quicksilver Mine Company (Salley, p. 113).

Knoxville Creek [NAPA]: *stream,* flows 4.25 miles to join Foley Creek and form Eticuera Creek 2.25 miles southeast of Knoxville (lat. 38°47'55" N, long. 122°18'45" W; sec. 16, T 11 N, R 4 W); the stream goes past Knoxville. Named on Knoxville (1958) 7.5' quadrangle.

Kohute Gulch [SONOMA]: *canyon,* drained by a stream that flows nearly 2 miles to Austin

Creek 3.5 miles west-southwest of Guerneville (lat. 38°28'55" N, long. 123°03'15" W). Named on Duncans Mills (1979) 7.5' quadrangle. Called Crinkley Gulch on Duncans Mills (1921) 15' quadrangle.

Kolmer Gulch [SONOMA]: *canyon,* drained by a stream that flows 3 miles to the sea 1.25 miles west-northwest of Fort Ross (lat. 38° 31'25" N, long. 123°15'50" W). Named on Fort Ross (1978) and Plantation (1977) 7.5' quadrangles. The name commemorates Michael Kolmer, who settled at the place in 1848 (Gudde, 1949, p. 177).

Kolmer Valley: see **Coleman Valley** [SONOMA].

Korbel [SONOMA]: *locality,* nearly 2 miles east of Guerneville along Russian River (lat. 38°30'25" N, long. 122°57'50" W; on E line sec. 28, T 8 N, R 10 W). Named on Guerneville (1955) 7.5' quadrangle. Postal authorities established Korbel's Mills post office 4 miles east of Guerneville (SE quarter sec. 28, T 8 N, R 10 W) in 1876 and discontinued in 1881; the name was from Korbel Lumber Company (Salley, p. 113).

Korbel's Mills: see **Korbel** [SONOMA].

Kortum Canyon [NAPA]: *canyon,* less than 1 mile long, opens into lowlands at Calistoga (lat. 38°34'25" N, long. 122°34'50" W). Named on Calistoga (1958) 7.5' quadrangle.

Kreuse Canyon [NAPA]: *canyon,* nearly 2 miles long, along Kreuse Creek above a point 2.5 miles east-southeast of downtown Napa (lat. 38°16'50" N, long. 122°14'35" W; near W line sec. 18, T 5 N, R 3 W). Named on Mount George (1951) 7.5' quadrangle.

Kreuse Creek [NAPA]: *stream,* flows 3.25 miles to Tulacay Creek 1.25 miles east-southeast of downtown Napa (lat. 38°17'20" N, long. 122°15'35" W). Named on Mount George (1951) and Napa (1951) 7.5' quadrangles.

Krug [NAPA]: *locality,* 1 mile north-northwest of Saint Helena along Southern Pacific Railroad (lat. 38°31'05" N, long. 122°28'50" W). Named on Saint Helena (1960) 7.5' quadrangle.

Kuskov: see **Bodega** [SONOMA] (2).

— L —

Lac [SONOMA]: *land grant,* 2 miles east-northeast of Sonoma. Named on Sonoma (1951) 7.5' quadrangle. Damasco Rodriguez received 100 varas in 1844; Jacob P. Leese claimed 177 acres patented in 1872 (Cowan, p. 43).

Lacresta [SONOMA]: *locality,* 5 miles northwest of Sebastopol along Petaluma and Santa Rosa Railroad (lat. 38°27'25" N, long. 122° 53' W). Named on Sebastopol (1942) 15' quadrangle.

La Franchi: see **Santa Rosa** [SONOMA].

Lafranchi Creek [SONOMA]: *stream,* flows 2.5 miles to Redwood Creek (1) 5 miles west-

southwest of Mount Saint Helena in Knights Valley (lat. 38°38'15 N, long. 122°42'50" W). Named on Mount Saint Helena (1959) 7.5' quadrangle.

Laguna de los Gentiles: see **Caslamayomi** [SONOMA].

Laguna de San Antonio [SONOMA]: *land grant,* around Laguna Lake on Marin-Sonoma county line. Named on Cotati (1954), Petaluma (1953), Point Reyes NE (1954), and Two Rock (1954) 7.5' quadrangles. Bartolo Bojorquez received 6 leagues in 1845 and claimed 24,903 acres patented in 1871 (Cowan, p. 72).

Laguna de San Antonio: see **Laguna Lake** [SONOMA].

Laguna de Santa Rosa [SONOMA]: *water feature,* stream, with associated ponds and marsh, that joins Mark West Creek nearly 5 miles north of Sebastopol (lat. 38°28'15" N, long. 122°50'25" W). Named on Cotati (1954), Sebastopol (1954), and Two Rock (1954) 7.5' quadrangles. Called The Lagunas on Santa Rosa (1916) 15' quadrangle. A diseño of Llano de Santa Rosa grant has the Indian name "Livantuliyume" for the feature (Becker, 1969).

Laguna Lake [SONOMA]: *intermittent lake,* 2 miles long, 6 miles west-southwest of the city of Petaluma on Marin-Sonoma county line. 38°12'45" N, long. 122°44'50" W). Named on Petaluma (1953) and Point Reyes NE (1954) 7.5' quadrangles. Mason (1976, p. 163) called the feature Laguna de San Antonio.

Lagunas: see **The Lagunas**, under **Laguna de Santa Rosa** [SONOMA].

La Jota [NAPA]: *land grant,* 5 miles north-northeast of Saint Helena around Angwin. Named on Saint Helena (1960) 7.5' quadrangle. George C. Yount received 1 league in 1843 and claimed 4454 acres patented in 1857 (Cowan, p. 42-43).

La Jota: see **Angwin** [NAPA].

Lake Berryessa [NAPA]: *lake,* behind a dam on Putah Creek 11.5 miles south-southeast of Berryessa Peak (lat. 38°30'50" N, long. 122°06'10" W; sec. 29, T 8 N, R 2 W); the lake covers most of Berryessa Valley, including the site of the town of Monticello. Named on Aetna Springs (1958), Brooks (1959), Capell Valley (1951, photorevised 1968), Chiles Valley (1958), Lake Berryessa (1959), Monticello Dam (1959), Mount Vaca (1951), and Walter Springs (1959) 7.5' quadrangles. United States Board on Geographic Names (1957, p. 1) rejected the name "Monticello Reservoir" for the lake, and noted that the name "Lake Berryessa" was approved by congress on April 27, 1956.

Lake Camille [NAPA]: *lake,* 650 feet long, 2.25 miles southeast of downtown Napa (lat. 38°16'40" N, long. 122°15'10" W; sec. 13, T 5 N, R 4 W). Named on Napa (1951) 7.5' quadrangle.

Lake Curry [NAPA]: *lake,* behind a dam on

Suisun Creek 3.25 miles south-southwest of Mount Vaca (lat. 38°21'25" N, long. 122°07'25" W). Named on Fairfield North (1951) and Mount George (1951) 7.5' quadrangles. The name, given about 1925, honors Charles F. Curry; a congressman (Gudde, 1949, p. 86).

Lake Ellen [NAPA]: *lake,* 1800 feet long, 4.25 miles northeast of Saint Helena (lat. 38°33'20" N, long. 122°25'20" W). Named on Saint Helena (1960) 7.5' quadrangle.

Lake Henne [NAPA]: *lake,* 1250 feet long, nearly 6 miles north of Saint Helena (lat. 38°35'15" N, long. 122°27'40" W; sec. 31, T 9 N, R 5 W). Named on Saint Helena (1960) 7.5' quadrangle.

Lake Hennessey [NAPA]: *lake,* behind a dam on Conn Creek 5 miles north of Yountville (lat. 38°28'50" N, long. 122°22'20" W; near SW cor. sec. 1, T 7 N, R 5 W); water of the lake covers most of Conn Valley. Named on Chiles Valley (1958), Rutherford (1951), Saint Helena (1960), and Yountville (1951) 7.5' quadrangles. Davis' (1948) map has the name "Conn Valley Res." for the feature.

Lake Hinman [NAPA]: *lake,* 500 feet long, 5.25 miles south-southeast of Rutherford (lat. 38°23'30" N, long. 122°22'40" W; sec. 2, T 6 N, R 5 W). Named on Rutherford (1951) 7.5' quadrangle.

Lake Idell [SONOMA]: *lake,* 350 feet long, 0.5 mile west-northwest of Glen Ellen (lat. 38°22'05" N, long. 122°32'05" W). Named on Glen Ellen (1954) 7.5' quadrangle.

Lake Josephine [SONOMA]: *lake,* 700 feet long, 2.25 miles south of Glen Ellen (lat. 38°19'45" N, long. 122°31'20" W). Named on Glen Ellen (1954) 7.5' quadrangle.

Lake Marie [NAPA]: *lake,* 1200 feet long, 12 miles south-southwest of Mount Vaca (lat. 38°15'30" N, long. 122°13'35" W; at SE cor. sec. 19, T 5 N, R 3 W). Named on Mount George (1951) 7.5' quadrangle.

Lake Newton [NAPA]: *lake,* 1000 feet long, 6 miles north of Saint Helena (lat. 38°35'35" N, long. 122°28'10" W; near NE cor. sec. 36, T 9 N, R 6 W). Named on Saint Helena (1960) 7.5' quadrangle.

Lake Oliver [SONOMA]: *lake,* 1600 feet long, 0.25 mile north-northwest of Plantation (lat. 38°35'40" N, long. 123°18'45" W). Named on Plantation (1977) 7.5' quadrangle. Plantation (1943) 7.5' quadrangle shows an intermittent lake.

Lake Orth [SONOMA]: *lake,* 800 feet long, 4 miles east-northeast of Mark West Springs (lat. 38°34'10" N, long. 122°39'10" W; sec. 5, T 8 N, R 7 W). Named on Mark West Springs (1958) 7.5' quadrangle.

Lake Orville [NAPA]: *lake,* 1050 feet long, 6 miles north of Saint Helena (lat. 38°35'25" N, long. 122°27'55" W; at W line sec. 31, T 9 N, R 5 W). Named on Saint Helena (1960) 7.5' quadrangle.

Lake Ralphine [SONOMA]: *lake,* 1750 feet long, 2.5 miles east-northeast of downtown Santa Rosa (lat. 38°27'20" N, long. 122° 40' W). Named on Santa Rosa (1954) 7.5' quadrangle.

Lake Sonoma [SONOMA]: *intermittent lake,* behind a dam on Dry Creek 2 miles northnortheast of Skaggs Springs (lat. 38°43'10" N, long. 123°00'30" W). Named on Warm Springs Dam (1978) 7.5' quadrangle.

Lake Suttonfield [SONOMA]: *lake,* 1700 feet long, 0.5 mile southeast of Glen Ellen (lat. 38°21'20" N, long. 122°30'55" W). Named on Glen Ellen (1954) 7.5' quadrangle.

Lake Tolay: see **Lakeville** [SONOMA].

Lakeville [SONOMA]: *village,* 5.5 miles east-southeast of the city of Petaluma on the east bank of Petaluma River (lat. 38°11'55" N, long. 122°32'50" W). Named on Petaluma River (1954) 7.5' quadrangle. Postal authorities established Lakeville post office in 1859, discontinued it in 1874, reestablished it in 1875, and discontinued it in 1920 (Salley, p. 116). Lakeville was one of the earliest landing places along the river and was named for Lake Tolay, a large lake that lay in the hills east of the river (Miller, J.T., p. 19). William Bihler drained the lake after 1859 and planted potatoes and corn there—Lake Tolay was named for an Indian chief (Heig, p. 2).

Lake Whitehead [NAPA]: *lake,* 700 feet long, 6 miles north of Saint Helena (lat. 38°35'35" N, long. 122°27'55" W; near W line sec. 31, T 9 N, R 5 W). Named on Saint Helena (1960) 7.5' quadrangle.

Lambert: see **Healdsburg** [SONOMA].

Lancel Creek [SONOMA]: *stream,* flows 1.25 miles to Dutch Bill Creek 1 mile north-northwest of Occidental (lat. 38°25'20" N, long. 122°57'05" W; sec. 27, T 7 N, R 10 W). Named on Camp Meeker (1954) 7.5' quadrangle. North Fork enters from the north less than 0.5 mile above the mouth of the main stream; it is 1.5 miles long and is named on Camp Meeker (1954) 7.5' quadrangle.

Larkmead [NAPA]: *locality,* 3.25 miles east-southeast of Calistoga along Southern Pacific Railroad (lat. 38°33'30" N, long. 122°31'20" W). Named on Calistoga (1958) 7.5' quadrangle.

Las Lomas [SONOMA]: *locality,* 2.25 miles south-southeast of Big Mountain (lat. 38°40'40" N, long. 123°08'05" W; near N line sec. 36, T 10 N, R 12 W). Named on Tombs Creek (1978) 7.5' quadrangle. Postal authorities established Las Lomas post office in 1915 and discontinued it in 1916 (Frickstad, p. 196).

Las Putas [NAPA]: *land grant,* at and near Lake Berryessa. Named on Brooks (1959), Chiles Valley (1958), Lake Berryessa (1959), and Walter Springs (1959) 7.5' quadrangles. Jose de Jesus Berryessa and Sixto Berryessa received 8 leagues in 1843; M. Anastasio Higuera de Berryessa and others claimed 35,516 acres patented in 1863 (Cowan, p. 65-66).

Lathrop Hot Sulphur and Mud Spring: see **Calistoga** [NAPA].

Laton [SONOMA]: *locality,* 2 miles east-north-east of present Jenner at the end of a branch of Northwestern Pacific Railroad (lat. 38°27'55" N, long. 123°04'55" W). Named on Duncans Mills (1921) 15' quadrangle.

Lawhead Canyon: see **Lawhead Creek** [SONOMA].

Lawhead Creek [SONOMA]: *stream,* flows 1 mile to Gray Creek 6 miles northeast of Cazadero (lat. 38°35'30" N, long. 123°00'20" W). Named on Cazadero (1978) 7.5' quadrangle. On Guerneville (1955) 7.5' quadrangle, the canyon of the stream is called Lawhead Canyon.

Lawndale [SONOMA]: *locality,* 1.25 miles west-northwest of Kenwood (lat. 38°25'10" N, long. 122°39'15" W). Named on Kenwood (1954) 7.5' quadrangle.

Leddy: see **Santa Rosa** [SONOMA].

Ledgewood Creek [NAPA]: *stream,* heads in Napa County and flows 12 miles to marsh 1.5 miles south-southwest of downtown Fairfield in Solano County (lat. 38°13'45" N, long. 122°03'15" W). Named on Fairfield North (1951) and Fairfield South (1949) 7.5' quadrangles.

Lee Lake [SONOMA]: *lake,* 300 feet long, 5.5 miles north-northwest of Sears Point (lat. 38°13'10" N, long. 122°29'45" W). Named on Sears Point (1951) 7.5' quadrangle.

Lemon Hill [NAPA]: *peak,* 3.5 miles south of Mount Vaca (lat. 38° 21' N, long. 122°07'10" W). Altitude 1060 feet. Named on Fairfield North (1951) 7.5' quadrangle.

Leoma Lakes [NAPA]: *lakes,* two connected, 1050 feet long, 7 miles southwest of Mount Vaca along White Creek (lat. 38°20'35" N, long. 122°12'25" W; near NE cor. sec. 29, T 6 N, R 3 W). Named on Mount George (1951) 7.5' quadrangle.

Letton Springs: see **Lytton** [SONOMA].

Levantahyume: see **Molinos** [SONOMA].

Lewis Creek [SONOMA]: *stream,* flows 1.25 miles to Felder Creek 6.25 miles south of Glen Ellen (lat. 38°16'20" N, long. 122°30'35" W). Named on Glen Ellen (1954) 7.5' quadrangle.

Libantiliyami: see **Russian River** [SONOMA].

Liberty [SONOMA]: *locality,* 3 miles south of Cotati along Petaluma and Santa Rosa Railroad (lat. 38°17'05" N, long. 122°42'05" W). Named on Cotati (1954) 7.5' quadrangle. California Division of Highways' (1934) map shows a place called Merritt located along the railroad between Liberty and Denman, and a place called Dangers located along the railroad between Liberty and Divide.

Lichau Creek [SONOMA]: *stream,* flows 8.5 miles to Petaluma River 4 miles south-south-east of Cotati (lat. 38°16'25" N, long. 122°40'35" W). Named on Cotati (1954) and Glen Ellen (1954) 7.5' quadrangles.

Lidell: see **Aetna Springs** [NAPA].

Linda Falls [NAPA]: *waterfall,* nearly 4 mile north-northeast of Saint Helena along Conn Creek (lat. 38°33'20" N, long. 122°26'30" W). Named on Saint Helena (1960) 7.5' quadrangle.

Lion Canyon [NAPA]: *canyon,* drained by a stream that flows 1.25 miles to Gosling Canyon 5.5 miles south-southeast of Berryessa Peak (lat. 38°35'25" N, long. 122°09'10" W). Named on Lake Berryessa (1959) 7.5' quadrangle.

Lions Head Rock [SONOMA]: *relief feature,* 3 miles north-northwest of Cazadero (lat. 38°34'15" N, long. 123°06'05" W; sec. 5, T 8 N, R 11 W). Named on Cazadero (1978) 7.5' quadrangle.

Little Austin Creek: see **Gray Creek** [SONOMA].

Little Black Mountain [SONOMA]:
(1) *peak,* 3 miles northwest of Jenner (lat. 38°29'05" N, long. 123° 09'20" W). Altitude 865 feet. Named on Arched Rock (1977) 7.5' quadrangle.
(2) *peak,* 2 miles southwest of Cazadero (lat. 38°30'50" N, long. 123°07'10" W; near NW cor. sec. 30, T 8 N, R 11 W). Named on Cazadero (1978) 7.5' quadrangle.

Little Briggs Creek [SONOMA]: *stream,* flows 3 miles to Briggs Creek 5 miles west of Mount Saint Helena (lat. 38°40'40" N, long. 122°43'35" W; near NE cor. sec. 34, T 10 N, R 8 W). Named on Mount Saint Helena (1959) 7.5' quadrangle.

Little Creek [SONOMA]: *stream,* flows about 2.5 miles to Buckeye Creek (2) 5.5 miles north of the village of Stewarts Point (lat. 38° 44'05" N, long. 123°24'25" W; near S line sec. 3, T 10 N, R 14 W). Named on Annapolis (1977) and Stewarts Point (1978) 7.5' quadrangles.

Little Geysers: see **Calistoga** [NAPA]; **The Geysers** [SONOMA].

Little Island [NAPA]: *island,* 2 miles long, 5.5 miles west of Napa Junction between Napa Slough, Devils Slough, China Slough, and South Slough (lat. 38°10'45" N, long. 122°21' W). Named on Cuttings Wharf (1949) 7.5' quadrangle.

Little Oat Mountain [SONOMA]: *peak,* 2 miles west-northwest of Cazadero (lat. 38°32'45" N, long. 123°07'15" W; near SW cor. sec. 7, T 8 N, R 11 W). Named on Cazadero (1978) 7.5' quadrangle.

Little Portuguese Canyon [NAPA]: *canyon,* 2.25 miles long, opens into the canyon of Putah Creek 9.5 miles south-southeast of Berryessa Peak (lat. 38°32' N, long. 122°08'25" W; near S line sec. 13, T 8 N, R 3 W). Named on Lake Berryessa (1959) 7.5' quadrangle. Water of Lake Berryessa covers the lower part of the canyon.

Little Rancheria Creek [SONOMA]: *stream,* flows 2 miles to Rancheria Creek 5 miles west-northwest of Skaggs Springs (lat. 38°43'20" N, long. 123°06'20" W; near S line sec. 8, T 10 N, R 11 W). Named on Tombs

Creek (1978) and Warm Springs Dam (1978) 7.5' quadrangles.

Little Strawberry Creek [SONOMA]: *stream,* flows 1.25 miles to Warm Springs Creek 4.5 miles west of Skaggs Springs (lat. 38°41'30" N, long. 123°06'30" W; near NW cor. sec. 29, T 10 N, R 11 W). Named on Warm Springs Dam (1978) 7.5' quadrangle.

Little Sugarloaf Peak [NAPA]: *peak,* 10 miles south-southwest of Berryessa Peak (lat. 38°31'25" N, long. 122°15' W); the peak is 0.5 mile south-southwest of Sugarloaf Peak. Altitude 1647 feet. Named on Chiles Valley (1958) and Lake Berryessa (1959) 7.5' quadrangles.

Little Sulphur Creek [SONOMA]: *stream,* flows 16 miles to Big Sulphur Creek 4 miles northeast of Asti (lat. 38°48'35" N, long. 122°55'30" W). Named on Asti (1959), Jimtown (1955), Mount Saint Helena (1959), and The Geysers (1959) 7.5' quadrangles. North Branch enters from the east 2.25 miles from the mouth of the main stream; it is 5.5 miles long and is named on Asti (1959) and The Geysers (1959) 7.5' quadrangles.

Little Valley [NAPA]: *canyon,* drained by a stream that flows 1.5 miles to Moskowite Reservoir 6 miles northwest of Mount Vaca (lat. 38°27'25" N, long. 122°11'15" W; near E line sec. 16, T 7 N, R 3 W). Named on Capell Valley (1951) 7.5' quadrangle.

Little Warm Springs Creek [SONOMA]: *stream,* flows 2.25 miles to Warm Springs Creek near Skaggs Springs (lat. 38°41'40" N, long. 123°01'35" W; sec. 24, T 10 N, R 11 W). Named on Warm Springs Dam (1978) 7.5' quadrangle.

Litton Springs: see **Lytton** [SONOMA].

Livantuliyume: see **Laguna de Santa Rosa** [SONOMA].

Live Oaks: see **Divide** [SONOMA].

Livereau Creek [SONOMA]: *stream,* flows 2 miles to Russian River at Guerneville (lat. 38°30' N, long. 123°15' W; sec. 31, T 8 N, R 10 W). Named on Cazadero (1978) 7.5' quadrangle.

Llajome: see **Yajome** [NAPA].

Llano [SONOMA]: *locality,* 1.5 miles east-northeast of Sebastopol (lat. 38°24'45" N, long. 122°47'35" W); the place is on Llano de Santa Rosa grant. Named on Sebastopol (1954) 7.5' quadrangle.

Llano de Santa Rosa [SONOMA]: *land grant,* southwest of Santa Rosa. Named on Cotati (1954), Santa Rosa (1954), Sebastopol (1954), and Two Rock (1954) 7.5' quadrangles. Joaquin Carillo received 3 leagues in 1844 and claimed 13,316 acres patented in 1865 (Cowan, p. 95).

Locallome: see **Locoallomi** [NAPA].

Locoallomi [NAPA]: *land grant,* at and around Pope Valley (1). Named on Aetna Springs (1958), Chiles Valley (1958), and Saint Helena (1960) 7.5' quadrangles. Julian Pope received 2 leagues in 1841; Joseph Pope and others claimed 8873 acres patented in 1862 (Cowan, p. 45; Cowan used the form "Locallome" for the name). The grant name is from an Indian village (Kroeber, p. 46).

Lokoya [NAPA]: *settlement,* 9 miles northwest of downtown Napa (lat. 38°22'20" N, long. 122°25'25" W; around NW cor. sec. 16, T 6 N, R 5 W). Named on Sonoma (1951) 7.5' quadrangle, Postal authorities established Solid Comfort post office in 1918, changed the name to Lokoya in 1925, and discontinued it in 1951 (Frickstad, p. 111, 112). Sonoma (1951) 7.5' quadrangle shows Redwood cemetery situated southeast of Lokoya (near E line sec. 16, T 6 N, R 5 W). According to Salley (p. 211), postal authorities established Spruce Hill post office in 1874 and discontinued it in 1875; it was located 7 miles northeast of Sonoma [SONOMA] in Napa County at a site called Redwood (SE quarter sec. 16, T 6 N, R 5 W).

Lombard [NAPA]: *locality,* 0.5 mile west-north-west of Napa Junction along Southern Pacific Railroad (lat. 38°11'30" N, long. 122°15'35" W; sec. 13, T 4 N, R 4 W). Named on Cuttings Wharf (1949) 7.5' quadrangle.

Lomitas: see **Rutherford** [NAPA].

Lone Pine Thicket [NAPA]: *area,* 3.25 miles south of Knoxville (lat. 38°46'30" N, long. 122°20'30" W; sec. 30, T 11 N, R 4 W). Named on Knoxville (1958) 7.5' quadrangle.

Lookout Point [NAPA]: *peak,* 6 miles north of Saint Helena (lat. 38°35'40" N, long. 122°28'30" W; near S line sec. 25, T 9 N, R 6 W). Named on Saint Helena (1960) 7.5' quadrangle.

Lookout Point [SONOMA]: *peak,* 4 miles west of Big Mountain (lat. 38°42'30" N, long. 123°13'15" W; near SE cor. sec. 18, T 10 N, R 12 W). Named on Tombs Creek (1978) 7.5' quadrangle.

Lookout Rock [SONOMA]: *relief feature,* 0.5 mile northwest of Big Mountain (lat. 38°43' N, long. 123°09'10" W; sec. 14, T 10 N, R 12 W). Named on Tombs Creek (1978) 7.5' quadrangle.

Los Guilicos [SONOMA]:
(1) *land grant,* at and near Kenwood. Named on Glen Ellen (1954), Kenwood (1954), Rutherford (1951), and Santa Rosa (1954) 7.5' quadrangles. John Wilson received 4 leagues in 1837 and claimed 18,834 acres patented in 1866 (Cowan, p. 39). The name is from an Indian village that was at the head of Sonoma Creek (Kroeber, p. 42).
(2) *locality,* 2 miles west-northwest of Kenwood along Southern Pacific Railroad (lat. 38°25'40" N, long. 122°34'50" W); the place is on Los Guilicos grant. Named on Santa Rosa (1916) 15' quadrangle.

Los Guilicos: see **Kenwood** [SONOMA].

Los Guilicos Warm Springs [SONOMA]: *spring,* 1.5 miles south of Kenwood along Sonoma Creek (lat. 38°23'40" N, long. 122°33' W); the spring is on Los Guilicos grant.

Named on Kenwood (1954) 7.5' quadrangle. Water from two springs was the basis of a resort at the place (Waring, p. 114).

Lovall Valley [NAPA]: *valley,* 6 miles west of downtown Napa on the headwaters of Huichica Creek (lat. 38°17'30" N, long. 122°23'45" W). Named on Sonoma (1951) 7.5' quadrangle. On Napa (1902) 30' quadrangle, the name has the form "Loveall Valley," and it extends west over a divide into Sonoma County. Sonoma (1942) 15' quadrangle has the name "Loveall Canyon" for the same extended feature.

Loveall Canyon: see **Lovall Valley** [NAPA].

Loveall Valley: see **Lovall Valley** [NAPA].

Lovers Gulch Creek [SONOMA]: *stream,* flows 1.5 miles to Little Sulphur Creek 9 miles north of Healdsburg (lat. 38°44'50" N, long. 122°50'40" W). Named on Jimtown (1955) 7.5' quadrangle.

Lowell [NAPA]: *locality,* 1 mile south of Napa Junction (lat. 38°10'25" N, long. 122°15'10" W; sec. 24, T 4 N, R 4 W). Named on Cuttings Wharf (1949) 7.5' quadrangle.

Lower Lake [SONOMA]: *lake,* 1450 feet long, less than 1 mile northwest of Plantation (lat. 38°36' N, long. 123°19'05" W). Named on Plantation (1977) 7.5' quadrangle, which shows a marshy lake. Plantation (1943) 7.5' quadrangle has marsh at the place.

Lyle Ridge [SONOMA]: *ridge,* east-southeast-trending, 1 mile long, 9.5 miles west-southwest of Cloverdale (lat. 38°45'05" N, long. 123°11' W). Named on Hopland (1960) 15' quadrangle, and on Tombs Creek (1978) 7.5' quadrangle.

Lynch Creek [SONOMA]: *stream,* flows 6 miles to Petaluma River 1 mile north of downtown Petaluma (lat. 38°14'50" N, long. 122°38'10" W). Named on Cotati (1954), Glen Ellen (1954), and Petaluma (1953) 7.5' quadrangles.

Lytton [SONOMA]: *village,* 3 miles north of Healdsburg (lat. 38°39'35" N, long. 122°52'15" W). Named on Jimtown (1955) 7.5' quadrangle. Postal authorities established Letton Springs post office in 1887, discontinued it in 1888, reestablished it with the name "Litton Springs" in 1889, discontinued it in 1891, reestablished it with the name "Lytton" in 1895, moved it 0.5 mile east in 1897, and discontinued it in 1954 (Salley, p. 130). Lytton Springs are 0.5 mile west of Lytton; a resort at the springs was known as Geysers Spa (Waring, p. 165). The misspelled name "Lytton" is for Captain Litton, developer of the resort in 1875 (Gudde, 1949, p. 198).

— M —

Maacama: see **Camp Maacama** [SONOMA].

Maacama Creek [SONOMA]: *stream,* formed by the confluence of McDonnell Creek and

Briggs Creek, flows 7 miles to Russian River 4.5 miles east of Healdsburg (lat. 38°36'50" N, long. 122°46'55" W). Named on Healdsburg (1955), Jimtown (1955), and Mount Saint Helena (1959) 7.5' quadrangles.

Macauley: see **Santa Rosa** [SONOMA].

Madrone [SONOMA]: *locality,* nearly 2 miles south-southeast of Glen Ellen along Northwestern Pacific Railroad (lat. 38°20'25" N, long. 122°30'25" W). Named on Santa Rosa (1916) 15' quadrangle.

Magnesite: see **Cazadero** [SONOMA].

Magoon: see **Eaton H. Magoon Lake**, under **Aetna Springs** [NAPA].

Malacomas Range: see **Mayacmas Mountains** [NAPA].

Mallacomes or Morristul [SONOMA]: *land grant,* around the northwest end of Knights Valley. Named on Mount Saint Helena (1959) 7.5' quadrangle. Jose de los Santos Berryessa received 2 leagues in 1843; Martin E. Cook and Rufus Ingalls claimed 2560 acres patented in 1859 (Cowan, p. 46—Cowan listed the grant under the designation "Malacomes, (or) Moristal"; Perez, p. 72). The name "Mallacomes" is from an Indian village that was situated 1 mile south of present Calistoga; another Indian village in the region had the name "Moristul" (Kroeber, p. 46, 49).

Mallacomes or Moristul y Plan de Agua Caliente [NAPA-SONOMA]: *land grant,* at and around the southeast end of Alexander Valley on Napa-Sonoma county line, mainly in Sonoma County. Named on Calistoga (1958), Detert Reservoir (1958), Mark West Springs (1958), and Mount. Saint Helena (1959) 7.5' quadrangles. Jose de los Santos Berryessa received 4 leagues in 1843 and claimed 17,743 acres patented in 1873 (Cowan, p. 46; Cowan listed the grant under the designation "Seno de Malacomes, (or) Moristal y Plan de Agua Caliente").

Mannings Flats [SONOMA]: *area,* 3.5 miles north-northeast of Cazadero along East Austin Creek (lat. 38°34'45" N, long. 123°03'50" W; sec. 34, T 9 N, R 11 W). Named on Cazadero (1978) 7.5' quadrangle

Mantua Gulch [SONOMA]: *canyon,* drained by a stream that flows 1 mile to Cheney Gulch 1.5 miles southeast of the village on Bodega Bay (lat. 38°19'05" N, long. 123°01'35" W). Named on Bodega Head (1972) 7.5' quadrangle.

Manzana [SONOMA]: *locality,* 4 miles northwest of Sebastopol along Petaluma and Santa Rosa Railroad (lat. 38°26'40" N, long. 122°52'15" W). Named on Sebastopol (1954) 7.5' quadrangle.

Maple Spring [NAPA]: *spring,* 4 miles north-northeast of Calistoga (lat. 38°37'45" N, long. 122°32'50" W; sec. 17, T 9 N, R 6 W). Named on Detert Reservoir (1958) 7.5' quadrangle.

Marble Mine Ridge [SONOMA]: *ridge,* east-southeast to east-trending, 1 mile long, 5.5

miles northeast of Cazadero (lat. 38°34'55" N, long. 123°00'30" W). Named on Cazadero (1978) 7.5' quadrangle. Marble Mine Ridge and Thompson Ridge (2) together are called Dutton Ridge on California Division of Forestry's (1945) map.

Marie: see **Lake Marie** [NAPA].

Markham [SONOMA]: *locality,* 1.25 miles east of present Jenner along Northwestern Pacific Railroad (lat. 38°27'10" N, long. 123° 05'45" W). Named on Duncans Mills (1921) 15' quadrangle. Postal authorities established Markham post office in 1883, discontinued it in 1900, reestablished it in 1903, and discontinued it in 1910; the name was for Andrew Markham, first postmaster (Salley, p. 133).

Markle's Place: see **Cloverdale** [SONOMA].

Markleville: see **Cloverdale** [SONOMA].

Markley Canyon [NAPA]: *canyon,* 3 miles long, opens into the canyon of Putah Creek 11.5 miles south-southeast of Berryessa Peak (lat. 38°30'35" N, long. 122°07' W; near E line sec. 30, T 8 N, R 2 W). Named on Capell Valley (1951) and Monticello Dam (1959) 7.5' quadrangles. Called Martley Canyon on Capay (1945) 15' quadrangle. Water of Lake Berryessa now covers the lower part of the canyon.

Mark West [SONOMA]: *locality,* 8.5 miles southeast of Healdsburg along Northwestern Pacific Railroad (lat. 38°30'35" N, long. 122° 46'55" W; sec. 39, T 8 N, R 8 W); the place is near the railroad crossing of Mark West Creek. Named on Healdsburg (1955) 7.5' quadrangle. Postal authorities established Mark West post office in 1865, discontinued it in 1871, reestablished it in 1872, discontinued it in 1873, reestablished it in 1874, and discontinued it in 1917 (Salley, p. 134).

Mark West Creek [SONOMA]: *stream,* flows 28 miles to Russian River 5.5 miles east of Guerneville (lat. 38°29'35" N, long. 122°53'30" W; sec. 31, T 8 N, R 9 W). Named on Calistoga (1958), Camp Meeker (1954), Healdsburg (1955), Mark West Springs (1958), and Sebastopol (1954) 7.5' quadrangles. Called West C. [Creek] on Goddard's (1857) map. The name commemorates Mark West, owner of San Miguel grant (Gudde, 1949, p. 205).

Mark West Springs [SONOMA]: *locality,* 7.5 miles north of Santa Rosa (lat. 38°32'55" N, long. 122°48'10" W; near SW cor. sec. 11, T 8 N, R 8 W); the place is along Mark West Creek. Named on Mark West Springs (1958) 7.5' quadrangle. Mineralized water from springs at the site was the basis of a resort as early as 1880 (Waring, p. 115).

Marshall Creek [SONOMA]: *stream,* formed by the confluence of McKenzie Creek and Carson Creek, flows 6.5 miles to South Fork Gualala River 1.25 miles east-northeast of Plantation (lat. 38° 36' N, long. 123°17'15" W; sec. 27, T 9 N, R 13 W). Named on Fort Ross (1978) and Plantation (1977) 7.5' quadrangles. Called Sproule Creek on Fort Ross (1943) and Plantation (1943) 7.5' quadrangles, and United States Board on Geographic Names (1977a, p. 4) gave this name as a variant.

Marshall Gulch [SONOMA]: *canyon,* drained by a stream that flows 1 mile to the sea 3 miles north-northwest of the village of Bodega Bay (lat. 38°22'10" N, long. 123°04'20" W). Named on Bodega Head (1972) 7.5' quadrangle.

Martin Creek [SONOMA]: *stream,* flows 4 miles to Barnes Creek 6.5 miles east-southeast of Healdsburg (lat. 38°35'15" N, long. 122°45'20" W; sec. 33, T 9 N, R 8 W). Named on Healdsburg (1955) and Mark West Springs (1958) 7.5' quadrangles.

Martin Spring [NAPA]: *spring,* 6 miles north-northeast of Saint Helena (lat. 38°34'50" N, long. 122°25'10" W). Named on Saint Helena (1960) 7.5' quadrangle.

Martley Canyon: see **Markley Canyon** [NAPA].

Matanzas Creek [SONOMA]: *stream,* flows 10 miles to Santa Rosa Creek in downtown Santa Rosa (lat. 38°26'15" N, long. 122°42'40" W). Named on Glen Ellen (1954), Kenwood (1954), and Santa Rosa (1954) 7.5' quadrangles. South Fork enters from the south 5.5 miles east-southeast of downtown Santa Rosa; it is 4.5 miles long and is named on Glen Ellen (1954), Kenwood (1954), and Santa Rosa (1954) 7.5' quadrangles.

Maxwell Creek [NAPA]: *stream,* flows 9 miles to Pope Creek 1.5 miles southeast of Walter Springs (lat. 38°38'10" N, long. 122°20'35" W; sec. 18, T 9 N, R 4 W). Named on Chiles Valley (1958), Saint Helena (1960), and Walter Springs (1959) 7.5' quadrangles.

Mayacamas Mountains: see **Mayacmas Mountains** [NAPA-SONOMA].

Mayacmas Mountains [NAPA-SONOMA]: *range,* mainly in Sonoma and Lake Counties, but extends south along Napa-Sonoma county line. Named on Asti (1959), Detert Reservoir (1958), Mark West Springs (1958), Mount Saint Helena (1959), The Geysers (1959), and Whispering Pines (1958) 7.5' quadrangles. United States Board on Geographic Names (1933, p. 525) approved the name "Miyakma Range" for the feature, and rejected the names "Cobb Mountain Range," "Malacomas Range," "Mayacmis Range," and "St. Helena Range." Later the Board (1942, p. 35) approved the name "Mayacmas Mountains" for the same feature, and rejected the names "Miyakma Range," "Mayacamas Mountains," and "St. Helena Range."

Mayacmis Range: see **Mayacmas Mountains** [NAPA-SONOMA].

Mays Canyon [SONOMA]: *canyon,* drained by a stream that flows 2 miles to Pocket Canyon at the south edge of Guerneville (lat. 38°

29'50" N, long. 122°59'25" W; sec. 32, T 8 N, R 10 W). Named on Camp Meeker (1954) 7.5' quadrangle.

Mays Flat [NAPA]: *area,* 6.5 miles north-northwest of Berryessa Peak on Napa-Yolo county line (lat. 38°45' N, long. 122°14'30" W; near NE cor. sec. 1, T 10 N, R 4 W). Named on Brooks (1959) and Guinda (1959) 7.5' quadrangles.

McCauley [SONOMA]: *locality,* 4 miles east-northeast of Sebastopol along Petaluma and Santa Rosa Railroad (lat. 38°25'30" N, long. 122°45'30" W). Named on Sebastopol (1942) 15' quadrangle.

McChristian Creek [SONOMA]: *stream,* flows 1 mile to Mendocino County 6.5 miles west-northwest of Cloverdale (lat. 38°49'30" N, long. 123°08'05" W; near SW cor. sec. 6, T 11 N, R 11 W). Named on Hopland (1960) 15' quadrangle.

McClennon Gulch [SONOMA]: *canyon,* drained by a stream that flows 1 mile to Fisherman Bay 0.25 mile south-southeast of the village of Stewarts Point (lat. 38°38'50" N, long. 122°23'50" W). Named on Stewarts Point (1978) 7.5' quadrangle.

McCray Mountain [SONOMA]: *peak,* 4.25 miles north of Guerneville (lat. 38°33'50" N, long. 122°59'35" W; sec. 5, T 8 N, R 10 W). Altitude 1940 feet. Named on Guerneville (1955) 7.5' quadrangle.

McCrays: see **Cloverdale** [SONOMA].

McDonnell Creek [SONOMA]: *stream,* flows 4.25 miles to join Briggs Creek and form Maacama Creek 6 miles west of Mount Saint Helena (lat. 38°40'25" N, long. 122°44'30" W; near W line sec. 34, T 10 N, R 8 W). Named on Mount Saint Helena (1959) 7.5' quadrangle.

McGill [SONOMA]: *locality,* 3.25 miles north of Sears Point along Northwestern Pacific Railroad (lat. 38°11'55" N, long. 122°26'05" W). Named on Sears Point (1951) 7.5' quadrangle.

McKenzie Creek [SONOMA]: *stream,* flows 4 miles to join Carson Creek and form Marshall Creek 4 miles north-northeast of Fort Ross (lat. 38°33'50" N, long. 123°12'20" W; sec. 5, T 8 N, R 12 W). Named on Fort Ross (1978) 7.5' quadrangle.

McNear [SONOMA]: *locality,* 1.5 miles east-southeast of downtown Petaluma along Northwestern Pacific Railroad (lat. 38°13'45" N, long. 122°36'50" W). Named on Petaluma River (1954) 7.5' quadrangle.

Meacham Hill [SONOMA]: *ridge,* southeast-trending, 1.5 miles long, 2.25 miles south-southeast of Cotati (lat. 38°17'35" N, long. 122°41'35" W). Named on Cotati (1954) 7.5' quadrangle. Called Meachim Hill on Santa Rosa (1944) 15' quadrangle.

Meachim Hill: see **Meacham Hill** [SONOMA].

Meadows: see **The Meadows** [SONOMA].

Meeker: see **Camp Meeker** [SONOMA]; **Occidental** [SONOMA].

Melita [SONOMA]: *locality,* 4 miles east-northeast of downtown Santa Rosa (lat. 38°27'30" N, long. 122°38'20" W). Named on Santa Rosa (1954) 7.5' quadrangle. Called Melitta on Santa Rosa (1916) 15' quadrangle. Postal authorities established Melitta post office in 1891 and discontinued it in 1900 (Frickstad, p. 197).

Melitta: see **Melita** [SONOMA].

Mendosoma: see **Tobacco Creek** [SONOMA].

Merazo [SONOMA]: *locality,* 6.25 miles northeast of Sears Point along Southern Pacific Railroad (lat. 38°13' N, long. 122°22'10" W). Named on Cuttings Wharf (1949) 7.5' quadrangle.

Mercury: see **Guerneville** [SONOMA].

Mercuryville [SONOMA]: *locality,* 1.5 miles east-northeast of Geyser Peak (lat. 38°46'35" N, long. 122°49'15" W; near NW cor. sec. 25, T 11 N, R 9 W). Named on The Geysers (1959) 7.5' quadrangle.

Mercuryville: see **Guerneville** [SONOMA].

Mesa Grande [SONOMA]: *settlement,* 2.5 miles southwest of Guerneville along Russian River (lat. 38°28'35" N, long. 123°01'05" W). Named on Duncans Mills (1979) 7.5' quadrangle. Duncans Mills (1921) 15' quadrangle shows both Mesa Grande and Grandville P.O. at the place. Postal authorities established Grandville post office in 1907 and discontinued it in 1921 (Frickstad, p. 195).

Mesa Grande Gulch [SONOMA]: *canyon,* drained by a stream that flows 0.5 mile to Russian River nearly 3 miles southwest of Guerneville (lat. 38°28'10" N, long. 123°01'50" W). Named on Duncans Mills (1979) 7.5' quadrangle.

Meyer [SONOMA]: *locality,* 3 miles northwest of present Jenner (lat. 38°28'50" N, long. 123°09'50" W). Named on Duncans Mills (1921) 15' quadrangle.

Meyer Gulch [SONOMA]: *canyon,* drained by a stream that flows 0.5 mile to the sea 4.25 miles northwest of Jenner (lat. 38°29'05" N, long. 123°10'55" W). Named on Arched Rock (1977) 7.5' quadrangle.

Middle Creek [NAPA]: *stream,* flows nearly 2 miles to Capell Creek 9 miles northwest of Mount Vaca (lat. 38°28'30" N, long. 122°14'05" W; near N line sec. 7, T 7 N, R 3 W). Named on Capell Valley (1951) 7.5' quadrangle.

Middleton [NAPA]: *locality,* 1.5 miles north-northwest of Napa Junction along Southern Pacific Railroad (lat. 38°12'20" N, long. 122°15'45" W; at W line sec. 12, T 4 N, R 4 W). Named on Cuttings Wharf (1949) 7.5' quadrangle.

Midshipman Point [SONOMA]: *promontory,* 2.5 miles south of Sears Point along San Pablo Bay (lat. 38°07' N, long. 122°27' W). Named on Petaluma Point (1959) 7.5' quadrangle. Postal Route (1884) map has the name "Sonoma Ldg." along San Pablo Bay near present Midshipman Point at the end of Sonoma Valley Railroad.

Mile Rocks [SONOMA]: *rocks,* 1.5 miles west-southwest of Jenner, and nearly 1 mile offshore (lat. 38°26'25" N, long. 123°08'30" W). Named on Arched Rock (1977) 7.5' quadrangle.

Mill Creek [NAPA]: *stream,* flows 3.5 miles to Napa River 3 miles north-northwest of Saint Helena (lat. 38°32'40" N, long. 122°29'45" W). Named on Calistoga (1958) and Saint Helena (1960) 7.5' quadrangles. Calistoga (1958) 7.5' quadrangle shows Bale Mill historical monument by the stream.

Mill Creek [SONOMA]:

(1) *stream,* flows 11 miles to Dry Creek less than 2 miles south of Healdsburg (lat. 38°35'20" N, long. 122°52'10" W). Named on Guerneville (1955) and Healdsburg (1955) 7.5' quadrangles. The name is from March's Mill, a lumber mill of 1850 (LeBaron and others, p. 13).

(2) *stream,* flows 2.5 miles to Sonoma Creek 1 mile south-southeast of Glen Ellen (lat. 38°21' N, long. 122°30'50" W). Named on Glen Ellen (1954) 7.5' quadrangle.

(3) *stream,* flows 2.25 miles to Mark West Creek 1.25 miles east of Mark West Springs (lat. 38°32'50" N, long. 122°41'50" W; at N line sec. 13, T 8 N, R 8 W). Named on Mark West Springs (1958) 7.5' quadrangle.

Mill Creek: see **Redwood Canyon** [NAPA].

Miller Creek [SONOMA]:

(1) *stream,* flows 4.5 miles to Russian River 1 mile east of Geyserville (lat. 38°42'20" N, long. 122°53'05" W). Named on Geyserville (1955) and Jimtown (1955) 7.5' quadrangles.

(2) *stream,* flows 3 miles to the sea 1.5 miles west-southwest of Plantation (lat. 38°34'50" N, long. 123°20'05" W). Named on Plantation (1977) 7.5' quadrangle.

Miller Flat [NAPA]: *area,* 3.5 miles east-northeast of Calistoga in Dutch Henry Canyon (lat. 38°36'05" N, long. 122°31'20" W; sec. 28, T 9 N, R 6 W). Named on Calistoga (1958) 7.5' quadrangle.

Miller Ridge [SONOMA]: *ridge,* northwest-trending, 4 mile long, center 2.25 miles north-northeast of the village of Stewarts Point (lat. 38°41' N, long. 123°23' W). Named on Annapolis (1977) and Stewarts Point (1978) 7.5' quadrangles.

Mill Gulch [SONOMA]: *canyon,* drained by a stream that flows 1.5 miles to the sea 1.5 miles southeast of Fort Ross (lat. 38°30' N, long. 123°13'20" W). Named on Fort Ross (1978) 7.5' quadrangle.

Milliken Canyon [NAPA]: *canyon,* 6.25 miles long, along Milliken Creek above a point 4.25 miles north-northeast of downtown Napa (lat. 38°21'30" N, long. 122°15'30" W; sec. 24, T 6 N, R 4 W). Named on Capell Valley (1951), Mount George (1951), and Napa (1951) 7.5' quadrangles.

Milliken Creek [NAPA]: *stream,* flows 10.5 miles to Napa River 1.25 miles north-northeast of downtown Napa (lat. 38°19' N, long. 122°16'35" W); the stream drains Milliken Canyon. Named on Capell Valley (1951), Mount George (1951), Napa (1951), and Yountville (1951) 7.5' quadrangles.

Milliken Peak [NAPA]: *peak,* 4.5 miles west-southwest of downtown Napa (lat. 38°16'25" N, long. 122°21'35" W). Altitude 743 feet. Named on Napa (1951) 7.5' quadrangle.

Milliken Reservoir [NAPA]: *lake,* behind a dam on Milliken Creek 7 miles west-southwest of Mount Vaca (lat. 38°22'40" N, long. 122° 13'35" W; near E line sec. 7, T 6 N, R 3 W). Named on Capell Valley (1951) 7.5' quadrangle.

Mills [SONOMA]: *locality,* 1.25 miles northwest of Sebastopol along Petaluma and Santa Rosa Railroad (lat. 38°24'50" N, long. 122°50'30" W). Named on Sebastopol (1942) 15' quadrangle.

Mill Stream [SONOMA]: *stream,* flows 1.5 miles to Briggs Creek 2.5 miles west-northwest of Mount Saint Helena (lat. 38°41'25" N, long. 122°40'25" W; sec. 30, T 10 N, R 7 W). Named on Mount Saint Helena (1959) 7.5' quadrangle.

Mill Valley [NAPA]: *valley,* 5.5 miles north-northeast of Saint Helena (lat. 38°34'45" N, long. 122°25'35" W). Named on Saint Helena (1960) 7.5' quadrangle.

Mineral Spring [SONOMA]: *spring,* 4 miles north-northwest of Cazadero (lat. 38°35'05" N, long. 123°07'15" W). Named on Cazadero (1943) 7.5' quadrangle.

Mirabel Heights [SONOMA]: *settlement,* nearly 6 miles east of Guerneville along Russian River (lat. 38°29'30" N, long. 122°53'30" W; sec. 31, T 8 N, R 9 W). Named on Camp Meeker (1954) 7.5' quadrangle. Called Mirabell Heights on Sebastopol (1954) 15' quadrangle.

Mirabel Park [SONOMA]: *settlement,* 5.5 miles east of Guerneville along Russian River (lat. 38°29'35" N, long. 122°53'50" W; sec. 31, T 8 N, R 9 W). Named on Camp Meeker (1954) 7.5' quadrangle. Called Mirabell Park on Sebastopol (1954) 15' quadrangle. The earliest resort along Russian River was opposite present Mirabel Park and was called Wall Springs—six mineral springs were the chief attraction there (Hansen and Miller, p. 133).

Mira Monte Slough [SONOMA]: *water feature,* joins San Antonio Creek 7 miles southeast of downtown Petaluma (lat. 38°09'30" N, long. 122°33'05" W). Named on Petaluma River (1954) 7.5' quadrangle.

Mission Canyon [SONOMA]: *canyon,* 2 miles long, along Hulburt Creek (present Hulbert Creek) above a point 2.25 miles northwest of Guerneville (lat. 38°31'25" N, long. 123°01'50" W; sec. 24, T 8 N, R 11 W). Named on Cazadero (1943) 7.5' quadrangle.

45

Mission Creek [SONOMA]: *stream,* flows 1.5 miles to Hulbert Creek less than 2 miles west of Guerneville at Monte Rosa (lat. 38° 30'15" N, long. 123°01'35" W). Named on Cazadero (1978) 7.5' quadrangle.

Mission Highlands [SONOMA]: *settlement,* 2 miles north of Sonoma (lat. 38°19'15" N, long. 122°27'15" W; sec. 31, T 6 N, R 5 W). Named on Sonoma (1951) 7.5' quadrangle.

Mitchell Canyon: see **East Mitchell Canyon** [NAPA]; **West Mitchell Canyon** [NAPA].

Miwok Beach [SONOMA]: *beach,* 2.25 miles north-north-west of the village of Bodega Bay along the coast (lat. 38°21'35" N, long. 123° 04'05" W). Named on Bodega Head (1972) 7.5' quadrangle.

Miyakma Range: see **Mayacmas Mountains** [NAPA-SONOMA].

Mohrhardt Ridge [SONOMA]: *ridge,* generally east-trending, 3.5 miles long, 6.5 miles northeast of Fort Ross (lat. 38° 34'40" N, long. 123°09'15" W). Named on Fort Ross (1978) 7.5' quadrangle. On California Division of Forestry's (1945) map, a feature called Potatoe Patch Ridge extends south-southwest from Mohrhardt Ridge.

Molino [SONOMA]: *locality,* 2 miles northwest of Sebastopol along Petaluma and Santa Rosa Railroad (lat. 38°25'25" N, long. 122°50'50" W; sec. 27, T 7 N, R 9 W). Named on Sebastopol (1954) 7.5' quadrangle. Postal authorities established Molino post office in 1899 and discontinued it in 1902; the name is from Molinos grant (Salley, p. 143).

Molino: see **Molinos** [SONOMA].

Molinos [SONOMA]: *land grant,* north-north-west of Sebastopol around Graton and Forestville. Named on Camp Meeker (1954), Guerneville (1955), Healdsburg (1955), and Sebastopol (1954) 7.5' quadrangles. John Bautista Roger Cooper received 10.5 leagues in 1836 and claimed 17,892 acres patented in 1858 (Cowan, p. 48-49; Cowan listed the grant under the designation "Molino, (or) Rio Ayoska, (or) Levantahyume").

Monroe [SONOMA]: *locality,* 2 miles west-northwest of downtown Santa Rosa (lat. 38°27'10" N, long. 122°45' W). Named on Santa Rosa (1954) and Sebastopol (1954) 7.5' quadrangles.

Monte Cristo [SONOMA]: *settlement,* 2 miles southwest of Guerneville along Russian River (lat. 38°28'35" N, long. 123°01'10" W). Named on Duncans Mills (1979) 7.5' quadrangle.

Monte Cristo Creek [SONOMA]: *stream,* flows less than 1 mile to Russian River 2.25 miles southwest of Guerneville (lat. 38°29'40" N, long. 123°01'25" W); the stream is west of Monte Cristo. Named on Duncans Mills (1979) 7.5' quadrangle.

Monte Rio [SONOMA]: *town,* 2.25 miles south-southwest of Guerneville along Russian River (lat. 38°27'50" N, long. 123°00'35" W; sec. 7, T 7 N, R 10 W). Named on Duncans Mills (1979) 7.5' quadrangle. Postal authorities established Montrio post office in 1902 and changed the name to Monte Rio in 1924 (Frickstad, p. 197).

Monte Rosa [SONOMA]: *settlement,* 1.5 miles west of Guerneville (lat. 38°30'15" N, long. 123°01'35" W; sec. 25, 36, T 8 N, R 11 W). Named on Cazadero (1978) 7.5' quadrangle.

Montesano [SONOMA]: *settlement,* 1.5 miles southwest of Guerneville along Russian River (lat. 38°29'10" N, long. 123°00'50" W; near NW cor. sec. 6, T 7 N, R 10 W). Named on Duncans Mills (1979) 7.5' quadrangle.

Montgomery Creek [NAPA]: *stream,* flows 1.5 miles to Dry Creek nearly 4 miles south-southwest of Rutherford (lat. 38°24'20" N, long. 122°26'25" W). Named on Rutherford (1951) 7.5' quadrangle.

Montgomery Village [SONOMA]: *district,* 1.5 miles east-northeast of downtown Santa Rosa (lat. 38°26'40" N, long. 122°41'15" W). Named on Santa Rosa (1954) 7.5' quadrangle.

Monti: see **Fisherman Bay** [SONOMA].

Monticello [NAPA]: *town,* 6 miles south of Berryessa Peak in Berryessa Valley (lat. 38°34'45" N, long. 122°12'20" W). Named on Capay (1945) 15' quadrangle. Postal authorities established Monticello post office in 1867 and discontinued it in 1956 (Salley, p. 145). Water of Lake Berryessa now covers the site.

Monticello Reservoir: see **Lake Berryessa** [NAPA].

Montrio: see **Monte Rio** [SONOMA].

Moonshine Pond [SONOMA]: *lake,* 200 feet long, 1.5 miles northwest of Cazadero (lat. 38°32'55" N, long. 123°06'05" W; sec. 8, T 8 N, R 11 W). Named on Cazadero (1978) 7.5' quadrangle.

Moore: see **Camp C.C. Moore**, under **Camp Royaneh** [SONOMA].

Moore Creek [NAPA]: *stream,* flows 8 miles to Chiles Creek 6.25 miles east of Saint Helena (lat. 38°30'30" N, long. 122°21'15" W; near NE cor. sec. 31, T 8 N, R 4 W). Named on Chiles Valley (1958) and Saint Helena (1960) 7.5' quadrangles.

Moore Flat [NAPA]: *area,* 5.5 miles northeast of Walter Springs along lower reaches of Nevada Creek (lat. 38°42'45" N, long. 122° 17'30" W; near W line sec. 15, T 10 N, R 4 W). Named on Walter Springs (1959) 7.5' quadrangle.

Moristul y Plan de Agua Caliente: see **Mallacomes or Moristul y Plan de Agua Caliente** [NAPA-SONOMA].

Morrison Ridge [SONOMA]: *ridge,* west-southwest-trending, 1.5 miles long, 4.5 miles northeast of Cazadero (lat. 38°34'25" N, long. 123°01'30" W). Named on Cazadero (1978) 7.5' quadrangle.

Morris Peak [SONOMA]: *peak,* 6 miles west-northwest of Cloverdale (lat. 38°49'40" N, long. 123°07'15" W; sec. 6, T 11 N, R 11 W).

Altitude 1843 feet. Named on Cloverdale (1960) 7.5' quadrangle.

Morristal: see **Mallacomes or Morristul** [SONOMA].

Moscow [SONOMA]: *locality,* 4.25 miles southwest of Guerneville along Northwestern Pacific Railroad (lat. 38°27'20" N, long. 123° 02'55" W); the place is near Russian River. Named on Duncans Mills (1921) 15' quadrangle.

Moskowite Reservoir [NAPA]: *lake,* 1650 feet long, 6 miles northwest of Mount Vaca (lat. 38°27'30" N, long. 122°11'30" W; sec. 16, T 7 N, R 3 W). Named on Capell Valley (1951) 7.5' quadrangle.

Mountain Rock [SONOMA]: *relief feature,* 2 miles west of the village of Bodega Bay (lat. 38°20' N, long. 123°00'45" W). Named on Bodega Head (1942) 7.5' quadrangle.

Mount George [NAPA]: *peak,* 7.5 miles southwest of Mount Vaca (lat. 38°20'30" N, long. 122°13'10" W; sec. 29, T 6 N, R 3 W). Altitude 1877 feet. Named on Mount George (1951) 7.5' quadrangle. Called George Mt. on Napa (1902) 30' quadrangle.

Mount Helen: see **Mount Saint Helena** [SONOMA].

Mount Heller [SONOMA]: *peak,* nearly 3 miles south of Guerneville (lat. 38°27'40" N, long. 123°00'10" W; sec. 7, T 7 N, R 10 W). Altitude 865 feet. Named on Duncans Mills (1979) 7.5' quadrangle.

Mount Henry: see **Mount Saint John** [NAPA].

Mount Hood [SONOMA]: *peak,* 3 miles north of Kenwood (lat. 38° 27'35" N, long. 122°33'10" W; near S line sec. 8, T 7 N, R 6 W). Altitude 2730 feet. Named on Kenwood (1954) 7.5' quadrangle. The name commemorates William Hood, who arrived in California in 1846 and later bought part of Los Guilicos grant (Gudde, 1949, p. 152).

Mount Jackson [SONOMA]:

(1) *peak,* 3.25 miles northeast of Guerneville (lat. 38°32'20" N, long. 122°57'35" W; sec. 15, T 8 N, R 10 W). Altitude 1652 feet. Named on Guerneville (1955) 7.5' quadrangle.

(2) *settlement,* 5 miles east of Guerneville (lat. 38°30'50" N, long. 122°54'15" W; sec. 30, T 8 N, R 9 W). Named on Guerneville (1955) 7.5' quadrangle.

Mount Nebo: see **Bismark Knob** [NAPA-SONOMA].

Mount Olivet: see **Fulton** [SONOMA].

Mount Pisgah [SONOMA]:

(1) *ridge,* east-northeast-trending, 1 mile long, 3 miles northeast of Occidental (lat. 38°25'50" N, long. 122°53'55" W). Named on Camp Meeker (1954) 7.5' quadrangle.

(2) *peak,* 3.5 miles north of Sonoma (lat. 38°20'40" N, long. 122°27'35" W; near SW cor. sec. 19, T 6 N, R 5 W). Altitude 1349 feet. Named on Sonoma (1951) 7.5' quadrangle.

Mount Roscoe [SONOMA]: *peak,* 1 mile north-

northeast of the village of Bodega Bay (lat. 38°20'45" N, long. 123°02'30" W). Altitude 621 feet. Named on Bodega Head (1972) 7.5' quadrangle.

Mount Saint Helena [SONOMA]: *peak,* 13 miles east-northeast of Healdsburg near the junction of Sonoma County, Lake County, and Napa County (lat. 38°40'10" N, long. 122°37'55" W; near E line sec. 33, T 10 N, R 7 W). Altitude 4343 feet. Named on Mount Saint Helena (1959) 7.5' quadrangle. Called Mt. St. Hellens on Goddard's (1857) map. Trask (p. 10) called the feature Mount Helen. Whitney (p. 86-87) claimed that a Russian naturalist named Wosnessensky climbed the peak in 1841 and named it. It was called Devil's Mount in the early days of American settlement in California (Gudde, 1949, p. 295).

Mount Saint John [NAPA]: *peak,* 2.5 miles southwest of Rutherford (lat. 38°26'15" N, long. 122°27'35" W; sec. 19, T 7 N, R 5 W). Altitude 2375 feet. Named on Rutherford (1951) 7.5' quadrangle. Called St. John Mt. on Napa (1902) 30' quadrangle. Members of the Whitney survey named the peak Mount Henry for Joseph Henry of Princeton University and Smithsonian Institution, but the name was not adopted (Brewer, p. 224-225, 238).

Mount Tom [SONOMA]: *ridge,* east-southeast-trending, 1.25 miles long, 12.5 miles west-southwest of Cloverdale (lat. 38°46' N, long. 123°14'30" W). Named on Hopland (1960) 15' quadrangle.

Mount Vaca [NAPA]: *peak,* 12 miles northeast of Napa on Blue Ridge (2) on Napa-Solano county line (lat. 38°24' N, long. 122°06'20" W; sec. 5, T 6 N, R 2 W); the peak is in Vaca Mountains. Altitude 2819 feet. Named on Mount Vaca (1951) 7.5' quadrangle. United States Board on Geographic Names (1970, p. 3) gave the names "Blue Mountain" and "Vaca Peak" as variants, and pointed out that the feature is the highest point in Vaca Mountains.

Mount Veeder [NAPA-SONOMA]: *peak,* 5.5 miles south-southwest of Rutherford on Napa-Sonoma county line (lat. 38°22'45" N, long. 122°26'50" W; sec. 7, T 6 N, R 5 W). Named on Rutherford (1951) and Sonoma (1951) 7.5' quadrangles. Called Veeder Mt. on Napa (1902) 30' quadrangle. The name commemorates Peter V. Veeder, minister of the Presbyterian church in Napa from about 1858 until 1861 (Gudde, 1949, p. 377).

Mud Hen Slough [SONOMA]: *water feature,* joins San Antonio Creek 6.5 miles southeast of downtown Petaluma (lat. 38°10'10" N, long. 122°33'10" W). Named on Petaluma River (1954) 7.5' quadrangle.

Mudholes [SONOMA]: *water feature,* 7 miles north of Fort Ross (lat. 38°36'55" N, long. 123°13'30" W; at N line sec. 19, T 9 N, R 12 W). Named on Fort Ross (1978) 7.5' quadrangle.

Mud Lake [NAPA]: *lake,* 550 feet long, 3 miles west of Mount Vaca (lat. 38°24' N, long. 122°09'30" W). Named on Capell Valley (1951, photorevised 1968) 7.5' quadrangle.

Mud Slough [NAPA]: *water feature,* joins Napa River 3.5 miles west of Napa Junction (lat. 38°11'25" N, long. 122°18'50" W). Named on Cuttings Wharf (1949) 7.5' quadrangle.

Mud Spring [NAPA]: *spring,* 4.5 miles east-northeast of Calistoga on Rattlesnake Ridge (lat. 38°36'30" N, long. 122°30'20" W; sec. 22, T 9 N, R 6 W). Named on Calistoga (1958) 7.5' quadrangle.

Muñis: see **Muniz** [SONOMA].

Muniz [SONOMA]: *land grant,* along the coast from Russian River to northwest of Fort Ross. Named on Arched Rock (1977), Duncans Mills (1979), Fort Ross (1978), and Plantation (1977) 7.5' quadrangles. Manuel Torres received 4 leagues in 1845 and claimed 17,761 acres patented in 1860 (Cowan, p. 50; Cowan used the form "Muñis" for the name).

Murphy Creek [NAPA]: *stream,* flows 3 miles to join Spencer Creek and form Tulucay Creek 10.5 miles southwest of Mount Vaca (lat. 38°17'35" N, long. 122°14'15" W). Named on Mount George (1951) 7.5' quadrangle.

Murphy Mill [SONOMA]: *locality,* 4.5 miles east of Fort Ross (lat. 38°30'55" N, long. 123°09'20" W; near N line sec. 26, T 8 N, R 12 W). Named on Fort Ross (1943) 7.5' quadrangle. Fort Ross (1978) 7.5' quadrangle has the name "Black Mountain Conservation Camp" at the site.

Mussel Point [SONOMA]: *promontory,* nearly 2 miles west-southwest of the village of Bodega Bay along the coast (lat. 38°19'20" N, long. 123°04'35" W). Named on Bodega Head (1972) 7.5' quadrangle.

Mysterious Creek [NAPA]: *stream,* flows nearly 2 miles to Putah Creek 6.25 miles south-southwest of Knoxville (lat. 38°45'05" N, long. 122°24'10" W; near N line sec. 3, T 10 N, R 5 W); the stream drains Mysterious Valley. Named on Jericho Valley (1958) and Knoxville (1958) 7.5' quadrangles.

Mysterious Valley [NAPA]: *valley,* 5.25 miles south-southwest of Knoxville (lat. 38°45'05" N, long. 122°22'05" W); Mysterious Creek drains the valley. Named on Knoxville (1958) and Walter Springs (1959) 7.5' quadrangles.

— N —

Napa [NAPA]:

(1) *land grant,* mainly in Napa Valley at and northwest of the city of Napa. Named on Napa (1951), Rutherford (1951), Sonoma (1951), and Yountville (1951) 7.5' quadrangles. Salvador Vallejo received 4 leagues in 1838 and claimed 3178 acres patented in 1866; six other claimants received parcels ranging from 260 to 680 acres patented from 1866 to 1880

(Cowan, p. 51; Perez, p. 77-78). The name "Napa" may be from an Indian word for the detachable points of native fish harpoons (Kroeber, p. 50).

(2) *city,* near the south end of Napa Valley along Napa River (lat. 38°17'50" N, long. 122°17' W); the city is on Napa grant. Named on Napa (1951) 7.5' quadrangle. Called Nappa on Trask's (1853) map. Postal authorities established Napa City post office in 1850, and changed the name to Napa in 1890 (Frickstad, p. 111). Grigsby and Combs laid out the community in 1848 at what was known as the embarcadero at the head of navigation on Napa River (Bancroft, 1888, p. 510).

Napa City: see **Napa** [NAPA] (2).

Napa Creek [NAPA]: *stream,* formed by the confluence of Redwood Creek and Browns Valley Creek, flows 2 miles to Napa River in downtown Napa (lat. 38°17'55" N, long. 122°17' W). Named on Napa (1951) 7.5' quadrangle. On Napa (1902) 30' quadrangle, present Browns Valley Creek is called South Fork [Napa Creek], and the stream in present Pickel Canyon is called North Branch [Napa Creek].

Napa Creek: see **Napa River** [NAPA]; **Redwood Creek** [NAPA].

Napa Junction [NAPA]: *locality,* 7.5 miles south-southeast of Napa along Southern Pacific Railroad (lat. 38°11'15" N, long. 122°15' W; near S line sec. 13, T 4 N, R 4 W). Named on Cordelia (1951) and Cuttings Wharf (1949) 7.5' quadrangles. Postal authorities established Adelante post office at the place in 1869 and discontinued it in 1871; they established Napa Junction post office in 1875, discontinued it for a time in 1880, and discontinued it finally in 1933 (Salley, p. 1, 150). California Division of Highways' (1934) map shows a place called Kelly located about 1.5 miles north of Napa Junction along San Francisco, Napa, and Calistoga Railway (sec. 12, T 4 N, R 4 W), and a place called Napa Wye nearly 1 mile farther north (sec. 1, T 4 N, R 4 W), apparently at a highway junction. California Mining Bureau's (1917) map shows a place called Guthrie halfway from Napa Junction to Napa along a railroad.

Napa Reservoir: see **East Napa Reservoir** [NAPA]; **West Napa Reservoir** [NAPA].

Napa River [NAPA]: *stream,* heads in Napa County and flows 58 miles to Carquinez Strait (by way of Mare Island Strait) 2 miles south-southeast of downtown Vallejo in Solano County (lat. 38°04'30" N, long. 122°14'40" W). Named on Calistoga (1958), Cuttings Wharf (1949), Mare Island (1959), Napa (1951), Rutherford (1951), Saint Helena (1960), and Yountville (1951) 7.5' quadrangles. Called Nappa C.[Creek] on Trask's (1853) map, and called Napa Cr. on Eddy's (1854) map. United States Board on Geographic Names (1933, p. 544) rejected the name "Napa Creek" for the stream.

Napa Rock Soda Springs: see **Samuel Springs** [NAPA].

Napa Slough [NAPA-SONOMA]: *water feature,* forms part of Napa-Sonoma county line, joins Napa River 3.5 miles west of Napa Junction (lat. 38°11'05" N, long. 122°18'45" W). Named on Cuttings Wharf (1949) and Sears Point (1951) 7.5' quadrangles.

Napa Slough: see **Second Napa Slough** [SONOMA]; **Third Napa Slough** [SONOMA].

Napa Soda Springs [NAPA]: *locality,* 5 miles east-southeast of Yountville (lat. 38°23'30" N, long. 122°16'40" W; near SW cor. sec. 2, T 6 N, R 4 W). Named on Yountville (1951) 7.5' quadrangle. Postal authorities established Napa Soda Springs post office in 1882 and discontinued it in 1929 (Frickstad, p. 111). The place also was called Jacksons Napa Soda Springs (Waring, p. 155).

Napa Valley [NAPA]: *valley,* along Napa River above the city of Napa. Named on Calistoga (1958), Napa (1951), Rutherford (1951), Saint Helena (1960), and Yountville (1951) 7.5' quadrangles. Called Nappa Valley on Jefferson's (1849) map, and called Valley of Nappa by Wilkes (p. 86) in 1841.

Napa Vichy Spring: see **Vichy Springs** [NAPA].

Napa Wye: see **Napa Junction** [NAPA].

Nappa: see **Napa** [NAPA] (2).

Nappa Creek: see **Napa River** [NAPA].

Nappa Valley: see **Napa Valley** [NAPA].

Nash Creek [NAPA]: *stream,* flows 2 miles to Napa River 2.5 miles east-southeast of Calistoga (lat. 38°33'50" N, long. 122°31'55" W). Named on Calistoga (1958) 7.5' quadrangle. William Nash built a house by the stream in or before 1848 (Archuleta, p. 16).

Nathanson Creek [SONOMA]: *stream,* flows 7.25 miles to Schell Creek 2.5 miles south of Sonoma (lat. 38°15'30" N, long. 122° 27' W). Named on Sonoma (1951) 7.5' quadrangle.

Neal Creek [SONOMA]: *stream,* flows 0.5 mile to Mark West Creek 7.5 miles east-southeast of Mark West Springs (lat. 38°31' N, long. 122°34'55" W; sec. 25, T 8 N, R 7 W). Named on Calistoga (1958) 7.5' quadrangle.

Nebo: see **Mount Nebo**, under **Bismark Knob** [NAPA].

Neeley Hill [SONOMA]: *peak,* less than 1 mile south-southwest of Guerneville (lat. 38°29'25" N, long. 123°00' W; at E line sec. 31, T 8 N, R 10 E). Named on Camp Meeker (1954) and Duncans Mills (1979) 7.5' quadrangles.

Neese Ridge [SONOMA]: *ridge,* south-south-west-trending, 1 mile long, 4 miles west-southwest of Big Mountain (lat. 38°40'45" N, long. 123°12'30" W). Named on Tombs Creek (1978) 7.5' quadrangle.

Negro Canyon [NAPA]: *canyon,* drained by a stream that flows 1 mile to Lake Berryessa 8 miles northwest of Mount Vaca (lat. 38° 29'35" N, long. 122°12'10" W; near W line sec. 33, T 8 N, R 3 W). Named on Capell Val-

ley (1951, photorevised 1968) 7.5' quadrangle.

Neils Island [SONOMA]: *hill,* 4.5 miles southeast of downtown Petaluma in marsh southwest of Petaluma River (lat. 38°11'25" N, long. 122°34'40" W). Named on Petaluma River (1954) 7.5' quadrangle. Called Nell Island on Petaluma (1914) 15' quadrangle.

Nell Island: see **Neils Island** [SONOMA].

Nervo [SONOMA]: *locality,* 2 miles southeast of Geyserville along Northwestern Pacific Railroad (lat. 38°41'15" N, long. 122°52'45" W). Named on Geyserville (1955) 7.5' quadrangle.

Nevada Creek [NAPA]: *stream,* flows 7.5 miles to Adams Creek 5 miles northeast of Walter Springs (lat. 38°42'15" N, long. 122°17'30" W; near N line sec. 22, T 10 N, R 4 W). Named on Knoxville (1958) and Walter Springs (1959) 7.5' quadrangles.

Newgate Ridge [SONOMA]: *ridge,* south-trending, 1 mile long, 5 miles northeast of Guerneville (lat. 38°33'25" N, long. 122°56'30" W). Named on Guerneville (1955) 7.5' quadrangle.

New Philadelphia: see **Sonoma** [SONOMA].

Newtown [SONOMA]: *locality,* nearly 2 miles east of downtown Petaluma along Northwestern Pacific Railroad (lat. 38°13'55" N, long. 122°36'20" W). Named on Petaluma (1914) 15' quadrangle.

Nob Hill [SONOMA]: *peak,* 2.25 miles southeast of Annapolis (lat. 38°41'45" N, long. 123°20'20" W; sec. 20, T 10 N, R 13 W). Named on Annapolis (1977) 7.5' quadrangle.

Noel Heights [SONOMA]: *settlement,* 2 miles east-southeast of Guerneville in Picket Canyon (lat. 38°29'30" N, long. 122°57'30" W; sec. 34, T 8 N, R 10 W). Named on Camp Meeker (1954) 7.5' quadrangle.

Nolan Creek [SONOMA]: *stream,* flows about 3.5 miles to Salmon Creek (1) 2.5 miles northwest of Valley Ford (lat. 38°20'35" N, long. 122°57'45" W). Named on Camp Meeker (1954) and Valley Ford (1954) 7.5' quadrangles.

North Gap [SONOMA]: *pass,* 8.5 miles northeast of Fort Ross (lat. 38°36'55" N, long. 123°08'50" W; near SE cor. sec. 14, T 9 N, R 12 W). Named on Fort Ross (1978) 7.5' quadrangle.

North Salmon Creek Beach [SONOMA]: *beach,* 2 miles northwest of the village of Bodega Bay along the coast (lat. 38°21'25" N, long. 123°04' W); the beach is north of the mouth of Salmon Creek (1). Named on Bodega Head (1972) 7.5' quadrangle.

North Slough [NAPA]: *water feature,* enters lowlands along Napa River 1.5 miles west of Napa Junction (lat. 38°11'05" N, long. 122° 16'35" W; sec. 23, T 4 N, R 4 W). Named on Cuttings Wharf (1949) 7.5' quadrangle.

Northwest Cape [SONOMA]: *promontory,* 0.5 mile west of Fort Ross along the coast (lat.

38°30'45" N, long. 123°15'15" W). Named on Fort Ross (1978) and Plantation (1977) 7.5' quadrangles.

Northwood [SONOMA]: *settlement,* 2 miles south of Healdsburg along Russian River (lat. 38°28'30" N, long. 123°00'05" W; sec. 6, T 7 N, R 10 W). Named on Duncans Mills (1979) 7.5' quadrangle. Postal authorities established Northwood post office in 1929 and discontinued it in 1938; the name is from nearby Northwood Heights (Salley, p. 157).

Northwood: see **Northwood Heights** [SONOMA].

Northwood Heights [SONOMA]: *settlement,* 1.5 miles south of Guerneville along Russian River (lat. 38°28'45" N, long. 122°59'50" W; sec. 5, 6, T 7 N, R 10 W). Named on Camp Meeker (1954) 7.5' quadrangle. Called Northwood on Sebastopol (1942) 15' quadrangle.

Northwood Lodge [SONOMA]: *locality,* nearly 2 miles south of Guerneville along Russian River (lat. 38°28'35" N, long. 122°59'45" W; sec. 5, T 7 N, R 10 W). Named on Camp Meeker (1954) 7.5' quadrangle.

Nubble: see **The Nubble** [SONOMA].

Nunns Canyon [SONOMA]: *canyon,* 3 miles long, along Calabazas Creek above a point 2.25 miles southeast of Kenwood (lat. 38°23'30" N, long. 122°31' W). Named on Kenwood (1954) and Rutherford (1951) 7.5' quadrangles. Called Nuns Canyon on Santa Rosa (1944) and Sonoma (1951) 15' quadrangles.

Nunns Iron Spring [SONOMA]: *spring,* 4.25 miles east of Kenwood (lat. 38°24'30" N, long. 122°29'10" W; sec. 35, T 7 N, R 6 W); the spring is in Nunns Canyon. Named on Rutherford (1951) 7.5' quadrangle. Santa Rosa (1944) 15' quadrangle shows Nuns Iron Spring located 2.5 miles east-southeast of Kenwood in Nuns Canyon (present Nunns Canyon).

Nuns Canyon: see **Nunns Canyon** [SONOMA].

Nuns Iron Spring: see **Nunns Iron Spring** [SONOMA].

– O –

Oak Knoll [NAPA]: *locality,* 5 miles north-northwest of downtown Napa along Southern Pacific Railroad (lat. 38°21'30" N, long. 122° 20' W). Named on Napa (1951) 7.5' quadrangle.

Oak Knolls [SONOMA]: *peak,* 2.25 miles north-northwest of Skaggs Springs (lat. 38°43'15" N, long. 123°02'45" W; at S line sec. 11, T 10 S, R 11 W). Named on Warm Springs Dam (1978) 7.5' quadrangle.

Oakmont [SONOMA]: *locality,* 3 miles west-northwest of Kenwood (lat. 38°26'20" N, long. 122°35'35" W). Named on Kenwood (1954, photorevised 1980) 7.5' quadrangle.

Oak Moss Creek [NAPA]: *stream,* flows 3.25 miles to Capell Creek 7 miles west-northwest of Mount Vaca (lat. 38°27'15" N, long. 122°12'50" W; sec. 17, T 7 N, R 3 W). Named on Capell Valley (1951) 7.5' quadrangle.

Oak Mountain [SONOMA]: *peak,* 5.25 miles south-southwest of Big Mountain (lat. 38°38'10" N, long. 123°10'05" W; sec. 10, T 9 N, R 12 W). Altitude 1693 feet. Named on Tombs Creek (1978) 7.5' quadrangle.

Oak Ridge [SONOMA]:

(1) *ridge,* northwest-trending, 2.25 miles long, 5.5 miles east of Annapolis (lat. 38°42'50" N, long. 123°15'50" W). Named on Annapolis (1977) 7.5' quadrangle.

(2) *ridge,* southwest-trending, 0.5 mile long, 7.5 miles southeast of Jenner (lat. 38°22'45" N, long. 123°00'40" W). Named on Duncans Mills (1979) 7.5' quadrangle.

Oakville [NAPA]: *village,* 2 miles southeast of Rutherford (lat. 38° 26'10" N, long. 122°24'05" W). Named on Rutherford (1951) 7.5' quadrangle. Postal authorities established Oakville post office in 1857, discontinued it in 1859, and reestablished it in 1867 (Frickstad, p. 111).

Oat Creek: see **Big Oat Creek** [SONOMA].

Oat Hill [NAPA]:

(1) *peak,* 8 miles north-northeast of Calistoga (lat. 38°41'05" N, long. 122°30'50" W; sec. 27, T 10 N, R 6 W). Named on Detert Reservoir (1958) 7.5' quadrangle. California Mining Bureau's (1909) map shows a locality called Oat Hill located 12 miles by stage line north-northeast of Calistoga near present Oat Hill (1). Postal authorities established Oat Hill post office in 1891 and discontinued it in 1910; the name also had the form "Oathill" (Salley, p. 159).

(2) *hill,* less than 1 mile west-southwest of Napa Junction (lat. 38° 11'05" N, long. 122°15'45" W; near NW cor. sec. 24, T 4 N, R 4 W). Named on Cuttings Wharf (1949) 7.5' quadrangle.

Oat Mountain: see **Big Oat Mountain** [SONOMA]; **Little Oat Mountain** [SONOMA].

Oat Valley [SONOMA]: *valley,* 1.5 miles north-northwest of Cloverdale (lat. 38°49'35" N, long. 123°01'45" W). Named on Cloverdale (1960) 7.5' quadrangle.

Oat Valley Creek [SONOMA]: *stream,* flows 4.5 miles to Russian River less than 1 mile north-northeast of Cloverdale (lat. 38°49' N, long. 123°00'40" W); the stream goes through Oat Valley. Named on Cloverdale (1960) 7.5' quadrangle.38° 24'25" N, long. 122°56'45" W; sec. 34, T 7 N, R 10 W). Named on Camp Meeker (1954) 7.5' quadrangle. Postal authorities established Occidental post office in 1876; the name was from Occidental Methodist Church, the first building at the site (Salley, p. 159). In 1876 a narrow-gauge railroad reached the place, which then was called Howard's Station, Summit, and Meeker, as well as Occidental (Mullen). The name "Howard's" was for William Howard, an early settler; the name "Meeker" was for M.C. Meeker, who laid out the town (Gudde, 1949, p. 240). The name "Summit" reflects the position of the site at the highest point on the line of North Pacific Coast Railroad that ran up Dutch Bill Creek (Goodyear, 1890b, p. 678). A resort called Altamont Medical Springs was located at Occidental (Bradley, p. 335).

Ocean Cove [SONOMA]: *embayment,* 2.5 miles south of Plantation along the coast (lat. 38°33'20" N, long. 123°18'15" W). Named on Plantation (1977) 7.5' quadrangle.

Ocean View [SONOMA]: *settlement,* 4 miles south-southeast of Jenner (lat. 38°23'50" N, long. 123°05'35" W); the place is near the coast. Named on Duncans Mills (1979) 7.5' quadrangle.

Ocean View: see **Irish Hill** [SONOMA] (1).

Oceanview: see **Irish Hill** [SONOMA] (1).

Odd Fellows Park [SONOMA]: *settlement,* 2.5 miles east of Guerneville along Russian River (lat. 38°30'10" N, long. 122°56'45" W; on S line sec. 27, T 8 N, R 10 W). Named on Guerneville (1955) 7.5' quadrangle.

Ohmen Resort [SONOMA]: *locality,* 2.25 miles north-northwest of Cazadero (lat. 38°33'45" N, long. 123°06'05" W; sec. 5, T 8 N, R 11 W). Named on Cazadero (1943) 7.5' quadrangle.

Ohms Spring [SONOMA]: see **Boyes Hot Springs** [SONOMA].

Oil Well Canyon [NAPA]:
(1) *canyon,* drained by a stream that flows 1.5 miles to Lake Berryessa 5.5 miles south of Berryessa Peak (lat. 38°35'10" N, long. 122°12' W). Named on Lake Berryessa (1959) 7.5' quadrangle.
(2) *canyon,* drained by a stream that flows 1.25 miles to Gosling Canyon 5.25 miles south-southeast of Berryessa Peak (lat. 38°35'40" N, long. 122°09'05" W). Named on Lake Berryessa (1959) 7.5' quadrangle, which shows an oil well in the canyon.

Okell Hill [NAPA]: *peak,* 5.25 miles south of Mount Vaca (lat. 38° 19'35" N, long. 122°07'15" W). Altitude 1129 feet. Named on Fairfield North (1951) 7.5' quadrangle.

Old Baldy [NAPA]: *peak,* 4.5 miles east-north-east of Calistoga on Rattlesnake Ridge (lat. 38°36'45" N, long. 122°30'15" W; near E line sec. 22, T 9 N, R 6 W). Named on Calistoga (1958) 7.5' quadrangle.

Oliver: see **Lake Oliver** [SONOMA].

Olivet: see **Mount Olivet**, under **Fulton** [SONOMA].

Omus [SONOMA]: *locality,* 1.25 miles northwest of Geyserville along Northwestern Pacific Railroad (lat. 38°43'10" N, long. 122° 55'05" W). Named on Geyserville (1955) 7.5' quadrangle.

Onion Pond [SONOMA]: *lake,* 50 feet long, 3 miles north-northwest of Cazadero (lat. 38°34'10" N, long. 123°06'25" W; sec. 6, T 8 N, R 11 W). Named on Cazadero (1943) 7.5' quadrangle.

Orchard [SONOMA]: *locality,* 4.5 miles east-northeast of Bloomfield along Petaluma and Santa Rosa Railroad (lat. 38°20'10" N, long. 122°46'20" W). Named on Sebastopol (1942) 15' quadrangle.

Oregon Canyon [SONOMA]: *canyon,* drained by a stream that flows 1.25 miles to Pocket Canyon nearly 5 miles north of Occidental (lat. 38°28'35" N, long. 122°57'05" W; sec. 3, T 7 N, R 10 W). Named on Camp Meeker (1954) 7.5' quadrangle.

Original White Sulphur Springs: see **Sulphur Canyon** [NAPA].

Orrs Creek [SONOMA]: *stream,* flows nearly 2 miles to Russian River 3.25 miles east of Jenner (lat. 38°26'55" N, long. 123°03'25" W). Named on Duncans Mills (1979) 7.5' quadrangle.

Orth: see **Lake Orth** [SONOMA].

Orville: see **Lake Orville** [NAPA].

Osborne Creek [SONOMA]: *stream,* flows 1 mile to Porter Creek (1) 4 miles northeast of Guerneville (lat. 38°33' N, long. 122°57'15" W; sec. 10, T 8 N, R 10 W). Named on Guerneville (1955) 7.5' quadrangle.

Osser Creek [SONOMA]: *stream,* flows nearly 4 miles to North Fork Buckeye Creek (2) 10 miles north-northeast of the village of Stewarts Point (lat. 38°46'55" N, long. 123°18'45" W; sec. 21, T 11 N, R 13 W). Named on Ornbaun Valley (1960) 15' quadrangle.

– P –

Pacific Home: see **Healdsburg** [SONOMA].

Page's Station: see **Cotati** [SONOMA].

Palisades: see **The Palisades** [NAPA].

Palmer Canyon [SONOMA]: *canyon,* drained by a stream that flows 2 miles to Marshall Creek 4.5 miles north-northeast of Fort Ross (lat. 38°34'40" N, long. 123°13'20" W; sec. 31, T 9 N, R 12 W). Named on Fort Ross (1978) 7.5' quadrangle.

Palmer Creek [SONOMA]: *stream,* flows 3.5 miles to Mill Creek (1) 6.25 miles north-northeast of Guerneville (lat. 38°35'05" N, long. 122°56'50" W). Named on Guerneville (1955) 7.5' quadrangle.

Pansey Valley [SONOMA]: *valley,* 2 miles east of Sonoma (lat. 38° 17'10" N, long. 122°25'05" W). Named on Sonoma (1951) 7.5' quadrangle.

Panther Beds [SONOMA]: *area,* 4.25 miles northeast of Cazadero (lat. 38°34'50" N, long. 123°02'25" W; sec. 35, T 9 N, R 11 W). Named on Cazadero (1978) 7.5' quadrangle.

Panther Den [SONOMA]: *relief feature,* 0.5 mile north of Big Mountain (lat. 38°43'10"

N, long. 123°08'40" W; near NE cor. sec. 14, T 10 N, R 12 E). Named on Tombs Creek (1978) 7.5' quadrangle.

Paradise Valley [NAPA]: *valley,* 4 miles west-southwest of Knoxville along Hunting Creek on Napa-Lake county line (lat. 38°48'15" N, long. 122°24' W; sec. 15, T 11 N, R 5 W). Named on Jericho Valley (1958) 7.5' quadrangle.

Paso de las Trancas: see **Yajome** [NAPA].

Pasquini Canyon [SONOMA]: *canyon,* less than 1 mile long, 2 miles northeast of Guerneville (lat. 38°31'15" N, long. 122°57'45" W). Named on Guerneville (1955) 7.5' quadrangle.

Passion River: see **Russian River** [SONOMA].

Patty Clark Springs: see **Bald Hills** [SONOMA].

Peaches Creek: see **Pechaco Creek** [SONOMA].

Peachland: see **Sebastopol** [SONOMA].

Peaked Hill [SONOMA]: *peak,* 1.25 miles south of Jenner (lat. 38° 25'50" N, long. 123°07'05" W). Altitude 377 feet. Named on Duncans Mills (1979) 7.5' quadrangle.

Pearl Gap [NAPA]: *pass,* 3.25 miles south of Mount Vaca (lat. 38° 21'10" N, long. 122°05'40" W). Named on Fairfield North (1951) 7.5' quadrangle.

Pechaco Creek [SONOMA]: *stream,* flows nearly 3 miles to Pena Creek 3.5 miles south-southeast of Skaggs Springs (lat. 38°38'50" N, long. 123°00'25" W; sec. 7, T 9 N, R 10 W). Named on Geyserville (1955) and Warm Springs Dam (1978) 7.5' quadrangles. Called Peaches Creek on Healdsburg (1940) 15' quadrangle.

Pena Creek [SONOMA]: *stream,* flows 10.5 miles to Dry Creek 3.25 miles west of Geyserville on Tzabaco grant, which belonged to Jose German Peña (lat. 38°42'05" N, long. 122°57'40" W). Named on Geyserville (1955) and Warm Springs Dam (1978) 7.5' quadrangles. Chapman Branch enters 4.5 miles above the mouth of the main stream; it is 1.5 miles long and is named on Geyserville (1955) 7.5' quadrangle.

Penn: see **Penngrove** [SONOMA].

Penngrove [SONOMA]: *village,* 3 miles southeast of Cotati (lat. 38° 18'10" N, long. 122°39'55" W). Named on Cotati (1954) 7.5' quadrangle. Postal authorities established Penn post office in 1882, changed the name to Penns Grove in 1883, and to Penngrove in 1894 (Frickstad, p. 197).

Penns Grove: see **Penngrove** [SONOMA].

Penny Island [SONOMA]: *island,* 0.5 mile long, in Russian River at Jenner (lat. 38°26'50" N, long. 123°07'05" W). Named on Duncans Mills (1979) 7.5' quadrangle.

Pepperwood Creek [SONOMA]: *stream,* flows 4.5 miles to House Creek 6.5 miles southwest of Big Mountain (lat. 38°38'05" N, long. 123°13' W; near E line sec. 7, T 9 N, R 12 W). Named on Fort Ross (1978) and Tombs Creek (1978) 7.5' quadrangles.

Pepperwood Creek: see **Big Pepperwood Creek** [SONOMA].

Pepperwood Gulch [SONOMA]: *canyon,* drained by a stream that flows 1 mile to Salmon Creek (1) 1.5 miles north of the village of Bodega Bay (lat. 38°21'25" N, long. 123°02'25" W). Named on Bodega Head (1972) 7.5' quadrangle.

Petaluma [SONOMA]:

(1) *land grant,* east of Petaluma River and north of San Pablo Bay. Named on Cotati (1954), Glen Ellen (1954), Petaluma (1953), Petaluma River (1954), Sears Point (1951), and Sonoma (1951) 7.5' quadrangles. Mariano Guadalupe Vallejo received 15 leagues in 1834, and in 1843 and 1844; he claimed 66,622 acres patented in 1874 (Cowan, p. 60). The name is from an Indian village that was located east of Petaluma River (Kroeber, p. 54).

(2) *city,* 15 miles south-southeast of Santa Rosa (lat. 38°14' N, long. 122°38'15" W); the city is along Petaluma River. Named on Cotati (1954, photorevised 1980), Glen Ellen (1954, photorevised 1968), Petaluma (1953), and Petaluma River (1954) 7.5' quadrangles. Postal authorities established Petaluma post office in 1852 (Frickstad, p. 197), and the city incorporated in 1858. Settlement of the place began in 1851 with construction of a trading post at the head of navigation on Petaluma River; Garrett W. Keller then laid out the community in 1852 (Heig, p. 28-29). In 1903 a group of Petaluma businessmen established Petaluma and Santa Rosa Electric Railway, which ran for 37 miles from Petaluma to Santa Rosa by way of Sebastopol; between Petaluma and Stony Point were eight station about 1 mile apart: Dunn, Cinnabar, Corona, Denman, Liberty, Dangers, Divide, and Live Oak (Heig, p. 91, 94). California Division of Forestry's (1945) map shows a place called Staubeville situated 2 miles west-northwest of downtown Petaluma.

Petaluma Creek: see **Petaluma River** [SONOMA].

Petaluma Reservoir [SONOMA]: *lake,* 1050 feet long, 5.25 miles south-southwest of Glen Ellen (lat. 38°17'50" N, long. 122°34'35" W). Named on Glen Ellen (1954) 7.5' quadrangle.

Petaluma River [SONOMA]: *stream,* heads in Sonoma County and flows 21 miles to San Pablo Bay 3.5 miles southwest of Sears Point (lat. 38°06'40" N, long. 122°29'30" W). Named on Cotati (1954), Novato (1954), Petaluma (1953), Petaluma Point (1959), and Petaluma River (1954) 7.5' quadrangles. Called Petaluma Creek on Mare Island (1916) and Petaluma (1914) 15' quadrangles, but United States Board on Geographic Names (1959, p. 7) rejected this form of the name. The feature is called Estero de Petaluma on the diseño of Olompali grant made in 1843 (Becker, 1964).

The stream also had the Spanish names "Estero de las Mercedes" and "Estero de Nuestra Señora de la Merced" (Wagner, H.R., p. 472, 478). The river forms the Marin-Sonoma county line below the mouth of San Antonio Creek

Petaluma Valley [SONOMA]: *valley,* along Petaluma River from north of the city of Petaluma to San Pablo Bay; on Marin-Sonoma county line. Named on Santa Rosa (1958) 1°x 2° quadrangle. Tyson (p. 19) referred to Petaloma valley in 1850.

Peter Hill [SONOMA]: *peak,* 5.5 miles west of Mount Saint Helena (lat. 38°40'25" N, long. 122°44' W; sec. 34, T 10 N, R 8 W). Altitude 841 feet. Named on Mount Saint Helena (1959) 7.5' quadrangle.

Peters Creek: see **Rail Creek** [SONOMA].

Petersen: see **Roblar** [SONOMA].

Peterson Creek [SONOMA]: *stream,* flows 3.5 miles to Russian River 2 miles east-southeast of Geyserville (lat. 38°41'40" N, long. 122°52'05" W). Named on Geyserville (1955) 7.5' quadrangle.

Peters Springs [SONOMA]: *well,* 2.5 miles east of downtown Santa Rosa (lat. 38°26'45" N, long. 122°40'05" W). Named on Santa Rosa (1954) 7.5' quadrangle.

Petrified Forest [SONOMA]: *locality,* 4.5 miles east of Mark West Springs (lat. 38°33'20" N, long. 122°38'15" W; sec. 9, T 8 N, R 7 W). Named on Mark West Springs (1958) 7.5' quadrangle. William Travis discovered petrified trees at the site in 1857, and the place opened to the public in the 1870's (Miller, J.T., p. 32).

Philadelphia: see **New Philadelphia**, under **Sonoma** [SONOMA].

Phillips Gulch [SONOMA]: *canyon,* drained by a stream that flows 1.25 miles to the sea 1.5 miles west-southwest of Plantation (lat. 38°35'05" N, long. 123°20'20" W). Named on Plantation (1977) 7.5' quadrangle.

Phillips Soda Springs: see **Samuel Springs** [NAPA].

Phoenix Mine: see **Aetna Springs** [NAPA].

Pickle Canyon [NAPA]: *canyon,* drained by a stream that flows 4 miles to Redwood Canyon 5.25 miles west-northwest of downtown Napa (lat. 38°20'05" N, long. 122°22'10" W). Named on Napa (1951) and Sonoma (1951) 7.5' quadrangles. The stream in Pickle Canyon is called North Branch [Napa Creek] on Napa (1902) 30' quadrangle.

Pickle Canyon [SONOMA]: *canyon,* 2 miles long, along Mill Creek (1) above a point 6.5 miles north of Guerneville (lat. 38°35'50" N, long. 122°59'30" W; sec. 29, T 9 N, R 10 W). Named on Cazadero (1978) and Guerneville (1955) 7.5' quadrangles.

Picnic Creek [SONOMA]: *stream,* flows 1.5 miles to Warm Springs Creek nearly 1 mile west-northwest of Skaggs Springs (lat. 38°41'45" N, long. 123°02'25" W; sec. 23, T 10 N, R 11 W). Named on Warm Springs Dam (1978) 7.5' quadrangle.

Pilot Knob [SONOMA]: *peak,* 3 miles northwest of Mount Saint Helena (lat. 38°41'55" N, long. 122°40'25" W; sec. 19, T 10 N, R 7 W). Named on Mount Saint Helena (1959) 7.5' quadrangle.

Pine Creek Reservoir [SONOMA]: *lake,* 400 feet long, less than 2 miles north-northeast of downtown Santa Rosa (lat. 38°28' N, long. 122°42'15" W; on E line sec. 11, T 7 N, R 8 W. Named on Santa Rosa (1954, photorevised 1968 and 1973) 7.5' quadrangle.

Pine Flat [SONOMA]: *area,* 10 miles northeast of Healdsburg along Little Sulphur Creek (lat. 38°44'20" N, long. 122°45'50" W; sec. 5, T 10 N, R 8 W). Named on Jimtown (1955) 7.5' quadrangle.

Pine Flat: see **Healdsburg** [SONOMA].

Pine Grove: see **Sebastopol** [SONOMA].

Pine Hill [SONOMA]: *peak,* 7.25 miles northnortheast of Fort Ross (lat. 38°36'50" N, long. 123°11'50" W; at SW cor. sec. 16, T 9 N, R 12 W). Altitude 1572 feet. Named on Fort Ross (1978) 7.5' quadrangle.

Pine Mountain [SONOMA]: *peak,* 6 miles northwest of Mount Saint Helena on Sonoma-Lake county line (lat. 38°43'55" N, long. 122° 42'20" W; on E line sec. 11, T 10 N, R 8 W). Altitude 3614 feet. Named on Mount Saint Helena (1959) 7.5' quadrangle.

Pine Ridge Canyon [SONOMA]: *canyon,* drained by a stream that flows 2 miles to Dry Creek 1 mile west-northwest of Healdsburg (lat. 38°37'10" N, long. 122°53'20" W). Named on Guerneville (1955) 7.5' quadrangle.

Pine Station: see **Zinfandel** [NAPA].

Pinnacle Rock [SONOMA]: *rock,* 2.25 miles southeast of the village of Bodega Bay, and 300 feet offshore (lat. 38°18'25" N, long. 123° 01'10" W). Named on Bodega Head (1972) 7.5' quadrangle.

Pisgah: see **Mount Pisgah** [SONOMA].

Pitchers Range [SONOMA]: *locality,* 3 miles east-southeast of present Jenner along Willow Creek (lat. 38°25'50" N, long. 123°04'55" W). Named on Duncans Mills (1921) 15' quadrangle.

Plan de Agua Caliente: see **Mallacomes or Muristul y Plan de Agua Caliente** [NAPA-SONOMA].

Plantation [SONOMA]: *settlement,* 6.25 miles northwest of Fort Ross (lat. 38°35'25" N, long. 123°18'30" W). Named on Plantation (1977) 7.5' quadrangle. Postal authorities established Fisk's Mill post office in 1871, changed the name to Fisk in 1894, moved it 3 miles southeast in 1902 when they changed the name to Plantation, and discontinued it in 1933—the name "Fisk" was for Andrew J. Fisk, a lumber-mill operator, and the name "Plantation" was for Plantation House, a travelers stop (Salley, p. 75, 173).

Pluton Cañon: see **Big Sulphur Creek** [SONOMA].

Pluton River: see **Big Sulphur Creek** [SONOMA].

Pluton Valley: see **Big Sulphur Creek** [SONOMA].

Pocket Canyon [SONOMA]: *canyon,* drained by a stream that flows 5.5 miles to Russian River at Guerneville (lat. 38°30' N, long. 122°59'45" W; sec. 32, T 8 N, R 10 W). Named on Camp Meeker (1954) and Guerneville (1955) 7.5' quadrangles.

Pocket Opening [SONOMA]: *area,* 4.5 miles north-northeast of Guerneville (lat. 38°33'45" N, long. 122°58' W). Named on Guerneville (1955) 7.5' quadrangle.

Pocket Peak [SONOMA]: *peak,* 4.5 miles east-northeast of Asti (lat. 38°47' N, long. 122°53'40" W). Altitude 2269 feet. Named on Asti (1959) 7.5' quadrangle.

Pocock Creek [NAPA]: *stream,* flows 2 miles to Hunting Creek 4.5 miles southwest of Knoxville (lat. 38°47'15" N, long. 122°24'30" W; near E line sec. 21, T 11 N, R 5 W). Named on Jericho Valley (1958) 7.5' quadrangle.

Pole Mountain [SONOMA]: *peak,* 2.5 miles southwest of Cazadero (lat. 38°30'20" N, long. 123°07'10" W; sec. 30, T 8 N, R 11 W). Altitude 2204 feet. Named on Cazadero (1978) 7.5' quadrangle.

Pole Mountain Creek [SONOMA]: *stream,* flows 2.25 miles to Ward Creek 6 miles east-northeast of Fort Ross (lat. 38°32'05" N, long. 123°08'05" W; sec. 13, T 8 N, R 12 W); the stream heads north of Pole Mountain. Named on Cazadero (1978) and Fort Ross (1978) 7.5' quadrangles.

Pool Creek [SONOMA]: *stream,* flows 8 miles to Windsor Creek 6.5 miles south-southeast of Healdsburg (lat. 38°31'20" N, long. 122°49'50" W; sec. 23, T 8 N, R 9 W). Named on Healdsburg (1955) and Mark West Springs (1958) 7.5' quadrangles. United States Board on Geographic Names (1967, p. 5) approved the name "Wright Creek" for a stream that flows 3 miles to Pool Creek 2.4 miles east of Windsor (lat. 38°32'48" N, long. 122°46'17" W); the name commemorates John Wright, a pioneer rancher of the neighborhood.

Pool Ridge [SONOMA]: *ridge,* south-southeast-to south-trending, 1 mile long, 1.25 miles west-northwest of Guerneville (lat. 38°30'45" N, long. 123°01' W). Named on Cazadero (1978) 7.5' quadrangle. Duncans Mills (1943) 7.5' quadrangle has the name on a ridge located 2.25 miles west-southwest of Guerneville. The name "Pool" is for a pioneer family (Clar, p. 87).

Poor Man's Flat: see **Windsor** [SONOMA].

Pope Creek [NAPA]: *stream,* flows 17 miles to Putah Creek 14 miles east-northeast of Saint Helena in Lake Berryessa (lat. 38°37'25" N, long. 122°15'55" W); the stream goes through Pope Valley. Named on Aetna Springs (1958), Chiles Valley (1958), and Walter Springs (1959) 7.5' quadrangles.

Pope Mineral Spring: see **Samuel Springs** [NAPA].

Pope Valley [NAPA]:
(1) *valley,* 9 miles north-northeast of Saint Helena (lat. 38°37' N, long. 122°24'30" W); the valley is on Locoallomi grant, and partly along Pope Creek. Named on Aetna Springs (1958), Chiles Valley (1958), and Saint Helena (1960) 7.5' quadrangles. The name commemorates William Pope, who received Locoallomi grant in 1841 (Menefee, p. 170).
(2) *settlement,* 8 miles north-northeast of Saint Helena along the south edge of Pope Valley (1) (lat. 38°36'55" N, long. 122°25'35" W). Named on Saint Helena (1960) 7.5' quadrangle. Postal authorities established Pope Valley post office in 1863 (Frickstad, p. 111).

Porter Creek [SONOMA]:
(1) *stream,* flows 6.5 miles to Russian River 6.25 miles east of Guerneville (lat. 38°30'55" N, long. 122°52'55" W; sec. 29, T 8 N, R 9 W). Named on Guerneville (1955) 7.5' quadrangle.
(2) *stream,* flows 1 mile to Buckeye Creek (2) 2 miles north-northeast of Annapolis (lat. 38°44'50" N, long. 123°21'15" W; sec. 6, T 10 N, R 13 W). Named on Ornbaun Valley (1960) 15' quadrangle, and on Annapolis (1977) 7.5' quadrangle.
(3) *stream,* flows 8 miles to Mark West Creek 1 mile east of Mark West Springs (lat. 38°32'50" N, long. 122°42'10" W; near SW cor. sec. 12, T 8 N, R 8 W). Named on Calistoga (1958) and Mark West Springs (1958) 7.5' quadrangles. Jerry Porter was the first known settler in the neighborhood (Archuleta, p. 29).

Porterfield Creek [SONOMA]: *stream,* formed by the confluence of North Branch and South Branch, flows 1.5 miles to the flood plain of Russian River 1.25 miles southeast of Cloverdale (lat. 38°47'20" N, long. 123°00'05" W). Named on Cloverdale (1960) 7.5' quadrangle. North Branch is 1.25 miles long and South Branch is 1.5 miles long; both branches are named on Cloverdale (1960) 7.5' quadrangle.

Port Rumyantsev: see **Bodega Bay** [SONOMA].

Portuguese Beach [SONOMA]: *beach,* 5.25 miles south-southeast of Jenner along the coast (lat. 38°22'50" N, long. 123°04'50" W). Named on Duncans Mills (1979) 7.5' quadrangle.

Portuguese Canyon [NAPA]: *canyon,* 3.5 miles long, opens into the canyon of Putah Creek 10 miles south-southeast of Berryessa Peak (lat. 38°31'05" N, long. 122°08'20" W; sec. 24, T 8 N, R 3 W). Named on Lake Berryessa (1959) 7.5' quadrangle. Water of Lake Berryessa covers the lower part of the canyon.

Portuguese Canyon: see **Little Portuguese Canyon** [NAPA].

Potatoe Patch Ridge: see **Mohrhardt Ridge** [SONOMA].

Potato Hill [NAPA]: *peak,* 4.5 miles northeast of Calistoga (lat. 38° 37'10" N, long. 122°30'50" W; sec. 22, T 9 N, R 6 W). Named on Calistoga (1958) 7.5' quadrangle.

Pratt Valley [NAPA]: *valley,* 2.5 miles north-northwest of Saint Helena (lat. 38°32'25" N, long. 122°28'45" W). Named on Saint Helena (1960) 7.5' quadrangle.

Press Creek [SONOMA]: *stream,* flows about 2.25 miles to Porter Creek (1) 5.25 miles east-northeast of Guerneville (lat. 38°32'20" N, long. 122°54'45" W; sec. 13, T 8 N, R 10 W). Named on Guerneville (1955) 7.5' quadrangle.

Press Valley [SONOMA]: *area,* 5.5 miles northeast of Guerneville (lat. 38°32'50" N, long. 122°54'45" W); the place is along Press Creek. Named on Guerneville (1955) 7.5' quadrangle.

Preston [SONOMA]: *locality,* 2 miles north of Cloverdale along Northwestern Pacific Railroad (lat. 38°50'10" N, long. 123°00'55" W; near N line sec. 6, T 11 N, R 10 W). Named on Cloverdale (1960) 7.5' quadrangle. Postal authorities established Preston post office in 1890 and discontinued it in 1941; the name was for Madam Emily Preston, a cult leader (Salley, p. 178). Water from Barcal Spring, located 2 miles east of Preston (sec. 32, T 12 N, R 10 W), was bottled for sale (Bradley, p. 335).

Preston Lake [SONOMA]: *lake,* 500 feet long, 3 miles north of Cloverdale (lat. 38°51' N, long. 123°00'50" W; sec. 31, T 12 N, R 10 W); the lake is 1 mile north of Preston. Named on Cloverdale (1960) 7.5' quadrangle.

Priest Soda Springs: see **Samuel Springs** [NAPA].

Pritchard Hill [NAPA]: *settlement,* 5.5 miles north of Yountville (lat. 38°29'10" N, long. 122°20'45" W; sec. 6, T 7 N, R 4 W). Named on Yountville (1951) 7.5' quadrangle.

Pritchett Peaks [SONOMA]: *peaks,* along a ridge 4 miles north-northwest of Skaggs Springs (lat. 38°44'45" N, long. 123°03'30" W). Named on Cloverdale (1960) and Warm Springs Dam (1978) 7.5' quadrangles.

Proschold Resort [SONOMA]; *locality,* 1.25 mile east of Cazadero (lat. 38°31'40" N, long. 123°03'45" W; sec. 22, T 8 N, R 11 W). Named on Cazadero (1943) 7.5' quadrangle.

Puerto de la Bodega: see **Bodega Bay** [SONOMA].

Pumpkin Flat [NAPA]: *area,* nearly 4 miles south-southeast of Mount Vaca (lat. 38°20'55" N, long. 122°04'50" W; sec. 21, T 6 N, R 2 W). Named on Fairfield North (1951) 7.5' quadrangle.

Purrington Creek [SONOMA]: *stream,* flows 3.5 miles to Green Valley Creek 3.5 miles east-northeast of Occidental (lat. 38°26'15" N, long. 122°53'20" W). Named on Camp Meeker (1954) 7.5' quadrangle.

Puta Creek: see **Putah Creek** [NAPA].

Putah Creek [NAPA]: *stream,* heads in Lake County and flows 60 miles through Napa County and along Solano-Yolo county line to Yolo County 8.5 miles northeast of Dixon (lat. 38° 32'15" N, long. 121°42'35" W). Named on Aetna Springs (1958), Allendale (1953), Chiles Valley (1958), Davis (1952), Jericho Valley (1958), Lake Berryessa (1959), Merritt (1952), Monticello Dam (1959), Mount Vaca (1951), Walter Springs (1959) and Winters (1953) 7.5' quadrangles. Called Puta Cr. on Eddy's (1854) map, but United States Board on Geographic Names (1933, p. 625) rejected this form of the name. Williamson (p. 39) referred to Putos creek. According to Gudde (1949, p. 276), the name "Putah" is from the designation of Indians who lived along the stream, but Kroeber (p. 56) rejected an Indian origin for the name, and attributed it to *puta,* which means "harlot" in Spanish. South Fork diverges southeast from the main stream 6 miles north-northeast of Dixon and flows 5 miles to Yolo County 8.5 miles northeast of Dixon; it is named on Davis (1952) and Merritt (1952) 7.5' quadrangles.

Putos Creek: see **Putah Creek** [NAPA].

– Q –

Quarries [SONOMA]: *locality,* 2.5 miles north of Sears Point along Northwestern Pacific Railroad (lat. 38°11'10" N, long. 122°26'20" W). Named on Mare Island (1916) 15' quadrangle. Postal authorities established Quarries post office in 1908 and discontinued it in 1926 (Frickstad, p. 197).

Quarry: see **Roblar** [SONOMA].

Quarry Canyon [NAPA]: *canyon,* drained by a stream that flows 2.5 miles to Lake Berryessa 8.5 miles south-southwest of Berryessa Peak (lat. 38°32'50" N, long. 122°14'05" W). Named on Chiles Valley (1958) and Lake Berryessa (1959) 7.5' quadrangles.

Queens Peak [SONOMA]: *peak,* 5.5 miles north of Guerneville (lat. 38°34'50" N, long. 122°59'15" W; sec. 32, T 9 N, R 10 W). Altitude 1948 feet. Named on Guerneville (1955) 7.5' quadrangle.

Quicksilver Flat [SONOMA]: *area,* 3.5 miles west of Big Mountain (lat. 38°42'40" N, long. 123°12'45" W; sec. 17, T 10 N, R 12 W). Named on Tombs Creek (1978) 7.5' quadrangle.

Quinlan Gulch [SONOMA]: *canyon,* drained by a stream that flows 2 miles to Cheney Gulch 2 miles east-southeast of the village of Bodega Bay (lat. 38°19'05" N, long. 123°00'55" W). Named on Bodega Head (1972) 7.5' quadrangle.

– R –

Rabbit Knoll [SONOMA]: *relief feature,* 6.25 miles northeast of Cazadero (lat. 38°35'55" N, long. 122°00'25" W; sec. 30, T 9 N, R 10 W). Named on Cazadero (1978) 7.5' quadrangle.

Racetrack: see **The Racetrack** [SONOMA].

Rag Cañon: see **Wragg Canyon** [NAPA].

Rail Creek [SONOMA]: *stream,* flows 3.5 miles, partly in Mendocino County, to Dry Creek 7.5 miles west of Cloverdale (lat. 38°47'30" N, long. 123°09'15" W; near E line sec. 23, T 11 N, R 12 W). Named on Hopland (1960) 15' quadrangle. Called Peters Creek on Hopland (1944) 15' quadrangle.

Railroad Slough [SONOMA]: *water feature,* joins Steamboat Slough 5.5 miles north-north-east of Sears Point (lat. 38°13'40" N, long. 122°25'25" W). Named on Sears Point (1951) 7.5' quadrangle.

Rainbow Slough [SONOMA]: *water feature,* 4.5 miles northeast of Sears Point (lat. 38°11'25" N, long. 122°22'30" W). Named on Cuttings Wharf (1949) and Sears Point (1951) 7.5' quadrangles.

Ralphine: see **Lake Ralphine** [SONOMA].

Ramal [SONOMA]: *locality,* 5.5 miles north-northeast of Sears Point along Southern Pacific Railroad (lat. 38°13'20" N, long. 122°23'40" W). Named on Sears Point (1951) 7.5' quadrangle.

Rancheria Creek [SONOMA]: *stream,* flows 6 miles to Warm Springs Creek 3 miles west-northwest of Skaggs Springs (lat. 38° 42'25" N, long. 123°04'40" W; near S line sec. 16, T 10 N, R 11 W). Named on Tombs Creek (1978) and Warm Springs Dam (1978) 7.5' quadrangles.

Rancheria Creek: see **Little Rancheria Creek** [SONOMA].

Ranchero Hill [SONOMA]: *peak,* 4 miles west-southwest of Big Mountain (lat. 38°41'40" N, long. 123°13' W; near SE cor. sec. 19, T 10 N, R 12 W). Altitude 1013 feet. Named on Tombs Creek (1978) 7.5' quadrangle.

Rancho Monticello [NAPA]: *locality,* 13 miles east-northeast of Saint Helena along Lake Berryessa (lat. 38°35'25" N, long. 122° 15'20" W). Named on Chiles Valley (1958) 7.5' quadrangle.

Raney Rock [NAPA]: *relief feature,* 6 miles west-northwest of Mount Vaca (lat. 38°26'45" N, long. 122°11'55" W; sec. 21, T 7 N, R 3 W). Named on Capell Valley (1951) 7.5' quadrangle.

Rattlesnake Canyon [SONOMA]: *canyon,* 1.5 miles long, on upper reaches of Kellogg Creek above a point 1.25 miles west-southwest of Mount Saint Helena (lat. 38°39'40" N, long. 122°39'05" W; near NE cor. sec. 5, T 9 N, R 7 W). Named on Mount Saint Helena (1959) 7.5' quadrangle.

Rattlesnake Ridge [NAPA]: *ridge,* generally north-northwest-trending, 3.25 miles long, 6.5 miles north of Saint Helena (lat. 38° 36' N, long. 122°29'45" W). Named on Calistoga (1958) and Saint Helena (1960) 7.5' quadrangles.

Rattlesnake Spring [NAPA]: *spring,* 6.5 miles north of Calistoga (lat. 38°40'20" N, long. 122°35'20" W; sec. 36, T 10 N, R 7 W). Named on Detert Reservoir (1958) 7.5' quadrangle.

Ratto Landing [NAPA]: *locality,* 3.5 miles northwest of Napa Junction along Napa River (lat. 38°13'55" N, long. 122°17'20" W). Named on Cuttings Wharf (1949, photorevised 1968) 7.5' quadrangle.

Reclamation [SONOMA]: *locality,* 2 miles southwest of Sears Point along Northwestern Pacific Railroad (lat. 38°07'45" N, long. 122° 28'10" W). Named on Sears Point (1951) 7.5' quadrangle. Postal authorities established Reclamation post office in 1891 and discontinued it in 1903; the name was from a land-reclamation project (Salley, p. 182).

Recreation Flat [NAPA]: *area,* 5.5 miles northeast of Saint Helena (lat. 38°33'45" N, long. 122°24'10" W; sec. 10, T 8 N, R 5 W). Named on Saint Helena (1960) 7.5' quadrangle.

Rector [NAPA]: *locality,* 5.5 miles east of Yountville (lat. 38°25'05" N, long. 122°15'45" W). Named on Sonoma (1942) 15' quadrangle. Napa (1902) 30' quadrangle shows the place situated 1.5 miles farther west-northwest near the head of Rector Canyon (sec. 27, T 7 N, R 4 W). Postal authorities established Rector post office in 1896 and discontinued it in 1932; the name commemorates John P. Rector, an early settler in the neighborhood (Salley, p. 182).

Rector Canyon [NAPA]: *canyon,* nearly 4 miles long, opens into lowlands 2.5 miles north-northeast of Yountville (lat. 38°26'30" N, long. 122°20'55" W); Rector Creek drains the canyon. Named on Yountville (1951) 7.5' quadrangle.

Rector Creek [NAPA]: *stream,* flows 7 miles to Conn Creek 1.5 miles north of Yountville (lat. 38°25'45" N, long. 122°22'15" W). Named on Yountville (1951) 7.5' quadrangle.

Rector Reservoir [NAPA]: *lake,* behind a dam on Rector Creek 2.5 miles north-northeast of Yountville (lat. 38°26'30" N, long. 122°20'40" W; sec. 19, T 7 N, R 4 W). Named on Yountville (1951) 7.5' quadrangle.

Redbud Park [NAPA]: *locality,* 10.5 miles south-southeast of Berryessa Peak along Putah Creek (lat. 38°31'10" N, long. 122°08'10" W; near SE cor. sec. 24, T 8 N, R 3 W). Named on Capay (1945) 15' quadrangle. Water of Lake Berryessa now covers the site.

Red Hill [NAPA]: *peak,* nearly 5 miles north-northwest of Calistoga (lat. 38°38'25" N, long. 122°36'50" W; near E line sec. 10, T 9 N, R 7

W). Altitude 2156 feet. Named on Detert Reservoir (1958) 7.5' quadrangle.

Red Hill [SONOMA]:

(1) *peak,* 10 miles northeast of Healdsburg (lat. 38°43'45" N, long. 122°45'25" W; on W line sec. 9, T 10 N, R 8 W). Altitude 2527 feet. Named on Jimtown (1955) 7.5' quadrangle.

(2) *peak,* 3 miles southeast of Jenner (lat. 38°25'15" N, long. 123° 04'50" W). Altitude 1062 feet. Named on Duncans Mills (1979) 7.5' quadrangle.

(3) *peak,* 3 miles south of Big Mountain (lat. 38°39'55" N, long. 123°08'15" W; near S line sec. 36, T 10 N, R 12 W). Named on Tombs Creek (1978) 7.5' quadrangle.

Red Lake [NAPA]: *lake,* 550 feet long, 6 miles north of Saint Helena (lat. 38°35'25" N, long. 122°27'40" W; sec. 31, T 9 N, R 5 W). Named on Saint Helena (1960) 7.5' quadrangle.

Red Mountain [NAPA]: *peak,* 9 miles northwest of Mount Vaca (lat. 38°28'20" N, long. 122°14'35" W; near E line sec. 12, T 7 N, R 4 W). Altitude 1360 feet. Named on Capell Valley (1951) 7.5' quadrangle.

Red Mountain [SONOMA]:

(1) *peak,* 3.25 miles northeast of Kenwood (lat. 38°27'10" N, long. 122°30'30" W; sec. 15, T 7 N, R 6 W). Altitude 2548 feet. Named on Kenwood (1954) 7.5' quadrangle.

(2) *peak,* 2.5 miles west-southwest of Cloverdale (lat. 38°47'25" N, long. 123°03'25" W; sec. 23, T 11 N, R 11 W). Altitude 1494 feet. Named on Cloverdale (1960) 7.5' quadrangle.

(3) *peak,* 5.5 miles west of Cloverdale (lat. 38°47'50" N, long. 123° 06'55" W; at W line sec. 17, T 11 N, R 11 W). Named on Cloverdale (1960) 7.5' quadrangle.

Red Oat Ridge [SONOMA]: *ridge,* south- to southeast-trending, 1.5 miles long, 2.5 miles north of Cazadero (lat. 38°34' N, long. 123° 05'25" W). Named on Cazadero (1978) 7.5' quadrangle.

Red Slide [SONOMA]:

(1) *relief feature,* 5.25 miles north of Cazadero (lat. 38°36'20" N, long. 123°06' W). Named on Cazadero (1978) 7.5' quadrangle.

(2) *relief feature,* 3.25 miles south of Big Mountain (lat. 38°39'50" N, long. 123°08'20" W; on S line sec. 36, T 10 N, R 12 W); the feature is on the southwest side of present Red Hill (3). Named on Tombs Creek (1943) 7.5' quadrangle.

Red Slide Creek [SONOMA]: *stream,* flows 2 miles to Austin Creek 4 miles north-north-west of Cazadero (lat. 38°35'05" N, long. 123° 06'55" W; sec. 31, T 9 N, R 11 W); the stream heads near Red Slide (1). Named on Cazadero (1978) 7.5' quadrangle.

Redwood Canyon [NAPA]: *canyon,* 7 miles long, along Redwood Creek above a point 3.5 miles west-northwest of downtown Napa (lat. 38°19'15" N, long. 122°20'40" W). Named on Napa (1951) and Sonoma (1951) 7.5' quad-

rangles. On Napa (1902) 30' quadrangle, the stream in present Redwood Canyon above the mouth of present Pickle Canyon is called Mill Creek.

Redwood Canyon [SONOMA]: *canyon,* drained by a stream that flows nearly 1 mile to Pena Creek 3.5 miles south of Skaggs Springs (lat. 38°38'25" N, long. 123°01'35" W; sec. 12, T 9 N, R 11 W). Named on Warm Springs Dam (1978) 7.5' quadrangle.

Redwood Creek [NAPA]: *stream,* flows 9.5 miles to join Brown Valley Creek and form Napa Creek 1.5 miles west-northwest of downtown Napa (lat. 38°18'15" N, long. 122°18'45" W). Named on Napa (1951) 7.5' quadrangle. On Napa (1902) 30' quadrangle, the stream is called Napa Creek and North Branch [Napa Creek].

Redwood Creek [SONOMA]:

(1) *stream,* formed by the confluence of Kellogg Creek and Yellow Jacket Creek, flows 4.25 miles to Maacama Creek 6.5 miles west-southwest of Mount Saint Helena (lat. 38°38'30" N, long. 122°44'40" W; sec. 9, T 9 N, R 8 W); the stream originates in Knights Valley. Named on Mount Saint Helena (1959) 7.5' quadrangle. Bancroft's (1864) map has the name "Knights Cr.," apparently for present Redwood Creek (1) and for present Maacama Creek below its junction with Redwood Creek (1).

(2) *stream,* flows 2.5 miles to Fife Creek 1.5 miles north of Guerneville (lat. 38°31'35" N, long. 123°59'55" W; near E line sec. 19, T 8 N, R 10 W). Named on Guerneville (1955) 7.5' quadrangle.

(3) *stream,* flows 1.5 miles to Wheatfield Fork Gualala River 6.5 miles east of Annapolis (lat. 38°43'50" N, long. 123°14'55" W; at N line sec. 12, T 10 N, R 13 W). Named on Annapolis (1977) 7.5' quadrangle.

Redwood Hill [SONOMA]: *peak,* 1 mile south of Mark West Springs (lat. 38°32'05" N, long. 122°43'10" W; near SW cor. sec. 14, T 8 N, R 8 W). Named on Mark West Springs (1958) 7.5' quadrangle.

Redwood Lake [SONOMA]: *lake,* 450 feet long, 4.5 miles east-northeast of Cazadero (lat. 38°33'55" N, long. 123°00'35" W; sec. 6, T 8 N, R 10 W). Named on Cazadero (1978) 7.5' quadrangle.

Redwood Log Creek [SONOMA]: *stream,* flows 3.25 miles to Pena Creek 3.5 miles south of Skaggs Springs (lat. 38°38'40" N, long. 123°02' W; sec. 12, T 9 N, R 11 W). Named on Warm Springs Dam (1978) 7.5' quadrangle.

Redwood Mountain [SONOMA]: *peak,* 3.25 miles north-northwest of Cloverdale (lat. 38°50'50" N, long. 123°02'35" W; on E line sec. 35, T 12 N, R 11 W). Altitude 1675 feet. Named on Cloverdale (1960) 7.5' quadrangle.

Reese Gap [SONOMA]: *pass,* 4.5 miles south of Skaggs Springs (lat. 38°37'35" N, long. 123°02'05" W; near W line sec. 13, T 9 N, R

11 W). Named on Warm Springs Dam (1978) 7.5' quadrangle.

Renevar Gulch [SONOMA]: *canyon,* drained by a stream that flows 0.5 mile to Palmer Creek 6 miles north-northeast of Guerneville (lat. 38°34'40" N, long. 122°56'30" W). Named on Guerneville (1955) 7.5' quadrangle.

Riccas Corner [SONOMA]: *locality,* 2.5 miles northeast of Sebastopol (lat. 38°25'25" N, long. 122°47'15" W). Named on Sebastopol (1954) 7.5' quadrangle. Called Smith Corner on Sebastopol (1942) 15' quadrangle.

Rien [SONOMA]: *locality,* 1.5 miles southeast of present Jenner along Russian River (lat. 38°26'15" N, long. 123°06'10" W). Named on Duncans Mills (1921) 15' quadrangle.

Right-Hand Canyon [NAPA]: *canyon,* drained by a stream that flows 1.5 miles to Gosling Canyon 6.25 miles south-southeast of Berryessa Peak (lat. 38°34'35" N, long. 122°09'15" W). Named on Lake Berryessa (1959) 7.5' quadrangle.

Rincon Creek [SONOMA]: *stream,* flows 4.25 miles to Santa Rosa Creek 2 miles east-north-east of downtown Santa Rosa (lat. 38°27'10" N, long. 122°40'35" W). Named on Mark West Springs (1958) and Santa Rosa (1954) 7.5' quadrangles.

Rincon de los Carneros [NAPA]: *land grant,* south of the city of Napa. Named on Cuttings Wharf (1949) and Napa (1951) 7.5' quadrangles. The place is part of Entre Napa grant that Nicolas Higuera received in 1836; Julius Martin claimed 2557 acres patented in 1858 (Cowan, p. 24).

Rincon de Musalacon [SONOMA]: *land grant,* along Russian River near Cloverdale. Named on Asti (1959), Cloverdale (1960), and Geyserville (1955) 7.5' quadrangles. Francisco Berreyessa received 2 leagues in 1846; Johnson Horrel and others claimed 8867 acres patented in 1866 (Cowan, p. 50; Cowan gave the name "Rincon de Musulacon" as an alternate). The name "Musalacon" probably is of Indian origin (Kroeber, p. 49).

Rincon Valley [SONOMA]: *valley,* 3.5 miles northeast of downtown Santa Rosa (lat. 38°28'30" N, long. 122°40' W); the valley is along Rincon Creek. Named on Santa Rosa (1954) 7.5' quadrangle.

Rio Ayoska: see **Molinos** [SONOMA].

Rio Dell [SONOMA]: *settlement,* 5 miles east of Guerneville along Russian River (lat. 38°29'55" N, long. 122°54'15" W; sec. 31, T 8 N, R 9 W). Named on Camp Meeker (1954) and Guerneville (1955) 7.5' quadrangles.

Rio Nido [SONOMA]: *settlement,* 1.5 miles northeast of Guerneville on the north side of Russian River (lat. 38°31'15" N, long. 122°58'35" W; sec. 20, 21, T 8 N, R 10 W). Named on Guerneville (1955) 7.5' quadrangle. Called Rionido on Healdsburg (1940) 15' quadrangle, but United States Board on Geo-

graphic Names (1950, p. 6) rejected this form of the name. Postal authorities established Eaglenest post office in 1908, changed the name to Rionido in 1910, and changed it to Rio Nido in 1947; the name is from an eagle nest in a tree on the river bank—*rio nido* means "river nest" in Spanish (Salley, p. 63, 186).

Rio Rusa: see **Russian River** [SONOMA].

Ritchey Creek: see **Ritchie Creek** [NAPA].

Ritchie Creek [NAPA]: *stream,* flows nearly 4 miles to Napa River 4 miles east-southeast of Calistoga (lat. 38°33'30" N, long. 122°30'30" W). Named on Calistoga (1958) 7.5' quadrangle. The name commemorates one of the purchasers of land from Edward T. Bale, owner of Carne Humana grant (Archuleta, p. 105). United States Board on Geographic Names (1991, p. 6) approved the name "Ritchey Creek" for the stream, and pointed out that the name is for Matthew Dill Ritchey, an early settler.

River Slavianka: see **Russian River** [SONOMA].

Robinson: see **Cherry** [SONOMA].

Robinson Ridge [SONOMA]: *ridge,* west-south-west-trending, 2 miles long, 8.5 miles north-northwest of the village of Stewarts Point (lat. 38°46' N, long. 122°27'10" W). Named on Ornbaun Valley (1960) 15' quadrangle.

Robinson Rock [SONOMA]: *relief feature,* 2 miles north of the village of Bodega Bay (lat. 38°21'55" N, long. 123°02'50" W). Named on Bodega Head (1942) 7.5' quadrangle.

Roblar [SONOMA]: *locality,* 5 miles east of Bloomfield along Petaluma and Santa Rosa Railroad (lat. 38°19'20" N, long. 122°45'30" W); the place is on Roblar de la Miseria grant. Named on Two Rock (1954) 7.5' quadrangle. California Division of Highways' (1934) map shows two places, Vestal and Petersen, located along the railroad between Roblar and Stony Point, and a place called Quarry located along the railroad just north of Roblar.

Roblar de la Miseria [SONOMA]: *land grant,* west and northwest of the city of Petaluma. Named on Cotati (1954), Petaluma (1953), and Two Rock (1954) 7.5' quadrangles. Juan Nepomuceno Padilla received 4 leagues in 1845; David Wright and others claimed 16,887 acres patented in 1858 (Cowan, p. 68).

Rockpile Creek [SONOMA]: *stream,* heads in Mendocino County and flows 6 miles in Sonoma County to South Fork Gualala River 7.5 miles north-northwest of the village of Stewarts Point (lat. 38° 45'05' N, long. 123°28'10" W; sec. 31, T 11 N, R 14 W). Named on Ornbaun Valley (1960) 15' quadrangle.

Rock Point [SONOMA]: *promontory,* 4.25 miles south-southeast of Jenner along the coast (lat. 38°23'35" N, long. 123°05'20" W). Named on Duncans Mills (1979) 7.5' quadrangle. Called Rocky Point on Duncans Mills (1921) 15' quadrangle.

Rocktram [NAPA]: *locality,* nearly 3 miles south of downtown Napa along Southern Pacific Railroad (lat. 38°15'25" N, long. 122°16'45" W). Named on Napa (1951) 7.5' quadrangle. Called Rockfram on Sonoma (1942) 15' quadrangle.

Rockwell Gap [NAPA]: *pass,* 7.5 miles south-southeast of Berryessa Peak on Rocky Ridge on Napa-Yolo county line (lat. 38°34' N, long. 122°07'15" W; sec. 6, T 8 N, R 2 W). Named on Monticello Dam (1959) 7.5' quadrangle. Called Rosslyn Gap on Capay (1945) 15' quadrangle, but United States Board on Geographic Names (1962a), p. 15) rejected this name.

Rocky Mountain [SONOMA]:
(1) *peak,* 4.25 miles north-northeast of Guerneville (lat. 38°33'40" N, long. 122°58'45" W; near SW cor. sec. 4, T 8 N, R 10 W). Named on Guerneville (1955) 7.5' quadrangle.
(2) *peak,* nearly 5 miles north of Cazadero (lat. 38°36' N, long. 123° 04'20" W; sec. 28, T 9 N, R 11 W). Altitude 1482 feet. Named on Cazadero (1978) 7.5' quadrangle.

Rocky Point [SONOMA]: *promontory,* 1.5 miles south-southeast of the village of Stewarts Point along the coast (lat. 38°37'50" N, long. 123°23'20" W). Named on Stewarts Point (1978) 7.5' quadrangle.

Rocky Point: see **Rock Point** [SONOMA].

Rocky Ridge [NAPA]: *ridge,* extends south-southeast along Napa-Yolo county line for 12.5 miles from near Berryessa Peak to Putah Creek. Named on Brooks (1959), Lake Berryessa (1959), and Monticello Dam (1959) 7.5' quadrangles.

Rodgers Creek [SONOMA]: *stream,* flows 8 miles to Fowler Creek nearly 6.5 miles north of Sears Point (lat. 38°14'55" N, long. 122° 27'35" W). Named on Glen Ellen (1954), Sears Point (1951), and Sonoma (1951) 7.5' quadrangles.

Rohnert Park [SONOMA]: *town,* 1 mile north-northeast of Cotati (lat. 38°20'30" N, long. 122°41'45" W). Named on Cotati (1954, photorevised 1980) 7.5' quadrangle. Postal authorities established Rohnert Park post office in 1961 (Salley, p. 188), and the town incorporated in 1962. Development of the place began in 1957 on Waldo Rohnert seed farm (Mullen).

Rolands [SONOMA]: *settlement,* 1 mile northeast of Guerneville along Russian River (lat. 38°30'40" N, long. 122°58'50" W; on W line sec. 28, T 8 N, R 10 W). Named on Guerneville (1955) 7.5' quadrangle.

Romans Resort [SONOMA]: *locality,* 2.5 miles north-northwest of Cazadero (lat. 38°33'45" N, long. 123°06'25" W; near E line sec. 6, T 8 N, R 11 W). Named on Cazadero (1943) 7.5' quadrangle.

Romanzoff: see **Cape Romanzoff**, under **Bodega Head** [SONOMA].

Roscoe: see **Mount Roscoe** [SONOMA].

Rose [SONOMA]: *locality,* 3.25 miles southwest of Sears Point along Northwestern Pacific Railroad (lat. 38°07'15" N, long. 122°29'25" W). Named on Mare Island (1916) 15' quadrangle.

Rose: see **Camp Rose** [SONOMA].

Rosenberg: see **Camp Rosenberg** [SONOMA].

Ross [SONOMA]: *locality,* nearly 5 miles northeast of Occidental along Petaluma and Santa Rosa Railroad (lat. 38°27'30" N, long. 122°53'05" W). Named on Camp Meeker (1954) 7.5' quadrangle.

Ross: see **Fort Ross** [SONOMA].

Rosslyn Gap: see **Rockwell Gap** [NAPA].

Rough Creek [SONOMA]: *stream,* flows 2.25 miles to Scotty Creek 5.5 miles southeast of Jenner (lat. 38°23'05" N, long. 123°03'20" W). Named on Duncans Mills (1979) 7.5' quadrangle.

Roughs: see **The Roughs** [SONOMA].

Round Corral [NAPA]: *locality,* 6.5 miles southwest of Knoxville along Putah Creek in Big Basin (lat. 38°45'10" N, long. 122°25'05" W; near S line sec. 33, T 11 N, R 5 W). Named on Jericho Valley (1958) 7.5' quadrangle.

Routan Creek [NAPA]: *stream,* flows 4.25 miles to Butts Creek 6 miles northeast of Aetna Springs (lat. 38°41'55" N, long. 122°23'30" W; sec. 22, T 10 N, R 5 W). Named on Aetna Springs (1958) 7.5' quadrangle.

Royaneh: see **Camp Royaneh** [SONOMA].

Roy Creek [SONOMA]: *stream,* flows 2.5 miles to North Fork Buckeye Creek (2) 11 miles north-northeast of the village of Stewarts Point (lat. 38°48' N, long. 123°18'50" W; sec. 16, T 11 N, R 13 W). Named on Ornbaun Valley (1960) 15' quadrangle.

Rudesill's Landing: see **Haystack Landing**, under **Haystack** [SONOMA].

Rule [SONOMA]: *locality,* less than 1 mile north-northwest of present Jenner (lat. 38°27'50" N, long. 123°07'15" W). Named on Duncans Mills (1921) 15' quadrangle.

Rumsey Range: see **Blue Ridge** [NAPA].

Russian Gulch [SONOMA]: *canyon,* 1 mile long, opens to the sea 2.25 miles west-northwest of Jenner (lat. 38°28' N, long. 123°09'15" W). Named on Arched Rock (1977) 7.5' quadrangle. The canyon divides at the head into three branches called East, Middle, and West. East Branch is 2.5 miles long and is named on Arched Rock (1977) and Duncans Mills (1979) 7.5' quadrangles. Middle Branch and West Branch each are 4 miles long and are named on Arched Rock (1977) and Fort Ross (1978) 7.5' quadrangles.

Russian River [SONOMA]: *stream,* heads in Mendocino County and flows 68 miles in Sonoma County to the sea 0.5 mile west of Jenner (lat. 38°27'05" N, long. 123°07'40" W). Named on Santa Rosa (1958) 1°x 2° quadrangle. Called Rio Rusa on a diseño of San Miguel grant; the stream is designated by its

Indian name "Jauiyomi" on a diseño of Llano de Santa Rosa grant—the name "Jauiyomi" often has the spelling "Satiyome" or "Saliyome" (Becker, 1964). A map of 1850 produced by the Topographical Engineers has the names "Passion River" and "River Slavianka" for present Russian River (Wheat, p. 113). Ivan Kuskov, who explored the river in 1811, gave it the name "Slavyanka" (Schwartz, p. 43). Arguello passed through the valley of Russian River in 1821 and called it Libantiliyami (Bancroft, 1886, p. 449).

Russian River: see **Healdsburg** [SONOMA].

Russian River Heights [SONOMA]: *locality,* 1.5 miles south-southwest of Guerneville along Northwestern Pacific Railroad near Russian River (lat. 38°28'50" N, long. 123°00'30" W). Named on Duncans Mills (1921) 15' quadrangle.

Russian River Terrace [SONOMA]: *settlement,* 3.5 miles east of Guerneville along Russian River (lat. 38°30'15" N, long. 122°55'40" W; near SE cor. sec. 26, T 8 N, R 10 W). Named on Guerneville (1955) 7.5' quadrangle.

Russian Trough Spring [SONOMA]: *spring,* 2.25 miles northeast of Fort Ross (lat. 38°31'55" N, long. 123°12'25" W). Named on Fort Ross (1978) 7.5' quadrangle.

Russ Island [NAPA]: *island,* 3.25 miles west-southwest of Napa Junction between Napa River, South Slough, China Slough, and Devils Slough on Napa-Solano county line, mainly in Napa County (lat. 38°10'10" N, long. 122°18'30" W). Named on Cuttings Wharf (1949) 7.5' quadrangle. Called Knight Island on Mare Island (1916) 15' quadrangle.

Rutherford [NAPA]: *village,* 4 miles southeast of Saint Helena (lat. 38°27'30" N, long. 122°25'20" W). Named on Rutherford (1951) 7.5' quadrangle. Postal authorities established Rutherford post office in 1871 (Frickstad, p. 112). The name commemorates Thomas L. Rutherford, who married a granddaughter of George C. Yount (Gudde, 1949, p. 293). Postal authorities established Lomitas post office 10 miles northeast of Rutherford in 1894 and discontinued it in 1906 (Salley, p. 125).

– S –

Sacre Gap [SONOMA]: *pass,* 1 mile north of Mount Saint Helena on Sonoma-Lake county line (lat. 38°41'05" N, long. 122°38' W; sec. 28, T 10 N, R 7 W). Named on Mount Saint Helena (1959) 7.5' quadrangle.

Saddleback [NAPA]: *peak,* 2.5 miles east-northeast of Calistoga (lat. 38°35'40" N, long. 122°32'05" W; near SW cor. sec. 28, T 9 N, R 6 W). Named on Calistoga (1958) 7.5' quadrangle.

Sage Canyon [NAPA]: *canyon,* 4 miles long, opens into the canyon of Chiles Creek nearly 6 miles north of Yountville (lat. 38°29'25" N,

long. 122°20'50" W; sec. 6, T 7 N, R 4 W). Named on Chiles Valley (1958) and Yountville (1951) 7.5' quadrangles. Water of Lake Hennessey floods the lowermost part of the canyon.

Sage Creek [NAPA]: *stream,* flows 5.5 miles to Lake Hennessey 6 miles north-northeast of Yountville (lat. 38°29'30" N, long. 122°20'25" W; sec. 6, T 7 N, R 4 W); the stream goes through Sage Canyon. Named on Chiles Valley (1958) 7.5' quadrangle.

Sage Creek: see **Conn Creek** [NAPA].

Saint Elmo Creek [SONOMA]: *stream,* flows 2 miles to Austin Creek 0.25 mile south of Cazadero (lat. 38°31'30" N, long. 123°05'15" W; sec. 21, T 8 N, R 11 W). Named on Cazadero (1978) 7.5' quadrangle.

Saint Helena [NAPA]: *town,* 17 miles northwest of the city of Napa (lat. 38°30'15" N, long. 122°28'10" W). Named on Rutherford (1951) and Saint Helena (1960) 7.5' quadrangles. Postal authorities established Saint Helena post office in 1856 (Frickstad, p. 112), and the town incorporated in 1876. The community began in 1853 when Henry Still built a store and house there; the name is from the designation of a division of Sons of Temperance established at the place (Menefee, p. 186).

Saint Helena: see **Mount Saint Helena** [SONOMA].

Saint Helena Creek [NAPA]: *stream,* flows 2 miles to Lake County nearly 7 miles north of Calistoga (lat. 38°40'35" N, long. 122°35'25" W; sec. 36, T 10 N, R 7 W). Named on Detert Reservoir (1958) 7.5' quadrangle.

Saint Helena Range: see **Mayacmas Mountains** [NAPA-SONOMA].

Saint Helena White Sulphur Springs: see **Sulphur Canyon** [NAPA].

Saint Hellens: see **Mount Saint Hellens**, under **Mount Saint Helena** [SONOMA].

Saint John Mountain: see **Mount Saint John** [NAPA].

Saint Joseph Camp [SONOMA]: *locality,* 3.5 miles southwest of Guerneville along Russian River (lat. 38°27'40" N, long. 123°02'35" W). Named on Duncans Mills (1979) 7.5' quadrangle.

Saint Louis: see **Sonoma** [SONOMA].

Saliyome: see **Russian River** [SONOMA].

Salmon Creek [SONOMA]:

(1) *stream,* flows 17 miles to the sea 2 miles northwest of the village of Bodega Bay (lat. 38°21'20" N, long. 123°04' W). Named on Bodega Head (1972), Camp Meeker (1954), and Valley Ford (1954) 7.5' quadrangles. According to Bancroft (1886, p. 464), a party of Mexicans on the way to Fort Ross in 1822 called the stream Arroyo Verde for the color of the water after one of the party became ill and vomited into the stream—*verde* means "green" in Spanish.

(2) *village,* 1.5 miles northwest of the village of Bodega Bay (lat. 38°21'05" N, long.

123°03'40" W); the village is near the mouth of Salmon Creek (1). Named on Bodega Head (1972) 7.5' quadrangle.

Salmon Creek Beach: see **North Salmon Creek Beach** [SONOMA]; **South Salmon Creek Beach** [SONOMA].

Salt Creek [SONOMA]: *stream,* flows 1.5 miles to Santa Rosa Creek 5.25 miles north-north-west of Kenwood (lat. 38°29'25" N, long. 122°34' W; sec. 6, T 7 N, R 6 W). Named on Kenwood (1954) 7.5' quadrangle.

Salt Point [SONOMA]: *promontory,* 2 miles southwest of Plantation along the coast (lat. 38°33'55" N, long. 123°19'55" W). Named on Plantation (1977) 7.5' quadrangle.

Salt Tree Saddle [SONOMA]: *pass,* 3.25 miles north of Cazadero (lat. 38°34'40" N, long. 123°05'40" W; sec. 32, T 9 N, R 11 W). Named on Cazadero (1978) 7.5' quadrangle.

Salvador [NAPA]: *locality,* 3.5 miles north-northwest of downtown Napa (lat. 38°20'25" N, long. 122°19'10" W). Named on Napa (1951) 7.5' quadrangle.

Samuel Springs [NAPA]: *locality,* 11 miles northeast of Saint Helena (lat. 38°36'15" N, long. 122°18'40" W). Named on Chiles Valley (1958) 7.5' quadrangle. Springs at the place were the basis of a resort called Samuels' Soda Springs (Crawford, 1894, p. 341). Napa Rock Soda Springs, also known as Priest Soda Springs, were located about 6 miles south of Samuel Springs (Waring, p. 161)—water from these springs was bottled as early as 1898 (Bradley, p. 281). Phillips Soda Springs were situated about 350 yards north of Napa Rock Soda Springs; water there was used for bathing in the early days (Waring, p. 161). Pope Mineral Spring, also called Indian Spring, lies 1 mile west of Samuels Soda Springs; the proprietor began bottling the water in 1913 (Bradley, p. 281).

Samuels' Soda Springs: see **Samuel Springs** [NAPA].

San Antonio Creek [SONOMA]: *stream,* heads in Sonoma County and flows 17 miles, mainly along along Marin-Sonoma county line, to Petaluma River nearly 4 miles north-north-east of downtown Novato (lat. 38°09'30" N, long. 122°32'40" W). Named on Petaluma (1953) and Petaluma River (1954) 7.5' quadrangles. The stream was called Arroyo de San Antonio in Spanish days (Teather, p. 65).

Sandy Point [SONOMA]: *promontory,* 0.5 mile south of the village of Stewarts Point along the coast (lat. 38°38'40" N, long. 123°23'55" W). Named on Stewarts Point (1978) 7.5' quadrangle.

Sanitarium [NAPA]: *locality,* 2.5 miles north of Saint Helena (lat. 38°32'35" N, long. 122°28'25" W). Named on Saint Helena (1960) 7.5' quadrangle, which shows St. Helena Sanitarium at the place. Postal authorities established Sanitarium post office in 1901 and changed the name to Deer Park in 1970

(Salley, p. 195). Seventh-Day Adventists opened the sanitarium in 1878 and called the place Crystal Springs, but the community that developed there became known as Sanitarium (Gudde, 1949, p. 305).

San Miguel [SONOMA]: *land grant,* northwest of Santa Rosa. Named on Healdsburg (1955), Mark West Springs (1958), Santa Rosa (1954), and Sebastopol (1954) 7.5' quadrangles. William Mark West received 1.5 leagues in 1840 and 1844; Guadalupe V. West claimed 6663 acres patented in 1865 (Cowan, p. 85; Perez, p. 94).

San Pablo Bay [SONOMA]: *bay,* between San Francisco Bay and Carquinez Strait in Contra Costa County, Marin County, Solano County, and Sonoma County. Named on Cuttings Wharf (1949), Mare Island (1959), Petaluma Point (1959), Richmond (1959), San Quentin (1959), and Sears Point (1951) 7.5' quadrangles. Called Bahia de San Pablo on Beechey's (1827-1828) map, and called Pablo Bay on Wilkes' (1849) map. Canizares named the feature Bahia Redondo in 1775—*bahia redondo* means "round bay" in Spanish (Hanna, W.L., p. 44). Gudde (1969, p. 291) gave the names "Bahia Redonda" and "Bahia de Sonoma" as early designations of the feature.

Santa Nella [SONOMA]: *locality,* 1.5 miles east-southeast of Guerneville in Pocket Canyon (lat. 38°29'50" N, long. 122°57'55" W; near E line sec. 33, T 8 N, R 10 W). Named on Camp Meeker (1954) 7.5' quadrangle.

Santa Rosa [SONOMA]: *city,* in the east-central part of Sonoma County (downtown near lat. 38°26'25" N, long. 122°42'45" W). Named on Santa Rosa (1954) and Sebastopol (1954, photorevised 1968) 7.5' quadrangles. Postal authorities established Santa Rosa post office in 1852 (Frickstad, p. 198), and the city incorporated in 1868. The name is from Cabeza de Santa Rosa grant, where the city lies; an earlier settlement located nearby was called Franklin Town (Hanna, P.T., p. 292). Franklin Town disappeared when its buildings were moved to the site of the new community of Santa Rosa, located farther down Santa Rosa Creek (Hansen and Miller, p. 44). Cardwell's (1958) map has the name "Santa Rosa Valley" for lowlands around Santa Rosa, and *Californian* newspaper for August 15, 1846, used the name "Santa Rosa Plains" for the same lowlands. A resort called Santa Rosa Springs operated 2 miles from Santa Rosa about 1890 (Anderson, p. 231). Postal authorities established America post office 9 miles northeast of Santa Rosa in 1881, discontinued it for a time in 1887, and discontinued it finally in 1903; the name was from America S. Simpson, first postmaster (Salley, p. 6). California Division of Highways' (1934) map shows places called Wrights, Willow Grove, Macauley, Leddy, and La Franchi along

Petaluma and Santa Rosa Railroad between Santa Rosa and Llano.

Santa Rosa Creek [SONOMA]: *stream,* flows 21 miles to Laguna de Santa Rosa 3.5 miles north of Sebastopol (lat. 38°27'05" N, long. 122°50' W). Named on Calistoga (1958), Kenwood (1954), Santa Rosa (1954), and Sebastopol (1954) 7.5' quadrangles. Sebastopol (1954, photorevised 1968) 7.5' quadrangle shows the stream modified to form Santa Rosa Flood Control Channel. According to one account, a Spanish priest named the creek in the late 1820's for St. Rose of Lima after the priest had baptized an Indian girl at the stream (Hoover, Rensch, and Rensch, p. 533). Called Arroyo de Permanente on a diseño of Cabeza de Santa Rosa grant in 1838, and called Arroyo de Sta. Rosa on a diseño of San Miguel grant (Becker, 1969).

Santa Rosa Creek Reservoir [SONOMA]: *lake,* 3700 feet long, 3.5 miles east-northeast of downtown Santa Rosa (lat. 38°27'15" N, long. 122°39'05" W). Named on Santa Rosa (1954) 7.5' quadrangle.

Santa Rosa Flood Control Channel: see **Santa Rosa Creek** [SONOMA].

Santa Rosa Plains: see **Santa Rosa** [SONOMA].

Santa Rosa Springs: see **Santa Rosa** [SONOMA].

Santa Rosa Valley: see **Santa Rosa** [SONOMA].

Sarco Creek [NAPA]: *stream,* flows 4.5 miles to Milliken Creek nearly 2 miles north-north-east of downtown Napa (lat. 38°19'20" N, long. 122°16'25" W). Named on Mount George (1951) and Napa (1951) 7.5' quadrangles.

Sarlandt Resort [SONOMA]: *locality,* 2 miles south of Cazadero (lat. 38°30'05" N, long. 123°05'10" W). Named on Cazadero (1943) 7.5' quadrangle.

Satiyome: see **Russian River** [SONOMA].

Sausal Creek [SONOMA]: *stream,* flows 8 miles to Russian River 4 miles northeast of Healdsburg (lat. 38°39' N, long. 122°48'30" W). Named on Jimtown (1955) 7.5' quadrangle.

Sawmill Gulch [SONOMA]: *canyon,* 1 mile long, opens into the canyon of Russian River 1 mile east of Jenner (lat. 38°26'55" N, long. 123°05'45" W). Named on Duncans Mills (1979) 7.5' quadrangle.

Schell Creek [SONOMA]: *stream,* flows 3.5 miles to Schell Slough 6 miles north of Sears Point (lat. 38°14'20" N, long. 122°25'50" W). Named on Sears Point (1951) and Sonoma (1951) 7.5' quadrangles.

Schell Slough [SONOMA]: *water feature,* extends from Schell Creek to Steamboat Slough 5.5 miles north-northeast of Sears Point (lat. 38°13'40" N, long. 121°25'25" W). Named on Sears Point (1951) 7.5' quadrangle.

Schellville [SONOMA]: *settlement,* 6.5 miles north of Sears Point along Northwestern Pacific Railroad (lat. 38°14'45" N, long. 122°26'15" W); the place is near the mouth of Schell Creek. Named on Sears Point (1951) 7.5' quadrangle. Called Shellville on Mare Island (1916) 15' quadrangle. Postal authorities established Shellville post office in 1888 and discontinued it in 1931; the misspelled name was for Theodore L. Schell, pioneer rancher in the neighborhood (Salley, p. 203).

Schocken Hill [SONOMA]: *peak,* 1 mile north-northeast of Sonoma (lat. 38°18'15" N, long. 122°27' W). Altitude 658 feet. Named on Sonoma (1951) 7.5' quadrangle.

Schoolhouse Beach [SONOMA]: *beach,* 5.5 miles south-southeast of Jenner (lat. 38°22'35" N, long. 123°04'40" W). Named on Duncans Mills (1979) 7.5' quadrangle.

Schoolhouse Creek [SONOMA]:
(1) *stream,* flows 1.5 miles to Dry Creek 5 miles west of Geyserville (lat. 38°43'10" N, long. 123°59'30" W). Named on Geyserville (1955) and Warm Springs Dam (1978) 7.5' quadrangles.
(2) *stream,* flows 1 mile to Gilliam Creek 4 miles northeast of Cazadero (lat. 38°33'55" N, long. 123°01'55" W; sec. 1, T 8 N, R 11 W). Named on Cazadero (1978) 7.5' quadrangle.

Schoolhouse Gulch [SONOMA]: *canyon,* drained by a stream that flows 0.5 mile to Dutch Bill Creek 3 miles south-southwest of Guerneville (lat. 38°27'40" N, long. 123°00'35" W; sec. 7, T 7 N, R 10 W). Named on Duncans Mills (1979) 7.5' quadrangle.

Schoolhouse Point [SONOMA]: *ridge,* southwest-trending, 0.5 mile long, 1.5 miles northwest of Mount Saint Helena (lat. 38°41'25" N, long. 122°39'05" W). Named on Mount Saint Helena (1959) 7.5' quadrangle.

School Ridge [SONOMA]: *ridge,* south-trending, 1 mile long, 2 miles north of Annapolis (lat. 38°45' N, long. 123°22'20" W). Named on Annapolis (1977) 7.5' quadrangle.

Schultz Slough [SONOMA]: *water feature,* 4 miles southeast of downtown Petaluma in marsh southwest of Petaluma River (lat. 38°12' N, long. 122°34'35" W). Named on Petaluma River (1954) 7.5' quadrangle.

Scotts Creek [SONOMA]: *stream,* flows about 1.25 miles to Porter Creek (1) 4 miles northeast of Guerneville (lat. 38°32'50" N, long. 122°56'40" W; near SE cor. sec. 10, T 8 N, R 10 W); the stream is east of Scotts Ridge. Named on Guerneville (1955) 7.5' quadrangle.

Scotts Opening [SONOMA]: *area,* 4.5 miles northeast of Guerneville (lat. 38°33'25" N, long. 122°57' W); the place is on Scotts Ridge. Named on Guerneville (1955) 7.5' quadrangle.

Scotts Ridge [SONOMA]: *ridge,* south-trending, 1 mile long, 4.5 miles northeast of Guerneville (lat. 38°33'25" N, long. 122°57'

W). Named on Guerneville (1955) 7.5' quadrangle.

Scotty Creek [SONOMA]: *stream,* flows 2.5 miles to the sea 5 miles south-southeast of Jenner at Gleason Beach (lat. 38°23'05" N, long. 123°04'55" W). Named on Duncans Mills (1979) 7.5' quadrangle. On Duncans Mills (1921) 15' quadrangle, the canyon of the stream is called Gleason Gulch.

Scribner Mountain [NAPA]: *ridge,* west-north-west- to northwest-trending, 2.25 miles south-southwest of Berryessa Peak (lat. 38°38'05" N, long. 122°12'35" W). Named on Brooks (1959) 7.5' quadrangle.

Sea Ranch: see **German** [SONOMA].

Sears Point [SONOMA]: *locality,* 11 miles southeast of Petaluma along Northwestern Pacific Railroad (lat. 38°09' N, long. 122°26'45" W). Named on Sears Point (1951) 7.5' quadrangle. Postal authorities established Sears Point post office in 1903 and discontinued it in 1911; the name commemorates Franklin Sears, who settled near the place in 1851 (Salley, p. 200).

Seaview [SONOMA]: *locality,* 2.25 miles north-northeast of Fort Ross (lat. 38°32'45" N, long. 123°13'35" W; sec. 7, T 8 N, R 12 W). Named on Fort Ross (1943) 7.5' quadrangle. Skaggs (1921) 15' quadrangle has the form "Sea View" for the name. Postal authorities established Timber Cove post office in 1863, moved it 3 miles northeast and changed the name to Sea View in 1883, moved it 1 mile north in 1908, and discontinued it in 1914 (Salley, p. 200, 222).

Sebastopol [SONOMA]: *town,* 6.5 miles west-southwest of Santa Rosa (lat. 38°24'05" N, long. 122°49'25" W). Named on Sebastopol (1954) 7.5' quadrangle. Postal authorities established Sebastopol post office in 1867 (Salley, p. 200), and the town incorporated in 1902. The community began in 1852 with a store and settlement called Pine Grove; the name "Sebastopol" came in 1856 after a local quarrel was likened to the Crimean-War battle at Sebastopol (Miller, J.T., p. 32). California Mining Bureau's (1917) map shows a place called Kenilworth located northeast of Sebastopol along the railroad about halfway from Sebastopol to Santa Rosa. Postal authorities established Peachland post office 5 miles northwest of Sebastopol in 1891 and discontinued it in 1901; the site was in peach orchards (Salley, p. 168). They established Carillo post office 3 miles east of Sebastopol in 1897 and discontinued it in 1899; the name was for an early settler (Salley, p. 37).

Sebastopol: see **Yountville** [NAPA].

Second Napa Slough [SONOMA]: *water feature,* joins Sonoma Creek 3 miles north-north-east of Sears Point (lat. 38°11'15" N, long. 122°25'15" W). Named on Sears Point (1951) 7.5' quadrangle.

Secret Pasture [SONOMA]: *area,* 5.5 miles north-northwest of Sonoma (lat. 38°22'15" N, long. 122°29' W; near NE cor. sec. 14, T 6 N, R 6 W). Named on Sonoma (1951) 7.5' quadrangle.

Segassia Canyon [NAPA]: *canyon,* drained by a stream that flows 1.25 miles to Dry Creek 5 miles south of Rutherford (lat. 38°23'20" N, long. 122°24'30" W; near SE cor. sec. 4, T 6 N, R 5 W). Named on Rutherford (1951) and Sonoma (1951) 7.5' quadrangles.

Seno de Malacomes: see **Mallacomes or Moristul y Plan de Agua Caliente** [NAPA-SONOMA].

Sentinel Hill [NAPA]: *hill,* 4 miles north-north-east of Saint Helena (lat. 38°33'45" N, long. 122°26'50" W). Named on Saint Helena (1960) 7.5' quadrangle.

Seven Oaks Creek [SONOMA]: *stream,* flows 1.5 miles to Warm Springs Creek 1.5 miles west-northwest of Skaggs Springs (lat. 38°42'05" N, long. 123°03'05" W; sec. 23, T 10 N, R 11 W). Named on Warm Springs Dam (1978) 7.5' quadrangle.

Seven Springs [NAPA]: *locality,* 4.25 miles north-northeast of Saint Helena (lat. 38°33'20" N, long. 122°25'45" W). Named on Pope Valley (1921) 15' quadrangle.

Seventy Acre Canyon [NAPA]: *canyon,* drained by a stream that flows 2.25 miles to Lake Curry 2.5 miles south-southwest of Mount Vaca (lat. 38°22' N, long. 122°07'15" W). Named on Fairfield North (1951) and Mount Vaca (1951) 7.5' quadrangles.

Sheehy Creek [NAPA]: *stream,* flows nearly 4 miles to salt evaporators 3.25 miles north-northwest of Napa Junction (lat. 38°13'45" N, long. 121°16'40" W; near N line sec. 2, T 4 N, R 4 W). Named on Cuttings Wharf (1949, photorevised 1968) 7.5' quadrangle.

Sheephouse Creek [SONOMA]: *stream,* flows nearly 3 miles to Russian River 1.25 miles east of Jenner (lat. 38°26'55" N, long. 123°05'40" W). Named on Duncans Mills (1979) 7.5' quadrangle.

Sheep Repose Ridge [SONOMA]: *ridge,* north-to northwest-trending, 1 mile long, 4.25 miles west-northwest of Big Mountain (lat. 38°44'35" N, long. 123°12'35" W). Named on Tombs Creek (1978) 7.5' quadrangle.

Sheep Ridge [SONOMA]: *ridge,* south-trending, 2.5 miles long, 7 miles southeast of Jenner (lat. 38°22'55" N, long. 122°01'20" W). Named on Bodega Head (1972) and Duncans Mills (1979) 7.5' quadrangles.

Sheepskin Rock [SONOMA]: *peak,* 7 miles northwest of Mount Saint Helena (lat. 38°44'35" N, long. 122°43' W; sec. 2, T 10 N, R 8 W). Named on Mount Saint Helena (1959) 7.5' quadrangle.

Shell Beach [SONOMA]: *beach,* 2.5 miles south-southeast of Jenner along the coast (lat. 38°25' N, long. 123°06'15" W). Named on Duncans Mills (1979) 7.5' quadrangle.

Shellville: see **Schellville** [SONOMA].

Shellville Colony [SONOMA]: *settlement,* 6.5 miles north-northeast of Sears Point (lat. 38°14'35" N, long. 122°25' W); the place is 1.25 miles east-southeast of Shellville (present Schellville). Named on Mare Island (1916) 15' quadrangle.

Sheridan [SONOMA]: *locality,* 3.25 miles southwest of Guerneville along Russian River (lat. 38°27'55" N, long. 123°02'05" W). Named on Duncans Mills (1979) 7.5' quadrangle.

Sheridan Gulch [SONOMA]: *canyon,* drained by a stream that flows 0.5 mile to Russian River 3.25 miles southwest of Guerneville (lat. 38°27'50" N, long. 123°02'10" W). Named on Duncans Mills (1979) 7.5' quadrangle.

Shiloh [SONOMA]: *locality,* 7.5 miles southeast of Healdsburg along Northwestern Pacific Railroad (lat. 38°31'25" N, long. 122°47'40" W; sec. 19, T 8 N, R 8 W). Named on Healdsburg (1955) 7.5' quadrangle.

Shipyard Acres [NAPA]: *locality,* 2.5 miles south-southeast of downtown Napa (lat. 38°15'35" N, long. 122°16'20" W). Named on Napa (1951) 7.5' quadrangle.

Shoeheart Ridge: see **Britain Ridge** [SONOMA].

Shorttail Gulch [SONOMA]: *canyon,* drained by a stream that flows less than 1 mile to the sea nearly 3 miles southeast of the village of Bodega Bay (lat. 38°18'10" N, long. 123°00'45" W). Named on Bodega Head (1972) 7.5' quadrangle.

Signal Hill [NAPA]: *peak,* 2 miles south-southeast of Mount Vaca on Napa-Solano county line (lat. 38°22'35" N, long. 122°05' W; near S line sec. 9, T 6 N, R 2 W). Altitude 2394 feet. Named on Fairfield North (1951) and Mount Vaca (1951) 7.5' quadrangles.

Silverado City: see **Calistoga** [NAPA].

Simi [SONOMA]: *locality,* 1.5 miles north of Healdsburg along Northwestern Pacific Railroad (lat. 38°38'25" N, long. 122°52'25" W). Named on Jimtown (1955) 7.5' quadrangle.

Simmons Canyon [NAPA]: *canyon,* drained by a stream that flows 2 miles to lowlands nearly 2 miles east-northeast of Calistoga (lat. 38°35'30" N, long. 122°33' W). Named on Calistoga (1958) 7.5' quadrangle.

Skaggs: see **Skaggs Springs** [SONOMA].

Skaggs Springs [SONOMA]: *springs,* 7.5 miles south of Cloverdale along Little Warm Springs Creek (lat. 38°41'35" N, long. 123°01'30" W; near S line sec. 24, T 10 N, R 11 W). Named on Warm Springs Dam (1978) 7.5' quadrangle. Skaggs Springs (1943) 7.5' quadrangle shows buildings at the place before water of Lake Sonoma inundated the site. Postal authorities established Skaggs Springs post office in 1878, discontinued it in 1884, reestablished it in 1889, changed the name to Skaggs in 1895, changed the name back to Skaggs Springs in 1927, and discontinued it in 1943—the name commemorates Alexander Skaggs, first postmaster and developer of a

resort at the place (Salley, p. 205). The resort opened to the public in 1857, and by 1909 a hotel and cottages provided accommodations for 150 people to enjoy water from three hot springs (Waring, p. 81-82). Postal authorities established Groves post office 7 miles west of Skaggs post office in 1912 and discontinued it in 1914; the name was for James H. Groves, first postmaster (Salley, p. 90).

Skunk Creek [SONOMA]: *stream,* flows 3 miles to Cherry Creek 3.5 miles west-southwest of Cloverdale (lat. 38°47'35" N, long. 123° 04'55" W; near NE cor. sec. 21, T 11 N, R 11 W). Named on Cloverdale (1960) 7.5' quadrangle.

Sky High [SONOMA]: *peak,* 5.5 miles west of Cloverdale (lat. 38°48'35" N, long. 123°07'15" W; near S line sec. 7, T 11 N, R 11 W). Altitude 2041 feet. Named on Cloverdale (1960) 7.5' quadrangle.

Skyline Ridge [SONOMA]: *ridge,* southeast- to south-southeast-trending, 2.25 miles long, 8.5 miles southeast of Annapolis (lat. 38°38'10" N, long. 123°15' W). Named on Annapolis (1977), Fort Ross (1978), and Tombs Creek (1978) 7.5' quadrangles.

Slate Gap [SONOMA]: *pass,* 2.5 miles west-southwest of Guerneville (lat. 38°28'55" N, long. 123°02'10" W). Named on Duncans Mills (1979) 7.5' quadrangle.

Slaughterhouse Gulch [SONOMA]: *canyon,* drained by a stream that flows less than 1 mile to Russian River 3 miles east of Jenner (lat. 38°26'45" N, long. 123°03'45" W). Named on Duncans Mills (1979) 7.5' quadrangle.

Slavianka: see **River Slavianda**, under **Russian River** [SONOMA].

Slavyansk: see **Fort Ross** [SONOMA].

Smith Corner: see **Riccas Corner** [SONOMA].

Smith Creek [SONOMA]:

(1) *stream,* flows 5.5 miles to Dry Creek 5.5 miles southwest of Cloverdale (lat. 38°45' N, long. 123°05'40" W; near NE cor. sec. 5, T 10 N, R 11 W). Named on Hopland (1960) 15' quadrangle, and on Warm Springs Dam (1978) 7.5' quadrangle.

(2) *stream,* flows 2.5 miles to Russian River 2 miles south of Guerneville (lat. 38°28'30" N, long. 122°59'25" W; near S line sec. 5, T 7 N, R 10 W). Named on Camp Meeker (1954) 7.5' quadrangle.

Smith Ridge [SONOMA]: *ridge,* generally east-trending, 1.5 miles long, 3.25 miles east of Fort Ross (lat. 38°30'55" N, long. 123°10'50" W). Named on Fort Ross (1978) 7.5' quadrangle.

Smith's Ranch: see **Bodega** [SONOMA] (2).

Smittle Creek [NAPA]: *stream,* flows nearly 3 miles to Lake Berryessa 13 miles east-northeast of Saint Helena (lat. 38°34'40" N, long. 122°15'10" W). Named on Chiles Valley (1958) and Lake Berryessa (1959) 7.5' quadrangles.

Snell Creek [NAPA]: *stream,* flows 2 miles to

Butts Creek 5.25 miles northeast of Aetna Springs (lat. 38°42'15" N, long. 122°24'35" W; sec. 21, T 10 N, R 5 W); the stream heads near Snell Peak and joins Butts Creek in Snell Valley. Named on Aetna Springs (1958) 7.5' quadrangle.

Snell Peak [NAPA]: *peak,* 5 miles north-north-east of Aetna Springs (lat. 38°43'05" N, long. 122° 27' W; sec. 18, T 10 N, R 5 W). Altitude 1858 feet. Named on Aetna Springs (1958) 7.5' quadrangle.

Snell Valley [NAPA]: *valley,* 5 miles northeast of Aetna Springs along Snell Creek and Butts Creek (lat. 38°42'15" N, long. 122° 25' W). Named on Aetna Springs (1958) 7.5' quadrangle.

Snow Creek [SONOMA]: *stream,* flows 2 miles to Cherry Creek 4 miles west of Cloverdale (lat. 38°48'20" N, long. 123°05'15" W; sec. 16, T 11 N, R 11 W). Named on Cloverdale (1960) 7.5' quadrangle.

Snow Flat [NAPA]: *area,* 7.25 miles west-south-west of Mount Vaca (lat. 38°21'15" N, long. 122°13'15" W; sec. 20, T 6 N, R 3 W). Named on Mount George (1951) 7.5' quadrangle.

Soda Canyon [NAPA]: *canyon,* 4 miles long, opens into lowlands 5 miles north of downtown Napa (lat. 38°22' N, long. 122°17'05" W); Soda Creek (1) drains the canyon. Named on Napa (1951) and Yountville (1951) 7.5' quadrangles.

Soda Creek [NAPA]:
(1) *stream,* flows 5 miles to Napa River nearly 4 miles north of downtown Napa (lat. 38°21'10" N, long. 122°17'25" W); the stream goes through Soda Canyon. Named on Napa (1951) and Yountville (1951) 7.5' quadrangles.
(2) *stream,* flows 4.5 miles to Capell Creek 10 miles northwest of Mount Vaca (lat. 38°29'45" N, long. 122°14'30" W; near SE cor. sec. 36, T 8 N, R 4 W); the stream drains Soda Valley. Named on Capell Valley (1951), Chiles Valley (1958), and Yountville (1951) 7.5' quadrangles.

Soda Rock [SONOMA]: *relief feature,* nearly 4 miles northeast of Healdsburg on the south bank of Russian River (lat. 38°39'05" N, long. 122°49' W). Named on Jimtown (1955) 7.5' quadrangle. Postal authorities established Soda Rock post office, named for the feature, 6 miles east of Healdsburg in 1889 and discontinued it in 1892, when they moved it 1 mile northwest and changed the name to Alexander Valley (Salley, p. 207).

Soda Spring [NAPA]: *spring,* 11.5 miles east of Saint Helena (lat. 38°31'05" N, long. 122°15'35" W); the spring is at the head of a branch of Soda Creek (2). Named on Chiles Valley (1958) 7.5' quadrangle.

Soda Spring Creek [SONOMA]: *stream,* flows nearly 1 mile to House Creek 6.5 miles southwest of Big Mountain (lat. 38°38'55" N, long. 123°13'55" W; sec. 6, T 9 N, R 12 W). Named on Tombs Creek (1978) 7.5' quadrangle.

Soda Springs [SONOMA]: *locality,* 6.5 miles east-southeast of Annapolis along Wheatfield Fork Gualala River (lat. 38°40'20" N, long. 123°16' W; near NE cor. sec. 35, T 10 N, R 13 W). Site named on Annapolis (1977) 7.5' quadrangle.

Soda Springs Creek [SONOMA]: *stream,* flows 2 miles to Buckeye Creek (2) 2 miles north-northeast of Annapolis (lat. 38°44'50" N, long. 123°20'50" W; sec. 6, T 10 N, R 13 W). Named on Annapolis (1977) 7.5' quadrangle.

Soda Valley [NAPA]: *valley,* 11 miles east of Saint Helena on upper reaches of Soda Creek (2) (lat. 38°31'10" N, long. 122°16'10" W). Named on Chiles Valley (1958) 7.5' quadrangle.

Solid Comfort: see **Lokoya** [NAPA].

Sonoma [SONOMA]: *town,* 17 miles southeast of Santa Rosa (lat. 38°17'35" N, long. 122°27'25" W). Named on Sonoma (1951) 7.5' quadrangle. Postal authorities established Sonoma post office in 1849 (Frickstad, p. 198), and the town incorporated in 1900. San Francisco Solano mission was founded at the place about 1823, and Mariano Guadalupe Vallejo started Pueblo de Sonoma there in 1835 (Hoover, Rensch, and Rensch, p. 527, 528). The name "Sonoma" most probably is of Indian origin (Kroeber, p. 59). Gibbes' (1852) map has the name "St. Louis" for a place situated south of Sonoma on the west side of Sonoma Creek. A description of a trip from San Francisco to Sonoma published in *The California Star* newspaper for December 25, 1847, described a new city of St. Louis located on the east side of Sonoma Creek near the embarcadero, and a rival new city of New Philadelphia laid out across the creek on the west side.

Sonoma: see **Lake Sonoma** [SONOMA].

Sonoma Canyon: see **Adobe Canyon** [SONOMA].

Sonoma Creek [SONOMA]: *stream,* flows 32 miles to San Pablo Bay 2.25 miles east of Sears Point (lat. 38°09'10" N, long. 122°24'15" W); the mouth of the stream is near the intersection of Sonoma-Napa county line with Sonoma-Solano county line. Named on Glen Ellen (1954), Kenwood (1954), Rutherford (1951), Sears Point (1951), and Sonoma (1951) 7.5' quadrangles. Called Arroyo Grande on a diseño of Agua Caliente grant (Becker, 1969).

Sonoma Landing: see **Midshipman Point** [SONOMA].

Sonoma Mountain [SONOMA]: *ridge,* southeast-trending, 1.25 miles long, 4 miles southwest of Glen Ellen (lat. 38°19'30" N, long. 122° 34'30" W); the feature is in Sonoma Mountains. Named on Glen Ellen (1954) 7.5' quadrangle.

Sonoma Mountains [SONOMA]: *range,* extends for 25 miles northwest from San Pablo Bay to the vicinity of Santa Rosa, and lies northeast of Petaluma Valley and Cotati Valley. Named on Cotati (1954), Glen Ellen (1954), Kenwood (1954), Petaluma River (1954), Santa Rosa (1954), and Sears Point (1951) quadrangles.

Sonoma Valley [SONOMA]: *valley,* along Sonoma Creek from near Sonoma southeast toward San Pablo Bay. Named on Sears Point (1951) and Sonoma (1951) 7.5' quadrangles. On Goddard's (1857) map, the name extends north-northwest through present Valley of the Moon.

Soscol: see **Suscol** [NAPA].

Sotoyome [SONOMA]: *land grant,* near Healdsburg and the southeast end of Alexander Valley. Named on Geyserville (1955), Guerneville (1955), Healdsburg (1955), and Jimtown (1955) 7.5' quadrangles. Henry D. Fitch received 8 leagues in 1841; Fitch's heirs claimed 48,837 acres patented in 1858 (Cowan, p. 100; Cowan gave the name "Sotoyomi" as an alternate). According to Perez (p. 100), Fitch was the grantee in 1844. The name likely is an Indian place name derived in Spanish times from a personal name (Kroeber, p. 59-60).

Sousas Corner [SONOMA]: *locality,* 3.5 miles north-northwest of Sebastopol (lat. 38°26'45" N, long. 122°51'35" W). Named on Sebastopol (1954) 7.5' quadrangle. Called Sousa Corners on Sebastopol (1942) 15' quadrangle.

South Los Guilicos: see **Kenwood** [SONOMA].

South Salmon Creek Beach [SONOMA]: *beach,* 2.25 miles long, center 1.5 miles west-northwest of the village of Bodega Bay along the coast (lat. 38°20'15" N, long. 123°04'05" W); the beach is south of the mouth of Salmon Creek (1). Named on Bodega Head (1972) 7.5' quadrangle. Called Salmon Creek Beach on Bodega Head (1942) 7.5' quadrangle.

South Slough [NAPA]: *water feature,* on Napa-Solano county line, joins Napa River 3.25 miles north-northwest of downtown Vallejo (lat. 38°09'40" N, long. 122°17'15" W; sec. 34, T 4 N, R 4 W). Named on Cuttings Wharf (1949) 7.5' quadrangle.

Spanish Creek [SONOMA]: *stream,* flows 1.5 miles to Wolf Creek 3.5 miles southwest of Big Mountain (lat. 38°40'45" N, long. 123° 11'40" W; at S line sec. 28, T 10 N, R 12 W). Named on Tombs Creek (1978) 7.5' quadrangle.

Spanish Flat [NAPA]: *locality,* 9 miles south of Berryessa Peak (lat. 38°32'10" N, long. 122°13'20" W). Named on Lake Berryessa (1959) 7.5' quadrangle.

Spanish Flat Resort [NAPA]: *locality,* 10 miles south of Berryessa Peak on the west side of Lake Berryessa (lat. 38°31'10" N, long. 122°12'30" W; sec. 20, T 8 N, R 3 W); the place is 1 mile south-southeast of Spanish Flat. Named on Lake Berryessa (1959) 7.5' quadrangle.

Spanish Valley [NAPA]: *valley,* 5.5 miles east-

northeast of Aetna Springs along Stone Corral Creek (lat. 38°40'45" N, long. 122° 23' W; in and near sec. 26, T 10 N, R 5 W). Named on Aetna Springs (1958) 7.5' quadrangle.

Spanish Valley Creek: see **Stone Corral Creek** [NAPA].

Spencer Creek [NAPA]: *stream,* flows 3.25 miles to join Murphy Creek and form Tulucay Creek 10.5 miles southwest of Mount Vaca (lat. 38°17'35" N, long. 122°14'15" W). Named on Mount George (1951) 7.5' quadrangle. Called Cayetano Creek on Mount Vaca (1942) 15' quadrangle.

Spring Creek [SONOMA]:
(1) *stream,* flows about 0.5 mile to Ward Creek 5.5 miles east-northeast of Fort Ross (lat. 38°32'05" N, long. 123°08'40" W; sec. 14, T 8 N, R 12 W). Named on Fort Ross (1978) 7.5' quadrangle.
(2) *stream,* flows 5.5 miles to Matanzas Creek less than 1 mile east of downtown Santa Rosa (lat. 38°26'20" N, long. 122°41'55" W). Named on Kenwood (1954) and Santa Rosa (1954) 7.5' quadrangles.

Spring Valley [NAPA]: *valley,* 3 miles east of Saint Helena (lat. 38°30'05" N, long. 122°24'50" W; sec. 33, T 8 N, R 5 W). Named on Rutherford (1951) and Saint Helena (1960) 7.5' quadrangles.

Sproule Creek [SONOMA]: *stream,* flows 2.25 miles to Marshall Creek 5.5 miles north of Fort Ross (lat. 38°35'35" N, long. 123°14'55" W; sec. 25, T 9 N, R 11 W). Named on Plantation (1977) 7.5' quadrangle.

Sproule Creek: see **Marshall Creek** [SONOMA].

Spruce Hill: see **Lokoya** [NAPA].

Spud Point [SONOMA]: *promontory,* 0.5 mile southwest of the village of Bodega Bay on the west side of Bodega Harbor (lat. 38° 19'35" N, long. 123°03'15" W). Named on Bodega Head (1972) 7.5' quadrangle.

Squab [NAPA]: *locality,* 1.5 miles west-northwest of Napa Junction along Southern Pacific Railroad (lat. 38°11'55" N, long. 122°16'25" W; sec. 14, T 4 N, R 4 W). Named on Cuttings Wharf (1949) 7.5' quadrangle.

Squaw Creek [SONOMA]: *stream,* flows 7 miles to Big Sulphur Creek 6.5 miles northeast of Asti (lat. 38°49'25" N, long. 122°52'35" W; at W line sec. 4, T 11 N, R 9 W). Named on The Geysers (1959) 7.5' quadrangle.

Squirrel Rock [SONOMA]: *relief feature,* 3 miles north of Cazadero (lat. 38°34'30" N, long. 123°05'10" W; at NW cor. sec. 4, T 8 N, R 11 W). Named on Cazadero (1978) 7.5' quadrangle.

Stage Gulch [SONOMA]: *canyon,* 1 mile long, 5.25 miles east-southeast of downtown Petaluma (lat. 38°13'10" N, long. 122°32'35" W). Named on Petaluma River (1954) 7.5' quadrangle.

Stags Leap [NAPA]: *relief feature,* steep hillside 3 miles east-northeast of Yountville (lat. 38°25'10" N, long. 122°18'45" W; sec. 28, 33, T 7 N, R 4 W). Named on Yountville (1951) 7.5' quadrangle. Sonoma (1942) 15' quadrangle has the name for a feature situated about 1 mile farther southwest. California Division of Highways' (1934) map shows a place called Stags Leap located about 1.5 miles southwest of the relief feature shown on Yountville (1951) 7.5' quadrangle. Postal authorities established Stags Leap post office 11.5 miles north of Napa at a summer vacation resort in 1927 and discontinued it in 1944; the name "Stags Leap" is from a local legend (Salley, p. 211).

Staley Spring [SONOMA]: *spring,* 2 miles west-northwest of Big Mountain (lat. 38°43'25" N, long. 123°10'40" W; sec. 10, T 10 N, R 12 W). Named on Tombs Creek (1978) 7.5' quadrangle.

Stanley [NAPA]: *locality,* 4.5 miles north-northwest of Napa Junction (lat. 38°14'40" N, long. 122°17'30" W). Named on Cuttings Wharf (1949) 7.5' quadrangle. Mare Island (1916) 15' quadrangle shows the place situated along Southern Pacific Railroad.

Stanley Ridge [SONOMA]: *ridge,* north- to west-trending, 3 miles long, 7 miles north of the village of Stewarts Point (lat. 38°45'15" N, long. 123°26' W). Named on Ornbaun Valley (1960) 15' quadrangle, and on Stewarts Point (1978) 7.5' quadrangle.

Staubeville: see **Petaluma** [SONOMA] (2).

Steamboat Slough [NAPA]: *water feature,* passes around Bull Island and joins Napa River 4 miles northwest of Napa Junction (lat. 38° 13'10" N, long. 122°18'30" W; sec. 4, T 4 N, R 4 W). Named on Cuttings Wharf (1949) 7.5' quadrangle.

Steamboat Slough [SONOMA]: *water feature,* 5 miles north-northeast of Sears Point (lat. 38°13'15" N, long. 122°25'25" W). Named on Sears Point (1951) 7.5' quadrangle.

Steel Canyon [NAPA]: *canyon,* 3.5 miles long, opens into the canyon of Capell Creek 11 miles south of Berryessa Peak (lat. 38° 30'20" N, long. 122°12'20" W; near SE cor. sec. 29, T 8 N, R 3 W); water of Lake Berryessa covers the lower part of the canyon. Named on Capell Valley (1951) and Lake Berryessa (1959) 7.5' quadrangles.

Steel Canyon Resort [NAPA]: *locality,* 11 miles south of Berryessa Peak (lat. 38°30'30" N, long. 122°12' W; sec. 28, T 8 N, R 3 W); the place is near the mouth of Steel Canyon. Named on Lake Berryessa (1959) 7.5' quadrangle.

Steele Canyon [NAPA]: *canyon,* 1 mile long, 3 miles south-southeast of Mount Vaca (lat. 38°21'20" N, long. 122°05'20" W). Named on Fairfield North (1951) 7.5' quadrangle.

Stemple Creek [SONOMA]: *stream,* heads in Sonoma County and flows 15 miles to Estero de San Antonio 1.5 miles north of Tomales in

Marin County (lat. 38°16'15" N, long. 122°54'20" W). Named on Cotati (1954), Two Rock (1954) and Valley Ford (1954) 7.5' quadrangles. Teather (p. 75) associated the name with Henry M. Stemple, a rancher in the region. United States Board on Geographic Names (1943, p. 13) rejected the names "Aurora Creek," "Estero de San Antonio," and "Two Rock Creek" for the stream, or for any part of it.

Stewart Ridge [SONOMA]: *ridge,* south-trending, 1 mile long, 4.5 miles north-northeast of Fort Ross (lat. 38°34'20" N, long. 123°12'30" W). Named on Fort Ross (1978) 7.5' quadrangle.

Stewarts Creek [SONOMA]: *stream,* flows 1.25 miles to Fisherman Bay near the village of Stewarts Point (lat. 38°39' N, long. 123° 23'55" W). Named on Stewarts Point (1978) 7.5' quadrangle. Called Stewarts Point Creek on Annapolis (1943) and Stewarts Point (1943) 7.5' quadrangles.

Stewarts Point [SONOMA]:
(1) *promontory,* 0.5 mile north-northwest of the village of Stewarts Point along the coast (lat. 38°39'15" N, long. 123°24'25" W). Named on Stewarts Point (1978) 7.5' quadrangle. The name commemorates the Stewart family, who moved to the region in 1856 (Jackson, p. 8).
(2) *village,* 20 miles west of Healdsburg (lat. 38°39'05" N, long. 123°23'55" W); the village is near Stewarts Point (1). Named on Stewarts Point (1978) 7.5' quadrangle. Postal authorities established Stewarts Point post office in 1888, discontinued it in 1945, and reestablished it in 1946 (Frickstad, p. 198).

Stewarts Point Creek: see **Stewarts Creek** [SONOMA].

Stewarts Point Island [SONOMA]: *island,* 400 feet long, 0.5 mile west-northwest of the village of Stewarts Point (lat. 38°39'15" N, long. 123°24'30" W); the island is 50 feet offshore at Stewarts Point (1). Named on Stewarts Point (1978) 7.5' quadrangle.

Stillwater Cove [SONOMA]: *embayment,* 3 miles south of Plantation along the sea coast (lat. 38°32'15" N, long. 123°17'55" W). Named on Plantation (1977) 7.5' quadrangle. Santa Rosa (1958) 1°x 2° quadrangle shows Stillwater Cove located about 1 mile farther southeast along the coast; United States Board on Geographic Names (1984, p. 5) approved the name "Stillwater Cove" for this second place (lat. 38°32'20" N, long. 123°17'05" W), and at the same time rejected the name "Stillwater Harbor" for it.

Stillwater Harbor: see **Stillwater Cove** [SONOMA].

Stockhoff Creek [SONOMA]: *stream,* flows 2 miles to the sea 3 miles south of Plantation (lat. 38°32'50" N, long. 123°17'50" W). Named on Plantation (1977) 7.5' quadrangle.

Stone Corral [NAPA]: *locality,* 2 miles north-northwest of Walter Springs (lat. 38°41' N, long. 122°22'10" W; near W line sec. 25, T 10 N, R 5 W). Named on Walter Springs (1959) 7.5' quadrangle.

Stone Corral Creek [NAPA]: *stream,* flows 3.5 miles to Putah Creek 2 miles north-northeast of Walter Springs (lat. 38°40'40" N, long. 122°20'55" W; sec. 30, T 10 N, R 4 W); the stream goes past Stone Corral. Named on Aetna Springs (1958) and Walter Springs (1959) 7.5' quadrangles. The stream passes through Spanish Valley, but United States Board on Geographic Names (1962a, p. 17) rejected the name "Spanish Valley Creek" for it.

Stones: see **Cunningham** [SONOMA].

Stone Trough Canyon [NAPA]: *canyon,* 1 mile long, 3.5 miles south-southeast of Mount Vaca on upper reaches of Gordon Valley Creek (lat. 38°21' N, long. 122°05'10" W). Named on Fairfield North (1951) 7.5' quadrangle.

Stony Butte [SONOMA]: *peak,* 6 miles west-southwest of Glen Ellen (lat. 38°19'10" N, long. 122°37'05" W). Named on Glen Ellen (1954) 7.5' quadrangle.

Stony Creek [NAPA]: *stream,* flows 3 miles to Capell Creek nearly 7 miles west-northwest of Mount Vaca (lat. 38°26'55" N, long. 122°12'45" W; sec. 17, T 7 N, R 3 W). Named on Capell Valley (1951) 7.5' quadrangle.

Stony Point [SONOMA]: *locality,* 2 miles southwest of Cotati along Petaluma and Santa Rosa Railroad (lat. 38°18'40" N, long. 122°44'05" W). Named on Cotati (1954) 7.5' quadrangle. Postal authorities established Stony Point post office in 1857 and discontinued it in 1911; the name was from Stony Point hotel, where the post office was located (Salley, p. 213).

Strawberry Creek [SONOMA]: *stream,* flows 4 miles to Warm Springs Creek 3.5 miles west of Skaggs Springs (lat. 38°42'05" N, long. 123°05'35" W; near E line sec. 20, T 10 N, R 11 W). Named on Tombs Creek (1978) and Warm Springs Dam (1978) 7.5' quadrangles.

Strawberry Creek: see **Little Strawberry Creek** [SONOMA].

Stuart Canyon [SONOMA]: *canyon,* 3 miles long, along Stuart Creek above a point 1 mile east-northeast of Glen Ellen (lat. 38°22'10" N, long. 122°30'25" W). Named on Rutherford (1951) and Sonoma (1951) 7.5' quadrangles. Called Hooker Canyon on Napa (1902) 30' quadrangle.

Stuart Creek [SONOMA]: *stream,* flows 4.25 miles to Calabazas Creek in Glen Ellen (lat. 38°22'15" N, long. 122°31'25" W); the stream goes through Stuart Canyon. Named on Glen Ellen (1954) 7.5' quadrangle.

Stump Beach [SONOMA]: *beach,* 1.5 miles west-southwest of Plantation along the coast (lat. 38°34'55" N, long. 123°20'05" W). Named on Plantation (1977) 7.5' quadrangle.

Stump Gulch [SONOMA]: *canyon,* drained by a stream that flows 1.5 miles to the sea 4.5 miles south-southeast of present Jenner (lat.

35°23'40" N, long. 123°05'20" W). Named on Duncans Mills (1921) 15' quadrangle.

Sugarloaf [NAPA]: *peak,* 11.5 miles south-southwest of Mount Vaca (lat. 38°15'50" N, long. 122°13'15" W; sec. 20, T 5 N, R 3 W). Altitude 1630 feet. Named on Mount George (1951) 7.5' quadrangle.

Sugarloaf [SONOMA]:

(1) *peak,* 1 mile west of Big Mountain (lat. 38°42'45" N, long. 123° 09'45" W; on E line sec. 15, T 10 N, R 12 W). Altitude 1700 feet. Named on Tombs Creek (1978) 7.5' quadrangle.

(2) *peak,* 5 miles east of Mark West Springs (lat. 38°32'20" N, long. 122°37'50" W; at NW cor. sec. 22, T 8 N, R 7 W). Named on Mark West Springs (1958) 7.5' quadrangle.

(3) *peak,* 7 miles south of Guerneville (lat. 38°24'05" N, long. 123° 00'50" W). Altitude 1178 feet. Named on Duncans Mills (1979) 7.5' quadrangle.

Sugarloaf Creek [SONOMA]: *stream,* flows 1.5 miles to Tombs Creek 1.5 miles west of Big Mountain (lat. 38°42'30" N, long. 123° 10'15" W; near S line sec. 15, T 10 N, R 12 W); the stream is south of Sugarloaf (1). Named on Tombs Creek (1978) 7.5' quadrangle.

Sugarloaf Hill [SONOMA]: *peak,* 1.5 miles southwest of Mount Saint Helena (lat. 38°39'25" N, long. 122°39'20" W). Altitude 1717 feet. Named on Mount Saint Helena (1959) 7.5' quadrangle.

Sugarloaf Mountain [NAPA]: *peak,* 5 miles north-northeast of Calistoga (lat. 38°38'20" N, long. 122°31'45" W; sec. 9, T 9 N, R 6 W). Altitude 2988 feet. Named on Detert Reservoir (1958) 7.5' quadrangle.

Sugarloaf Park [NAPA]: *locality,* 9 miles south-southwest of Berryessa Peak (lat. 38°32'30" N, long. 122°14'15" W; sec. 18, T 8 N, R 3 W); the place is 1 mile north-northeast of Sugarloaf Peak. Named on Lake Berryessa (1959) 7.5' quadrangle.

Sugarloaf Peak [NAPA]: *peak,* 9.5 miles south-southwest of Berryessa Peak (lat. 38°31'50" N, long. 122°14'45" W). Altitude 1889 feet. Named on Lake Berryessa (1959) 7.5' quadrangle.

Sugarloaf Peak: see **Little Sugarloaf Peak** [NAPA].

Sugarloaf Ridge [SONOMA]: *ridge,* west-northwest- to west-trending, 2 miles long, 2 miles northeast of Kenwood (lat. 38°26'05" N, long. 122°31'15" W). Named on Kenwood (1954) 7.5' quadrangle.

Suisun Creek [NAPA]: *stream,* heads in Napa County and flows 20 miles, including through Lake Curry, to marsh 5 miles southwest of Fairfield in Solano County (lat. 38°11'35" N, long. 122°06'10" W). Named on Capell Valley (1951), Fairfield North (1951), Fairfield South (1949), and Mount George (1951) 7.5' quadrangles.

Suisun Valley [NAPA]: *valley,* 6 miles northwest

of Fairfield along Suisun Creek, mainly in Solano County, but extends north into Napa County (lat. 38°18'45" N, long. 122°07'30" W). Named on Fairfield North (1951) and Mount George (1951) 7.5' quadrangles.

Sullivan Creek [SONOMA]: *stream,* flows 1.5 miles to Fuller Creek 3.25 miles southeast of Annapolis (lat. 38°41'05" N, long. 123°19'40" W; sec. 29, T 10 N, R 13 W). Named on Annapolis (1977) 7.5' quadrangle.

Sulphur Banks: see **The Geysers** [SONOMA].

Sulphur Canyon [NAPA]: *canyon,* 4 miles long, opens into lowlands 1.25 miles south-southwest of Saint Helena (lat. 38°29'15" N, long. 122°28'40" W); Sulphur Creek drains the canyon. Named on Kenwood (1954) and Rutherford (1951) 7.5' quadrangles. Called Sulphur Sprs. Canyon on Napa (1902) 30' quadrangle. California Division of Highways' (1934) map shows a place called White Sulphur Springs situated along Sulphur Creek about 2 miles west-southwest of Saint Helena (sec. 2, T 7 N, R 6 W); the springs at the place were discovered in 1845 and were the basis of a resort called White Sulphur Springs and Original White Sulphur Springs (Bradley, p. 280)—the resort also was called St. Helena White Sulphur Springs (Waring, p. 254).

Sulphur Creek [NAPA]: *stream,* flows 6 miles to Napa River nearly 1 mile northeast of Saint Helena (lat. 38°30'40" N, long. 122°27'25" W). Named on Rutherford (1951) and Saint Helena (1960) 7.5' quadrangles.

Sulphur Creek [SONOMA]: *stream,* flows 2.25 miles to East Austin Creek 6 miles north of Cazadero (lat. 38°37'05" N, long. 123°05'30" W). Named on Cazadero (1978) 7.5' quadrangle.

Sulphur Creek: see **Big Sulphur Creek** [SONOMA]; **Little Sulphur Creek** [SONOMA].

Sulphur Peak: see **Geyser Peak** [SONOMA].

Sulphur Spring [NAPA]: *spring,* 2 miles southwest of Berryessa Peak (lat. 38°38'45" N, long. 122°13'15" W). Named on Brooks (1959) 7.5' quadrangle.

Sulphur Springs Canyon: see **Sulphur Canyon** [NAPA].

Sulphur Springs Mountain [NAPA]: *ridge,* south-southeast to south-trending, 4.5 miles long, 6 miles south-southwest of Cordelia (lat. 38°08' N, long. 122°10'50" W); the north end of the ridge is in Napa County. Named on Benicia (1959) and Cordelia (1951) 7.5' quadrangles.

Summerhome [SONOMA]: *settlement,* 3 miles east of Guerneville along Russian River (lat. 38°29'50" N, long. 122°56'20" W; sec. 35, T 8 N, R 10 W). Named on Camp Meeker (1954) and Guerneville (1955) 7.5' quadrangles. United States Board on Geographic Names (1992, p. 5) approved the name "Summerhome Park" for the place, and rejected the names "Summerhome" and "Summer Home Park."

Summerhome Park: see **Summerhome** [SONOMA].

Summit: see **Occidental** [SONOMA].

Summit Spring [NAPA]: *spring,* 4.5 miles east-northeast of Calistoga on Rattlesnake Ridge (lat. 38°36'45" N, long. 122°30'10" W; near E line sec. 22, T 9 N, R 6 W). Named on Calistoga (1958) 7.5' quadrangle.

Sunbeam Acres: see **Gates Canyon** [SONOMA].

Sunrise Mountain [SONOMA]: *peak,* 2 miles south-southeast of Cazadero (lat. 38°30'15" N, long. 123°04'45" W; near S line sec. 28, T 8 N, R 11 W). Named on Cazadero (1978) 7.5' quadrangle.

Sunset Point [NAPA]: *peak,* 3.5 miles north of Saint Helena (lat. 38° 33'25" N, long. 122°27'25" W; sec. 7, T 8 N, R 5 W). Named on Saint Helena (1960) 7.5' quadrangle.

Suscol [NAPA]: *locality,* 4.25 miles north-north-west of Napa Junction along Southern Pacific Railroad (lat. 38°14'40" N, long. 122° 17' W); the place is near the mouth of Suscol Creek. Named on Cuttings Wharf (1949) 7.5' quadrangle. Postal authorities established Suscol post office 4 miles south of Napa City post office in 1868, discontinued it in 1869, reestablished it with the name "Soscol" in 1872, and discontinued it finally in 1886 (Salley, p. 208).

Suscol Creek [NAPA]: *stream,* flows 4.5 miles to Napa River 4 miles north-northwest of Napa Junction (lat. 38°14'25" N, long. 122°17'05" W). Named on Cordelia (1951) and Cuttings Wharf (1949) 7.5' quadrangles. The name is from an Indian village (Kroeber, p. 60).

Suttonfield: see **Lake Suttonfield** [SONOMA].

Swallow City [SONOMA]: *relief feature,* 2 miles north-northeast of the village of Bodega Bay (lat. 38°21'45" N, long. 123°02'15" W). Named on Bodega Head (1942) 7.5' quadrangle.

Swartz Canyon [NAPA]: *canyon,* nearly 4 miles long, along Swartz Creek above a point 1 mile south-southwest of Aetna Springs (lat. 38°38'30" N, long. 122°29'15" W); sec. 11, T 9 N, R 6 W). Named on Detert Reservoir (1958) 7.5' quadrangle.

Swartz Creek [NAPA]: *stream,* flows 6 miles to Pope Creek 1.5 miles east-northeast of Aetna Springs in Popo Valley (lat. 38°39'35" N, long. 122°27'25" W; sec. 6, T 9 N, R 5 W). Named on Aetna Springs (1958) 7.5' quadrangle.

Sweetwater Creek [SONOMA]: *stream,* flows about 1 mile to Pena Creek 3.25 miles south of Skaggs Springs (lat. 38°38'45" N, long. 123°01'05" W; sec. 7, T 9 N, R 10 W). Named on Warm Springs Dam (1978) 7.5' quadrangle.

– T –

Table Mountain [NAPA]: *ridge,* northeast-trending, 1 mile long, 8 miles north-northeast of Calistoga (lat. 38°41'05" N, long. 122° 32' W). Named on Detert Reservoir (1958) 7.5' quadrangle.

Table Mountain [SONOMA]: *peak,* 5.5 miles north-northeast of Fort Ross (lat. 38°35'20" N, long. 123°12'35" W; sec. 29, T 9 N, R 12 W). Altitude 589 feet. Named on Fort Ross (1978) 7.5' quadrangle.

Table Rock [NAPA]: *peak,* 4.5 miles north of Calistoga (lat. 38°38'35" N, long. 122°34'45" W; sec. 12, T 9 N, R 7 W). Altitude 2462 feet. Named on Detert Reservoir (1958) 7.5' quadrangle.

Tanbark Canyon [SONOMA]: *canyon,* 1 mile long, 2.5 miles northwest of Mount Saint Helena along Mill Stream (lat. 38°41'45" N, long. 122°39'45" W). Named on Mount Saint Helena (1959) 7.5' quadrangle.

Tannery Creek [SONOMA]: *stream,* flows 2.5 miles to Salmon Creek (1) 4.25 miles northwest of Valley Ford (lat. 38°21'20" N, long. 122°59'20" W). Named on Camp Meeker (1954) and Valley Ford (1954) 7.5' quadrangles.

Tater Knoll [SONOMA]: *relief feature,* 5.5 miles north of Guerneville (lat. 38°35'05" N, long. 122°59'55" W; near W line sec. 32, T 9 N, R 10 W). Named on Guerneville (1955) 7.5' quadrangle.

Taylor Bluffs [NAPA]: *relief feature,* 2.5 miles south-southeast of Berryessa Peak on Napa-Yolo county line (lat. 38°37'50" N, long. 122°10' W). Named on Brooks (1959) and Lake Berryessa (1959) 7.5' quadrangles.

Taylor Mountain [SONOMA]: *peak,* 3.5 miles southeast of downtown Santa Rosa (lat. 38°24'05" N, long. 122°40'25" W; near N line sec. 6, T 6 N, R 7 W); the peak is 1.25 miles southeast of Kawana Springs, which formerly were known as Taylor's Springs. Altitude 1401 feet. Named on Santa Rosa (1954) 7.5' quadrangle.

Taylor's Springs: see **Kawana Springs** [SONOMA].

Taylor Sulphur Spring: see **Kawana Springs** [SONOMA].

Taylor's White Sulphur Springs: see **Kawana Springs** [SONOMA].

Telegraph Hill [SONOMA]: *peak,* 2 miles north-northeast of Mark West Springs (lat. 38°34'15" N, long. 122°42' W; sec. 1, T 8 N, R 8 W). Named on Mark West Springs (1958) 7.5' quadrangle.

Thayer: see **Camp Thayer** [SONOMA].

The Beehive [NAPA]: *peak,* 7 miles north-north-west of Saint Helena on Rattlesnake Ridge (lat. 38°36'15" N, long. 122°29'50" W; sec. 26, T 9 N, R 6 W). Altitude 2750 feet. Named on Saint Helena (1960) 7.5' quadrangle.

The Big Brush [SONOMA]: *area,* 6 miles north-northeast of Cazadero (lat. 38°36'50" N, long. 123°02'45" W). Named on Cazadero (1978) 7.5' quadrangle.

The Butcherknife [SONOMA]: *ridge,* south-trending, 1 mile long, 4.5 miles north-north-west of Cazadero (lat. 38°35'35" N, long. 123°06'55" W). Named on Cazadero (1978) 7.5' quadrangle.

The Cedars [SONOMA]: *area,* 7 miles north-northwest of Cazadero (lat. 38°37'30" N, long. 123°07'30" W). Named on Cazadero (1978), Fort Ross (1978), Tombs Creek (1978), and Warm Springs Dam (1978) 7.5' quadrangles.

The Cove [NAPA]: *relief feature,* 5.5 miles south of Rutherford (lat. 38°22'40" N, long. 122°26'15" W; sec. 8, T 6 N, R 5 W). Named on Rutherford (1951) 7.5' quadrangle.

The Geysers [SONOMA]: *water feature,* steam wells 3.25 miles northeast of Geyser Peak (lat. 38°48'05" N, long. 122°48'15" W; near E line sec. 13, T 11 N, R 9 W). Named on The Geysers (1959) 7.5' quadrangle. Called Hot Springs on Kelseyville (1921) 15' quadrangle. In 1847 William B. Elliott discovered the place where small hot springs and fumaroles occur on the north side of Big Sulphur Creek (Allen and Day, p. 11; Anderson, p. 138). Steam from wells at the site now generates electricity. United States Board on Geographic Names (1981, p. 2) approved the name "The Geysers" for an area of geothermal activity 10 miles long and 3 miles wide along the course of Big Sulphur Creek (NW end at lat. 38°49'40" N, long. 122°49'50" W; SE end at lat. 38°44'30" N, long. 122°41'45" W). An area of geothermal activity known as Little Geysers is in an amphitheater in a side canyon that opens into the canyon of Big Sulphur Creek from the northeast 5 miles above The Geysers (Allen and Day, p. 95). A mile downstream from The Geysers is a fumarole field known as Sulphur Banks (Allen and Day, p. 94), where extensive deposits of sulphur occur (Whitney, p. 94).

The Geysers: see **Geysers Resort** [SONOMA].

The Girdle [SONOMA]: *relief feature,* 0.5 mile west-northwest of Big Mountain (lat. 38°42'45" N, long. 122°09'15" W; sec. 14, T 10 N, R 12 W). Named on Tombs Creek (1978) 7.5' quadrangle.

The Horn [SONOMA]: *locality,* 9.5 miles north-east of Healdsburg along a road (lat. 38°43'30" N, long. 122°45'15" W; sec. 9, T 10 N, R 8 W). Named on Jimtown (1955) 7.5' quadrangle.

The Island [SONOMA]:
(1) *peak,* 7 miles north-northeast of Fort Ross (lat. 38°36'20" N, long. 123°10'50" W; sec. 21, T 9 N, R 12 W). Named on Fort Ross (1978) 7.5' quadrangle.
(2) *peak,* 5 miles north-northeast of Cazadero (lat. 38°36'05" N, long. 123°03'30" W). Altitude 1206 feet. Named on Cazadero (1978) 7.5' quadrangle.

The Lagunas: see **Laguna de Santa Rosa** [SONOMA].

The Meadows [SONOMA]: *area*, 3 miles south-southwest of Healdsburg (lat. 38°34'45" N, long. 122°54' W). Named on Guerneville (1955) 7.5' quadrangle.

The Nubble [SONOMA]: *relief feature*, nearly 4 miles west of Big Mountain (lat. 38°42'05" N, long. 123°12'45" W; sec. 20, T 10 N, R 12 W). Named on Tombs Creek (1978) 7.5' quadrangle.

The Palisades [NAPA]: *relief feature*, 4 miles north of Calistoga (lat. 38°38'10" N, long. 122°34' W; on N line sec. 18, T 9 N, R 6 W). Named on Detert Reservoir (1958) 7.5' quadrangle.

The Racetrack [SONOMA]: *area*, 1.25 miles west of Cazadero (lat. 38°32' N, long. 123°06'20" W; at W line sec. 17, T 8 N, R 11 W). Named on Cazadero (1943) 7.5' quadrangle.

The Roughs [SONOMA]: *area*, 2 miles north of Cazadero (lat. 38°33'40" N, long. 123°05'35" W; at SE cor. sec. 5, T 8 N, R 11 W). Named on Cazadero (1978) 7.5' quadrangle.

The Trees [NAPA]: *area*, 1.5 miles east-southeast of Berryessa Peak on Napa-Yolo county line (lat. 38°39'15" N, long. 122°09'50" W). Named on Brooks (1959) 7.5' quadrangle.

The Turnaround [SONOMA]: *locality*, 3.5 miles southwest of Skaggs Springs (lat. 38°39'15" N, long. 123°04'10" W). Named on Skaggs Springs (1943) 7.5' quadrangle.

Third Napa Slough [SONOMA]: *water feature*, joins Second Napa Slough 4.5 miles northeast of Sears Point (lat. 38°11'50" N, long. 122°23'30" W). Named on Sears Point (1951) 7.5' quadrangle.

Thoman [NAPA]: *locality*, 1.5 miles southeast of Saint Helena along Southern Pacific Railroad (lat. 38°29'30" N, long. 122°27'05" W). Named on Rutherford (1951) 7.5' quadrangle.

Thompson [NAPA]: *locality*, nearly 4 miles north-northwest of Napa Junction (lat. 38°14'15" N, long. 122°16'45" W; sec. 35, T 5 N, R 4 W). Named on Cuttings Wharf (1949) 7.5' quadrangle. Mare Island (1916) 15' quadrangle has the name nearby along Southern Pacific Railroad.

Thompson Creek [SONOMA]: *stream*, flows 2 miles to East Austin Creek 3.25 miles northeast of Cazadero (lat. 38°34'15" N, long. 123°02'55" W; sec. 2, T 8 N, R 11 W); the stream is south of Thompson Ridge (2). Named on Cazadero (1978) 7.5' quadrangle.

Thompson Ridge [SONOMA]:

(1) *ridge*, east- to east-southeast-trending, 4 miles long, 7 miles west-southwest of Cloverdale (lat. 38°46' N, long. 123°08' W). Named on Hopland (1960) 15' quadrangle.

(2) *ridge*, generally west-trending, 2 miles long, 4.25 miles northeast of Cazadero (lat. 38°34'45" N, long. 123°02'30" W). Named

on Cazadero (1978) 7.5' quadrangle. This ridge and Marble Mine Ridge together are called Dutton Ridge on California Division of Forestry's (1945) map.

Three Peaks [NAPA]: *peaks*, 7.5 miles north of Saint Helena (lat. 38°36'50" N, long. 122°29'45" W; sec. 23, T 9 N, R 6 W). Altitude of highest, 1889 feet. Named on Saint Helena (1960) 7.5' quadrangle.

Throop: see **Cloverdale** [SONOMA].

Thurston Creek [SONOMA]: *stream*, flows 2.5 miles to Nolan Creek 3.25 miles northwest of Valley Ford (lat. 38°21'10" N, long. 122°57'45" N). Named on Camp Meeker (1954) and Valley Ford (1954) 7.5' quadrangles.

Timber Cove [SONOMA]: *embayment*, 4.5 miles south-southeast of Plantation along the coast (lat. 38°31'45" N, long. 123°16'15" W). Named on Plantation (1977) 7.5' quadrangle. W.R. Miller operated a sawmill at Timber Cove in 1856; schooners carried lumber, cordwood, and tanbark from the place to San Francisco (Miller, J.T., p. 50).

Timber Cove: see **Seaview** [SONOMA].

Timber Cove Creek [SONOMA]: *stream*, flows 2 miles to the sea 4.5 miles south-southeast of Plantation at Timber Cove (lat. 38° 32' N, long. 123°16'20" W). Named on Plantation (1977) 7.5' quadrangle.

Timber Gulch [SONOMA]: *canyon*, drained by a stream that flows less than 1 mile to the sea 6 miles northwest of Jenner (lat. 38°29'50" N, long. 123°12'40" W). Named on Arched Rock (1977) and Fort Ross (1978) 7.5' quadrangles.

Tin Can Canyon [NAPA]: *canyon*, drained by a stream that flows 1.5 miles to lowlands along Lake Berryessa 4.5 miles south of Berryessa Peak (lat. 38°35'55" N, long. 122°12'30" W). Named on Lake Berryessa (1959) 7.5' quadrangle.

Tiny Creek [SONOMA]: *stream*, flows less than 1 mile to Conchea Creek 4 miles north of Cazadero (lat. 38°35'25" N, long. 123°05'20" W). Named on Cazadero (1978) 7.5' quadrangle. Called Canshea Creek on Cazadero (1943) 7.5' quadrangle.

Tobacco Creek [SONOMA]: *stream*, flows 1.5 miles to Wheatfield Fork Gualala River 5.5 miles southeast of Annapolis (lat. 38°40'15" N, long. 123°17'25" W; sec. 34, T 10 N, R 13 W). Named on Annapolis (1977) 7.5' quadrangle. California Division of Forestry's (1945) map shows a place called Mendosoma located along Wheatfield Fork Gualala River just downstream from the mouth of Tobacco Creek, where Annapolis (1977) 7.5' quadrangle shows Mendosoma Forest Fire Sta. (lat. 38°40'15" N, long. 123°17'40" W).

Tolay: see **Lake Tolay**, under **Lakeville** [SONOMA].

Tolay Creek [SONOMA]: *stream*, flows 11.5 miles to marsh along San Pablo Bay nearly 2 miles south-southwest of Sears Point (lat. 38°07'30" N, long. 122°27'10" W). Named on Petaluma River (1954) and Sears Point (1951) 7.5' quadrangles. The name is from former Lake Tolay (Gudde, 1949, p. 364). East Branch diverges from the main stream 1 mile north of Sears Point and extends nearly 2 miles to Sonoma Creek. North Branch enters East Branch from the north nearly 1.5 miles north-northeast of Sears Point. Both branches are named on Sears Point (1951) 7.5' quadrangle.

Toll Canyon [NAPA]: *canyon,* drained by a stream that flows 2 miles to Eticuera Creek 6.5 miles northeast of Walter Springs (lat. 38°42'40" N, long. 122°15'40" W). Named on Brooks (1959) and Walter Springs (1959) 7.5' quadrangles. Capay (1945) 15' quadrangle shows Old Toll Road on the north side of the canyon.

Tom: see **Mount Tom** [SONOMA].

Tombs Creek [SONOMA]: *stream,* flows 7.25 miles to Wheatfield Fork Gualala River 5.25 miles west of Big Mountain (lat. 38°43'05" N, long. 123°14'25" W; near W line sec. 18, T 10 N, R 12 W). Named on Tombs Creek (1978) 7.5' quadrangle.

Toole Pond [SONOMA]: *lake,* 350 feet long, 1.5 miles west-southwest of Cazadero (lat. 38°31'15" N, long. 123°06'30" W; near E line sec. 19, T 8 N, R 11 W). Named on Cazadero (1978) 7.5' quadrangle.

Tosca [SONOMA]: *locality,* less than 1 mile northwest of Geyserville along Northwestern Pacific Railroad (lat. 38°42'50" N, long. 122° 54'45" W). Named on Healdsburg (1940) 15' quadrangle.

Trees: see **The Trees** [NAPA].

Trenton [SONOMA]: *locality,* 6 miles north-northwest of Sebastopol (lat. 38°29'05" N, long. 122°51' W). Named on Sebastopol (1954) 7.5' quadrangle. Postal authorities established Trenton post office in 1887 and discontinued it in 1914 (Frickstad, p. 198).

Triniti: see **Glen Ellen** [SONOMA].

Trospers Resort [SONOMA]: *locality,* less than 2 miles north of Cazadero (lat. 38°33'25" N, long. 123°05'30" W; sec. 8, T 8 N, R 11 W). Named on Cazadero (1943) 7.5' quadrangle.

Trout Creek [NAPA]: *stream,* flows 5.25 miles to Pope Creek 11 miles northeast of Saint Helena (lat. 38°36'40" N, long. 122°18'50" W). Named on Chiles Valley (1958) 7.5' quadrangle.

Trout Creek Ridge [NAPA]: *ridge,* north-north-west-trending, 3 miles long, 12 miles east-northeast of Saint Helena (lat. 38°35'15" N, long. 122°16'55" W); the ridge is northeast of Trout Creek. Named on Chiles Valley (1958) 7.5' quadrangle.

Troutdale Creek [NAPA]: *stream,* flows 2.5 miles, partly in Lake County, to the canyon of Saint Helena Creek 6.25 miles north of Calistoga (lat. 38°40' N, long. 122°35'15" W; sec. 36, T 10 N, R 7 W). Named on Detert Reservoir (1958) 7.5' quadrangle.

Trubody [NAPA]: *locality,* nearly 6 miles north-northwest of downtown Napa along Southern Pacific Railroad (lat. 38°22'10" N, long. 122°20'20" W). Named on Napa (1902) 30' quadrangle. Postal authorities established Trubody post office in 1896 and discontinued it in 1906; the name was for members of the Trubody family, property owners at the place (Salley, p. 225).

Truitt Creek [SONOMA]: *stream,* flows 0.5 mile to Big Sulphur Creek 3.25 miles north of Geyser Peak (lat. 38°48'45" N, long. 122°51'20" W; sec. 10, T 11 N, R 9 W). Named on The Geysers (1959) 7.5' quadrangle.

Truth Home [SONOMA]: *locality,* 7.25 miles northeast of Fort Ross (lat. 38°34'50" N, long. 123°08'15" W; sec. 36, T 9 N, R 12 W). Named on Fort Ross (1943) 7.5' quadrangle.

Tubbs Island [SONOMA]: *island,* nearly 4 miles long, between Sears Point and the mouth of Sonoma Creek (lat. 38°09' N, long. 122°25'30" W). Named on Petaluma Point (1959) and Sears Point (1951) 7.5' quadrangles.

Tule Slough [SONOMA]: *water feature,* joins Petaluma River 6 miles east-southeast of downtown Petaluma (lat. 38°11'30" N, long. 122° 32'45" W). Named on Petaluma River (1954) 7.5' quadrangle.

Tulley Canyon: see **Tully Canyon** [NAPA].

Tully Canyon [NAPA]: *canyon,* drained by a stream that flows 4 miles to Lake Berryessa 4 miles south-southwest of Berryessa Peak (lat. 38°37' N, long. 122°13'25" W). Named on Brooks (1959) and Lake Berryessa (1959) 7.5' quadrangles. Called Tulley Canyon on Capay (1945) 15' quadrangle, but United States Board on Geographic Names (1962a, p. 18) rejected this form of the name. South Fork opens into the main canyon 2.5 miles south of Berryessa Peak; it is 1.5 miles long and is named on Brooks (1959) 7.5' quadrangle.

Tulucay [NAPA]: *land grant,* southeast of the city of Napa. Named on Cordellia (1951), Cuttings Wharf (1949), Mount George (1951), and Napa (1951) 7.5' quadrangles. Cayetano Juarez received 2 leagues in 1841 and claimed 8866 acres patented in 1861 (Cowan, p. 105-106). The name is from an Indian village that was located near present Napa (Kroeber, p. 63).

Tulucay Creek [NAPA]: *stream,* formed by the confluence of Murphy Creek and Spencer Creek, flows 3 miles to Napa River 1.25 miles south of downtown Napa (lat. 38°16'45" N, long. 122° 16'50" W); the stream is on Tulucay grant. Named on Mount George (1951) and Napa (1951) 7.5' quadrangles. United States Board on Geographic Names (1949, p. 3) rejected the name "Asylum Slough" for the stream, which is near Napa state hospital.

Turnaround: see **The Turnaround** [SONOMA].

Turner [SONOMA]: *locality,* 4.5 miles east-northeast of Bloomfield along Petaluma and Santa Rosa Railroad (lat. 38°20'30" N, long. 122°46'35" W). Named on Two Rock (1954) 7.5' quadrangle.

Turner Canyon [SONOMA]: *canyon,* drained by a stream that flows 1.25 miles to South Fork Gualala River 3.5 miles east-northeast of Fort Ross (lat. 38°31'50" N, long. 123°10'50" W; near SE cor. sec. 16, T 8 N, R 12 W). Named on Fort Ross (1978) 7.5' quadrangle. Called Turner Gl. on California Division of Forestry's (1945) map.

Turner Gulch: see **Turner Canyon** [SONOMA].

Turner Mountain [NAPA]: *peak,* 5.5 miles north of Walter Springs (lat. 38°44'10" N, long. 122°21'25" W; near SE cor. sec. 1, T 10 N, R 5 W). Altitude 1822 feet. Named on Walter Springs (1959) 7.5' quadrangle.

Twin Peaks [NAPA]: *peaks,* two, 1 mile apart, 5.25 miles north-northeast of Calistoga (the westernmost peak is near lat. 37°39' N, long. 122°32'55" W; at N line sec. 8, T 9 N, R 6 W). Altitudes 2719 feet and 2837 feet. Named on Detert Reservoir (1958) 7.5' quadrangle.

Two Rock [SONOMA]:
(1) *relief feature,* nearly 2 miles west-southwest of Cazadero (lat. 38°31'10" N, long. 123°06'50" W; sec. 19, T 8 N, R 11 W). Named on Cazadero (1978) 7.5' quadrangle.
(2) *village,* 4.5 miles southeast of Bloomfield (lat. 38°16' N, long. 122°47'30" W). Named on Two Rock (1954) 7.5' quadrangle. Postal authorities established Two Rocks post office in 1857, discontinued it in 1858, reestablished it in 1863, discontinued it in 1877, reestablished it with the name "Two Rock" in 1914, and discontinued it in 1953—the name is a translation of the designation of a nearby relief feature called Dos Piedras (Salley, p. 226).

Two Rock Ranch Station Military Reservation [SONOMA]: *military installation,* 5.5 miles southeast of Bloomfield near the village of Two Rock (lat. 38°15' N, long. 122°47'30" W). Named on Point Reyes NE (1954) and Two Rock (1954) 7.5' quadrangles. The installation is mainly in Sonoma County, but extends southwest into Marin County 6 miles east of Tomales

Two Rocks [SONOMA]: *relief feature,* 2 miles north of the village of Bodega Bay (lat. 38°21'45" N, long. 123°02'25" W). Named on Bodega Head (1942) 7.5' quadrangle.

Two Rocks: see **Two Rock** [SONOMA] (2).

Tyrone [SONOMA]: *locality,* 4 miles northwest of Occidental (lat. 38°26'55" N, long. 123°00' W; near SE cor. sec. 18, T 7 N, R 10 W). Named on Camp Meeker (1954) and Duncans Mills (1979) 7.5' quadrangles. Postal authorities established Tyrone post office in 1877, discontinued it in 1881, reestablished it in 1882, and discontinued it in 1883; the name is said to have been from a lumber mill (Salley, p. 227).

Tyrone Gulch [SONOMA]: *canyon,* 1 mile long, 4 miles south of Guerneville (lat. 38°26'30" N, long. 123°00'20" W); Tyrone is near the mouth of the canyon. Named on Duncans Mills (1979) 7.5' quadrangle

Tzabaco [SONOMA]: *land grant,* at and near Geyserville. Named on Geyserville (1955), Jimtown (1955), and Warm Springs Dam (1978) 7.5' quadrangles. Jose German Peña received 4 leagues in 1843, and his heirs claimed 15,439 acres patented in 1859 (Cowan, p. 106).

– U –

Uncle John Creek [NAPA]: *stream,* flows nearly 1 mile to Moore Creek 5.5 miles northeast of Saint Helena (lat. 38°33'35" N, long. 122°23'55" W; sec. 10, T 8 N, R 5 W). Named on Saint Helena (1960) 7.5' quadrangle.

Union [NAPA]: *locality,* 2.25 miles northwest of downtown Napa along Southern Pacific Railroad (lat. 38°19'20" N, long. 122°18'35" W). Named on Napa (1951) 7.5' quadrangle. California Mining Bureau's (1917) map has the name "Upton" at or near present Union.

Upper Bohn Lake: see **Aetna Springs** [NAPA].

Upton: see **Union** [NAPA].

– V –

Vaca: see **Mount Vaca** [NAPA].

Vaca Mountains [NAPA]: *range,* south of Putah Creek on Napa-Solano county line; Blue Ridge (2) is at the crest of the range. Named on Capell Valley (1951), Fairfield North (1951), Monticello Dam (1959), and Mount Vaca (1951) 7.5' quadrangles. United States Board on Geographic Names (1970, p. 3) gave the name "Blue Mountains" as a variant, and noted that the name "Vaca" commemorates the Vaca family, early residents of the region.

Vaca Peak: see **Mount Vaca** [NAPA].

Vacation: see **Vacation Beach** [SONOMA].

Vacation Beach [SONOMA]: *settlement,* 1.25 miles southwest of Guerneville along Russian River (lat. 38°29'20" N, long. 123°00'45" W; on S line sec. 31, T 8 N, R 10 W). Named on Duncans Mills (1979) 7.5' quadrangle. Postal authorities established Vacation post office, named for Vacation Beach, in 1904 and discontinued it in 1941 (Salley, p. 228).

Valley Crossing [SONOMA]: *locality,* 3.25 miles north-northwest of the village of Stewarts Point along South Fork Gualala River (lat. 38°42' N, long. 123°24'45" W). Named on Stewarts Point (1978) 7.5' quadrangle.

Valley Ford [SONOMA]: *village,* 8 miles southwest of Sebastopol (lat. 38°19'05" N, long. 122°55'25" W). Named on Valley Ford (1954) 7.5' quadrangle. Postal authorities established Valley Ford post office in 1876; the name is from the crossing of Estero Americano at the place (Salley, p. 229).

Valley of Nappa: see **Napa Valley** [NAPA].

Valley of the Moon [SONOMA]: *valley,* along Sonoma Creek from northwest of Sonoma to near Glen Ellen. Named on Glen Ellen (1954), Kenwood (1954), and Sonoma (1951) 7.5' quadrangles. On Goddard's (1857) map, the name "Sonoma Vy." extends north-northwest through present Valley of the Moon.

Van Buren Creek [SONOMA]: *stream,* flows 3 miles to Mark West Creek 5 miles east-southeast of Mark West Springs (lat. 38°30'40" N, long. 122°38'15" W; sec. 28, T 8 N, R 7 W). Named on Calistoga (1958) and Mark West Springs (1958) 7.5' quadrangles.

Van Ness Creek [NAPA]: *stream,* flows 3.5 miles to Saint Helena Creek 6.25 miles north of Calistoga (lat. 38°40'05" N, long. 122° 35'10" W; sec. 36, T 10 N, R 7 W). Named on Detert Reservoir (1958) 7.5' quadrangle.

Veeder Mountain: see **Mount Veeder** [NAPA-SONOMA].

Venado [SONOMA]: *locality,* 6.5 miles northeast of Cazadero (lat. 38°36'20" N, long. 123°00'25" W; near N line sec. 30, T 9 N, R 10 W). Named on Cazadero (1978) 7.5' quadrangle. Postal authorities established Venado post office in 1921 and discontinued it in 1941 (Frickstad, p. 199).

Verano [SONOMA]: *locality,* 1 mile northwest of Sonoma (lat. 38° 18'05" N, long. 122°28'25" W). Named on Sonoma (1951) 7.5' quadrangle.

Vestal: see **Roblar** [SONOMA].

Veteran Heights [NAPA]: *locality,* 5 miles north-northeast of Saint Helena (lat. 38°34'25" N, long. 122°26'05" W). Named on Saint Helena (1960) 7.5' quadrangle.

Veterans Home: see **Yountville** [NAPA].

Veterans Peak [NAPA]: *peak,* nearly 2 miles south-southwest of Yountville (lat. 38°23' N, long. 122°22'35" W); the peak is less than 1 mile south-southwest of State Veterans Home. Altitude 1209 feet. Named on Rutherford (1951) 7.5' quadrangle.

Vichy Springs [NAPA]: *locality,* 3 miles north-northeast of downtown Napa (lat. 38°20'20" N, long. 122°15'40" W). Named on Napa (1951) 7.5' quadrangle. A spring called Napa Vichy Spring was the basis of a resort and a water-bottling enterprise at the place (Bradley, p. 280).

Villa Grande [SONOMA]: *settlement,* 2.5 miles southwest of Guerneville along Russian River (lat. 38°38'25" N, long. 123°01'25" W). Named on Duncans Mills (1979) 7.5' quadrangle. Postal authorities established Villa Grande post office in 1921 (Salley, p. 232).

Vineburg [SONOMA]: *locality,* nearly 2 miles southeast of Sonoma (lat. 38°16'20" N, long. 122°26'15" W). Named on Sonoma (1951) 7.5' quadrangle. Called Vineyard on Napa (1902) 30' quadrangle. Postal authorities es-

tablished Vineburg post office in 1897, discontinued it in 1900, and reestablished it in 1902 (Frickstad, p. 199).

Vine Hill [SONOMA]: *ridge,* south-southeast-trending, 1.5 miles long, 5.25 miles north-northwest of Sebastopol (lat. 38°28'25" N, long. 122°51'45" W). Named on Sebastopol (1954) 7.5' quadrangle.

Vineyard: see **Vineburg** [SONOMA].

Vulture Ridge [SONOMA]: *ridge,* north- to northwest-trending, 0.5 mile long, 7 miles north-northeast of Cazadero (lat. 38°37'10" N, long. 123°00'50" W). Named on Cazadero (1978) 7.5' quadrangle.

– W –

Walalla River: see **Gualala River** [SONOMA].

Walbridge Ridge [SONOMA]: *ridge,* generally northwest-trending, 2.5 miles long, 5.25 miles west-southwest of Skaggs Springs (lat. 38°39'30" N, long. 123°07' W). Named on Tombs Creek (1978) and Warm Springs Dam (1978) 7.5' quadrangles.

Waldrue Heights [SONOMA]: *settlement,* 2.25 miles west of Glen Ellen (lat. 38°21'55" N, long. 122°33'55" W; sec. 18, T 6 N, R 6 W). Named on Glen Ellen (1954) 7.5' quadrangle.

Walker Canyon [SONOMA]: *canyon,* drained by a stream that flows 1.25 miles to Briggs Creek 4 miles west of Mount Saint Helena (lat. 38°40'35" N, long. 122°42'10" W; near N line sec. 36, T 10 N, R 8 W). Named on Mount Saint Helena (1959) 7.5' quadrangle.

Wallace Creek [SONOMA]: *stream,* flows 4 miles to Mill Creek (1) 2.5 miles west-southwest of Healdsburg (lat. 38°35'55" N, long. 122°54'40" W). Named on Geyserville (1955) and Guerneville (1955) 7.5' quadrangles.

Wallet Canyon [NAPA]: *canyon,* drained by a stream that flows less than 1 mile to Gosling Canyon 4.5 miles south-southeast of Berryessa Peak (lat. 38°36'20" N, long. 122°09'05" W). Named on Lake Berryessa (1959) 7.5' quadrangle.

Wall Springs: see **Mirabel Park** [SONOMA].

Walnut Flat [NAPA]: *area,* 7 miles north of Saint Helena (lat. 38° 36'15" N, long. 122°29' W; on W line sec. 25, T 9 N, R 6 W). Named on Saint Helena (1960) 7.5' quadrangle.

Walsh Landing [SONOMA]: *village,* 2.5 miles south-southeast of Plantation near the coast (lat. 38°33'20" N, long. 123°18' W). Named on Plantation (1977) 7.5' quadrangle.

Walter Springs [NAPA]: *locality,* 12 miles north-northeast of Saint Helena (lat. 38°39'10" N, long. 122°21'25" W; near NE cor. sec. 12, T 9 N, R 5 W). Named on Walter Springs (1959) 7.5' quadrangle. Bradley (p. 282) used the name "Walters Springs," and noted that springs discovered at the place about 1869 were the basis of a resort.

Walters Ridge [SONOMA]: *ridge,* generally

west-northwest-trending, 6 miles long, center 2.5 miles west-southwest of Big Mountain (lat. 38°42' N, long. 123°11'15" W). Named on Tombs Creek (1978) 7.5' quadrangle. Skaggs Springs (1943) and Tombs Creek (1943) 7.5' quadrangles have the name on a ridge located about 2 miles northeast of present Walters Ridge.

Walters Springs: see **Walter Springs** [NAPA].

Ward Creek [SONOMA]: *stream,* flows 6.5 miles to Austin Creek less than 1 mile north-northwest of Cazadero (lat. 38°32'30" N, long. 123°05'20" W; near W line sec. 16, T 8 N, R 11 W). Named on Cazadero (1978) and Fort Ross (1978) 7.5' quadrangles.

Warm Springs Creek [SONOMA]: *stream,* flows 13 miles to Dry Creek 2 miles north-northeast of Skaggs Springs (lat. 38°43'05" N, long. 123°00'25" W; sec. 18, T 10 N, R 10 W). Named on Warm Springs Dam (1978) 7.5' quadrangle.

Warm Springs Creek: see **Little Warm Springs Creek** [SONOMA].

Warren Creek [SONOMA]: *stream,* flows 1.5 miles to the sea 2 miles southwest of Plantation (lat. 38°34'15" N, long. 123°20'05" W). Named on Plantation (1977) 7.5' quadrangle.

Washoe [SONOMA]: *locality,* nearly 2 miles west-southwest of Cotati along Washoe Creek (lat. 38°18'50" N, long. 122°44'05" W). Named on Santa Rosa (1944) 15' quadrangle.

Washoe Creek [SONOMA]: *stream,* flows 2.5 miles to lowlands 1.5 miles west-northwest of Cotati (lat. 38°20' N, long. 122°44' W). Named on Cotati (1954) 7.5' quadrangle.

Watercress Gulch [SONOMA]: *canyon,* drained by a stream that flows less than 1 mile to Salmon Creek (1) nearly 2 miles north of the village of Bodega Bay (lat. 38°21'35" N, long. 123°03' W). Named on Bodega Head (1972) 7.5' quadrangle.

Watsons [SONOMA]: *locality,* 2 miles south-southeast of Cazadero along Northwestern Pacific Railroad (lat. 38°30'25" N, long. 123° 04'10" W). Named on Skaggs (1921) 15' quadrangle.

Weeks Creek [SONOMA]: *stream,* flows 3.25 miles to Mark West Creek 4.5 miles southeast of Mark West Springs (lat. 38°30'30" N, long. 122°38'55" W; at E line sec. 29, T 8 N, R 7 W). Named on Kenwood (1954), Mark West Springs (1958), and Santa Rosa (1954) 7.5' quadrangles.

West: see **John West Ridge** [SONOMA]; **Mark West** [SONOMA].

West Bull Canyon [NAPA]: *canyon,* 1 mile long, opens into Wragg Canyon 4.5 miles northwest of Mount Vaca (lat. 38°27'10" N, long. 122°09'10" W; near E line sec. 14, T 7 N, R 3 W); the mouth of the canyon is opposite the mouth of East Bull Canyon. Named on Capell Valley (1951) 7.5' quadrangle.

West Chapman Canyon [NAPA]: *canyon,* 1 mile long, opens into Wragg Canyon 5 miles

north-northwest of Mount Vaca (lat. 38°27'35" N, long. 122°09'15" W; near NE cor. sec. 14, T 7 N, R 3 W); the mouth of the canyon is opposite the mouth of East Chapman Canyon. Named on Capell Valley (1951) 7.5' quadrangle.

West Creek: see **Mark West Creek** [SONOMA].

West Guernewood [SONOMA]: *settlement,* 1 mile west-southwest of Guerneville along Russian River (lat. 38°29'35" N, long. 123°00'45" W; sec. 31, T 8 N, R 10 W). Named on Duncans Mills (1979) 7.5' quadrangle.

Westminister Woods [SONOMA]: *locality,* 2.5 miles northwest of Occidental (lat. 38°26'10" N, long. 122°58'20" W; sec. 21, T 7 N, R 10 W). Named on Camp Meeker (1954) 7.5' quadrangle.

West Mitchell Canyon [NAPA]: *canyon,* 1 mile long, opens into Wragg Canyon 5.5 miles north-northwest of Mount Vaca (lat. 38° 28'20" N, long. 122°09'25" W; sec. 11, T 7 N, R 3 W); the mouth of the canyon is opposite the mouth of East Mitchell Canyon. Named on Capell Valley (1951) 7.5' quadrangle.

West Napa Reservoir [NAPA]: *lake,* 225 feet long, 1.5 miles west-southwest of downtown Napa (lat. 38°17'35" N, long. 122°18'50" W). Named on Napa (1951) 7.5' quadrangle.

Wether Ridge [SONOMA]: *ridge,* west-north-west-trending, less than 1 mile long, 3.25 miles northwest of Big Mountain (lat. 38°44'45" N, long. 123°11'05" W). Named on Tombs Creek (1978) 7.5' quadrangle.

Whale Point [SONOMA]: *promontory,* 0.5 mile southwest of Jenner along the coast south of the mouth of Russian River (lat. 38°26'40" N, long. 123°07'30" W). Named on Duncans Mills (1979) 7.5' quadrangle.

Wheatfield Fork: see **Gualala River** [SONOMA].

White Cottage: see **Howell Mountain** [NAPA] (2).

White Creek [NAPA]: *stream,* flows 4 miles to Wooden Valley Creek 4.5 miles southwest of Mount Vaca (lat. 38°21'25" N, long. 122°10'15" W). Named on Mount George (1951) 7.5' quadrangle.

White Creek [SONOMA]: *stream,* flows 1.25 miles to Galloway Creek 10 miles west of Cloverdale (lat. 38°47'10" N, long. 123°11'55" W; sec. 21, T 11 N, R 12 W); the stream heads southwest of White Mountain. Named on Hopland (1960) 15' quadrangle.

Whitehead: see **Lake Whitehead** [NAPA].

White Mountain [SONOMA]: *peak,* 8.5 miles west of Cloverdale (lat. 38°47'10" N, long. 123°10'30" W; sec. 22, T 11 N, R 12 W). Altitude 1896 feet. Named on Hopland (1960) 7.5' quadrangle.

White Rock [SONOMA]: *relief feature,* 7 miles north-northeast of Jimtown (lat. 38°42'50" N, long. 123°49'50" W). Named on Jimtown (1955) 7.5' quadrangle.

White Sulphur Springs: see **Sulphur Canyon** [NAPA].

Whitman Canyon [SONOMA]: *canyon,* drained by a stream that flows 2 miles to Valley of the Moon 4 miles north-northwest of Sonoma (lat. 38°20'40" N, long. 122°29'30" W). Named on Sonoma (1951) 7.5' quadrangle.

Wiggins Hill [SONOMA]: *ridge,* northeast-trending, 1 mile long, 4 miles south-south-west of Cotati (lat. 38°16'15" N, long. 122°43'50" W). Named on Cotati (1954) 7.5' quadrangle.

Wildcat Canyon [NAPA]: *canyon,* drained by a stream that flows less than 1 mile to Moore Creek 5.25 miles northeast of Saint Helena (lat. 38°33'30" N, long. 122°24'05" W; sec. 10, T 8 N, R 5 W). Named on Saint Helena (1960) 7.5' quadrangle.

Wildcat Canyon [SONOMA]: *canyon,* drained by a stream that flows 1.25 miles to Woods Creek 4.5 miles south of Skaggs Springs (lat. 38°37'40" N, long. 123°01'30" W; sec. 13, T 9 N, R 11 W). Named on Cazadero (1978) and Warm Springs Dam (1978) 7.5' quadrangles.

Wildcat Creek [SONOMA]: *stream,* flows 1.25 miles to the sea 2.25 miles south of Plantation (lat. 38°33'30" N, long. 123°18'55" W). Named on Plantation (1977) 7.5' quadrangle.

Wildcat Mountain [SONOMA]: *peak,* 3.5 miles north-northwest of Sears Point (lat. 38°11'40" N, long. 122°28'20" W). Named on Sears Point (1951) 7.5' quadrangle.

Wild Cattle Canyon [SONOMA]: *canyon,* drained by a stream that flows 1.5 miles to Marshall Creek 5 miles north of Fort Ross (lat. 38°35'30" N, long. 123°14'20" W; near SW cor. sec. 30, T 9 N, R 12 W). Named on Fort Ross (1978) 7.5' quadrangle.

Wild Cattle Creek [SONOMA]: *stream,* flows nearly 3 miles to Warm Springs Creek 4.25 miles west of Skaggs Springs (lat. 38° 41' N, long. 123°06'20" W; sec. 29, T 10 N, R 11 W). Named on Tombs Creek (1978) and Warm Springs Dam (1978) 7.5' quadrangles.

Wild Hog Canyon [SONOMA]: *canyon,* drained by a stream that flows 1 mile to Carson Creek 4.5 miles north-northeast of Fort Ross (lat. 38°34'05" N, long. 123°11'55" W; sec. 5, T 8 N, R 12 W). Named on Fort Ross (1978) 7.5' quadrangle.

Wild Hog Hill [SONOMA]: *peak,* 5.5 miles northeast of Guerneville (lat. 38°33'35" N, long. 123°55'10" W). Altitude 1150 feet. Named on Guerneville (1955) 7.5' quadrangle.

Wildhorse Creek [SONOMA]: *stream,* heads in Mendocino and Lake Counties, flows 2.25 miles to Squaw Creek 5 miles north of Geysers Peak (lat. 38°50'20" N, long. 122°50'30" W; sec. 34, T 12 N, R 9 W). Named on The Geysers (1959) 7.5' quadrangle.

Wild Horse Ridge [SONOMA]: *ridge,* west-southwest-trending, 0.25 mile long, 3.5 miles west of Big Mountain (lat. 38°42'25" N, long. 123°12'45" W). Named on Tombs Creek (1978) 7.5' quadrangle.

Wild Horse Valley [NAPA]: *valley,* 8 miles southwest of Mount Vaca on Napa-Solano county line (lat. 38°19' N, long. 122° 11'45" W; on S line sec. 33, T 6 N, R 3 W). Named on Mount George (1951) 7.5' quadrangle.

Wild Lake [NAPA]: *lake,* 650 feet long, 7 miles north of Saint Helena (lat. 38°36'25" N, long. 122°29'10" W; near NE cor. sec. 26, T 9 N, R 6 W). Named on Saint Helena (1960) 7.5' quadrangle.

Wildwood [SONOMA]: *locality,* less than 1 mile south-southeast of Kenwood along Southern Pacific Railroad (lat. 38°24'25" N, long. 122°32'30" W). Named on Santa Rosa (1916) 15' quadrangle.

Wilfred [SONOMA]: *locality,* 3 miles north of Cotati along Northwestern Pacific Railroad (lat. 38°22'05" N, long. 122°42'54" W). Named on Cotati (1954) 7.5' quadrangle.

Williams [SONOMA]: *locality,* 4.5 miles northwest of Sebastopol along Petaluma and Santa Rosa Railroad (lat. 38°27' N, long. 122° 52'40" W). Named on Sebastopol (1942) 15' quadrangle.

Williams Cattle Station [SONOMA]: *locality,* 3.5 miles north-northeast of Cazadero (lat. 38°34'25" N, long. 123°03'05" W; sec. 2, T 8 N, R 11 W). Named on Cazadero (1943) 7.5' quadrangle.

Willow Brook [SONOMA]: *stream,* flows 5 miles to Lichau Creek 3.5 miles southeast of Cotati (lat. 38°17'05" N, long. 122°39'50" W). Named on Cotati (1954) and Glen Ellen (1954) 7.5' quadrangles. Called Haggin Creek on Santa Rosa (1916) 15' quadrangle.

Willow Creek [SONOMA]: *stream,* flows 5.5 miles to Russian River 1.5 miles east-south-east of Jenner (lat. 38°26'20" N, long. 123°05'45" W). Named on Duncans Mills (1979) 7.5' quadrangle.

Willow Grove: see **Santa Rosa** [SONOMA].

Willow Spring [SONOMA]: *spring,* 2.5 miles west of Skaggs Springs (lat. 38°41'20" N, long. 123°04'15" W; near W line sec. 27, T 10 N, R 11 W). Named on Warm Springs Dam (1978) 7.5' quadrangle.

Willow Springs Creek [SONOMA]: *stream,* flows 2.5 miles to Warm Springs Creek 4 miles west-southwest of Skaggs Springs (lat. 38°40'40" N, long. 123°05'55" W; at N line sec. 32, T 10 N, R 11 W); the stream heads at Willow Spring. Named on Warm Springs Dam (1978) 7.5' quadrangle.

Wilson Creek [SONOMA]: *stream,* flows 1.5 miles to Sonoma Creek 2.25 miles southeast of Glen Ellen (lat. 38°20'10" N, long. 122°30'05" W). Named on Glen Ellen (1954) and Sonoma (1951) 7.5' quadrangles.

Wilson Grove [SONOMA]: *locality,* 6.5 miles south of Healdsburg near Russian River (lat.

38°31' N, long. 122°51'15" W). Named on Healdsburg (1955) 7.5' quadrangle.

Windermere Point [SONOMA]: *promontory*, 5 miles south-southeast of Plantation along the coast (lat. 38°31'30" N, long. 123°16'05" W). Named on Plantation (1977) 7.5' quadrangle.

Windsor [SONOMA]: *town*, 5.5 miles southeast of Healdsburg (lat. 38°32'50" N, long. 122°48'55" W; around NE cor. sec. 14, T 8 N, R 9 W). Named on Healdsburg (1955) 7.5' quadrangle. Postal authorities established Windsor post office in 1855 (Frickstad, p. 199). The place also was known as Poor Man's Flat (Hansen and Miller, p. 48). The first postmaster chose the name "Windsor" for the fancied resemblance of the place to the oak-studded parks around Windsor Castle in England (Mullen).

Windsor: see **East Windsor** [SONOMA].

Windsor Creek [SONOMA]: *stream*, flows 8 miles to Mark West Creek 6.5 miles north of Sebastopol (lat. 38°29'45" N, long. 122°50'55" W); the stream goes past Windsor. Named on Healdsburg (1955) and Sebastopol (1954) 7.5' quadrangles.

Windy Flat [NAPA]: *area*, nearly 6 miles westsouthwest of Mount Vaca (lat. 38°22'25" N, long. 122°12'15" W; near NW cor. sec. 16, T 6 N, R 3 W). Named on Mount George (1951) 7.5' quadrangle.

Windy Point [NAPA]: *peak*, 2 miles southeast of Berryessa Peak on Napa-Yolo county line (lat. 38°38'40" N, long. 122°09'35" W). Named on Brooks (1959) 7.5' quadrangle.

Windy Point [SONOMA]: *peak*, 3.5 miles southwest of Big Mountain (lat. 38°40'30" N, long. 123°11'50" W; near NW cor. sec. 33, T 10 N, R 12 W). Named on Tombs Creek (1978) 7.5' quadrangle.

Wine Creek [SONOMA]: *stream*, flows 2.5 miles to Grape Creek 4.25 miles south-southwest of Geyserville (lat. 38°39'20" N, long. 123°56'45" W; near E line sec. 3, T 9 N, R 10 W). Named on Geyserville (1955) 7.5' quadrangle.

Wing Canyon [NAPA]: *canyon*, drained by a stream that flows nearly 2 miles to Dry Creek 4.5 miles south of Rutherford (lat. 38° 23'40" N, long. 122°25' W; sec. 4, T 6 N, R 5 W). Named on Rutherford (1951) 7.5' quadrangle. On Sonoma (1942) 15' quadrangle, the name "Wing Canyon" applies to the canyon of Dry Creek.

Wingo [SONOMA]: *locality*, 4.25 miles northnortheast of Sears Point (lat. 38°12'35" N, long. 122°25'35" W). Named on Sears Point (1951) 7.5' quadrangle.

Wire Gate Saddle [SONOMA]: *pass*, 4.5 miles north of Cazadero (lat. 38°35'50" N, long. 123°06'05" W; sec. 29, T 9 N, R 11 W). Named on Cazadero (1978) 7.5' quadrangle.

Wolf Creek [SONOMA]: *stream*, flows 5 miles to Wheatfield Fork Gualala River nearly 5 miles southwest of Big Mountain (lat. 38°

40'10" N, long. 123°12'55" W; at W line sec. 32, T 10 N, R 12 W). Named on Tombs Creek (1978) 7.5' quadrangle.

Woloki Slough [SONOMA]: *water feature*, joins Donahue Slough 6 miles southeast of downtown Petaluma (lat. 38°11' N, long. 122°32'45" W). Named on Petaluma River (1954) 7.5' quadrangle.

Wood Canyon [NAPA]: *canyon*, drained by a stream that flows nearly 1 mile to Chiles Valley 8 miles east-northeast of Saint Helena (lat. 38°32'40" N, long. 122°20'15" W). Named on Chiles Valley (1958) 7.5' quadrangle.

Wood Creek [SONOMA]: *stream*, flows nearly 3 miles to Russian River 0.5 mile east of Geyserville (lat. 38°42'30" N, long. 122°53'35" W). Named on Geyserville (1955) 7.5' quadrangle.

Wooden Valley [NAPA]: *valley*, 5 miles westsouthwest of Mount Vaca (lat. 38°22'30" N, long. 122°11'30" W). Named on Capell Valley (1951) and Mount George (1951) 7.5' quadrangles. The place was called Corral Valley before John Wooden purchased land there in 1850 (Gudde, 1949, p. 393).

Wooden Valley Creek [NAPA]: *stream*, flows 6.5 miles to Suisun Creek 5.25 miles southsouthwest of Mount Vaca (lat. 38°19'50" N, long. 122°08'10" W); the stream goes through Wooden Valley. Named on Capell Valley (1951) and Mount George (1951) 7.5' quadrangles.

Woodleaf [NAPA]: *locality*, 1.5 miles westnorthwest of Calistoga (lat. 38°35'20" N, long. 122°36'20" W). Named on Calistoga (1945) 15' quadrangle.

Woods Creek [SONOMA]: *stream*, flows 3 miles to Pena Creek 3.5 miles south of Skaggs Springs (lat. 38°38'25" N, long. 123°02'05" W; sec. 12, T 9 N, R 11 W). Named on Cazadero (1978) and Warm Springs Dam (1978) 7.5' quadrangles.

Woodworth [SONOMA]: *locality*, 5.25 miles east-northeast of Bloomfield along Petaluma and Santa Rosa Railroad (lat. 38°19'55" N, long. 122°45'35" W). Named on Sebastopol (1942) 15' quadrangle.

Woolsey [SONOMA]: *locality*, 5.5 miles north of Sebastopol (lat. 38° 29' N, long. 122°49'05" W). Named on Sebastopol (1942) 15' quadrangle.

Wragg Canyon [NAPA]: *canyon*, 8 miles long, opens into the canyon of Putah Creek 10 miles south of Berryessa Peak (lat. 38° 31'30" N, long. 122°09'30" W; sec. 23, T 8 N, R 3 W). Named on Capell Valley (1951, photorevised 1968) and Lake Berryessa (1959) 7.5' quadrangles. Water of Lake Berryessa covers the lower part of the canyon. The name commemorates the first settler in the neighborhood (Gudde, 1949, p. 393). Whitney (p. 105) called the feature Rag Cañon.

Wragg Creek [NAPA]: *stream*, flows nearly 6 miles to Lake Berryessa 6.25 miles north-

northwest of Mount Vaca (lat. 38°28'55" N, long. 122°09'25" W; sec. 2, T 7 N, R 3 W); the stream is in Wragg Canyon. Named on Capell Valley (1951, photorevised 1968) 7.5' quadrangle.

Wragg Ridge [NAPA]: *ridge,* south-trending, 8 miles long, 7.5 miles northwest of Mount Vaca (lat. 38°29'15" N, long. 122°10'40" W); the ridge is west of Wragg Canyon. Named on Capell Valley (1951) and Lake Berryessa (1959) 7.5' quadrangles.

Wright [SONOMA]: *locality,* nearly 2 miles south-southeast of present Jenner (lat. 38°25'50" N, long. 123°06'30" W). Named on Duncans Mills (1921) 15' quadrangle.

Wright Beach: see **Wrights Beach** [SONOMA].

Wright Creek: see **Pool Creek** [SONOMA].

Wright Gulch [SONOMA]: *canyon,* drained by a stream that flows 1.5 miles to the sea 3.5 miles south-southeast of present Jenner (lat. 38°24'20" N, long. 123°05'55" W); the mouth of the canyon is at present Wrights Beach. Named on Duncans Mills (1921) 15' quadrangle.

Wrights: see **Santa Rosa** [SONOMA].

Wrights Beach [SONOMA]: *beach,* 3.5 miles south-southeast of Jenner along the coast (lat. 38°24'15" N, long. 123°05'50" W). Named on Duncans Mills (1979) 7.5' quadrangle. Called Wright Beach on Duncans Mills (1943) 7.5' quadrangle.

Wye [SONOMA]: *locality,* 1 mile west-north-west of downtown Santa Rosa along Northwestern Pacific Railroad (lat. 38°27' N, long. 122°43'45" W). Named on Santa Rosa (1954) 7.5' quadrangle.

— X - Y —

Yajome [NAPA]: *land grant,* east of Napa River between Yountville and the city of Napa. Named on Napa (1951) and Yountville (1951) 7.5' quadrangles. Tomaso A. Rodriguez received 1.5 leagues in 1841; Salvador Vallejo and others claimed 6653 acres patented in 1864 (Cowan, p. 108; Cowan listed the grant under the designation "Yajome (or Llajome, or) Paso de las Trancas"). According to Perez (p. 104), Damaso Rodriguez was the grantee in 1841.

Yellow Jacket Creek [SONOMA]: *stream,* flows 3.5 miles to join Kellogg Creek and form Redwood Creek (1) 3 miles southwest of Mount Saint Helena (lat. 38°38'05" N, long. 122°40'15" W). Named on Mount Saint Helena (1959) 7.5' quadrangle. Calistoga (1945) 15' quadrangle, which shows Yellowjacket mine near the stream, has the form "Yellowjacket Creek" for the name.

Yellowjacket Springs [SONOMA]: *springs,* 1 mile east-southeast of Big Mountain (lat. 38°42'15" N, long. 123°07'45" W; sec. 24, T

10 N, R 12 W). Named on Tombs Creek (1978) 7.5' quadrangle.

York Creek [NAPA]: *stream,* flows 4.5 miles to Napa River 1.25 miles north-northwest of Saint Helena (lat. 38°31'20" N, long. 122° 28'30" W). Named on Calistoga (1958) and Saint Helena (1960) 7.5' quadrangles.

Yorty Creek [SONOMA]: *stream,* flows 3.25 miles to Dry Creek 5 miles southwest of Cloverdale (lat. 38°45'40" N, long. 123°05'25" W; sec. 33, T 11 N, R 11 W). Named on Cloverdale (1960) 7.5' quadrangle.

Young: see **George Young Creek** [SONOMA].

Yountville [NAPA]: *town,* 8.5 miles north-northwest of downtown Napa (lat. 38°24'25" N, long. 122°21'50" W). Named on Yountville (1951) 7.5' quadrangle, which shows the state veterans home located 1 mile south of Yountville. Postal authorities established Sebastopol post office in 1856, discontinued it in 1857, reestablished it in 1858, and changed the name to Yountville in 1867 (Frickstad, p. 112). The town incorporated in 1956. The name "Yountville" commemorates George C. Yount, first white settler in present Napa County, who arrived there in 1831 (Menefee, p. 19, 185). Postal authorities established Veterans Home post office at the state veterans home in 1892 (Frickstad, p. 112).

Yountville Hills [NAPA]: *range,* northwest of Yountville (lat. 38°25'10" N, long. 122°22'30" W). Named on Rutherford (1951) and Yountville (1951) 7.5' quadrangles.

Yulupa [SONOMA]: *locality,* nearly 2 miles southeast of Glen Ellen along Southern Pacific Railroad (lat. 38°20'30" N, long. 122°30'20" W). Named on Santa Rosa (1944) 15' quadrangle. Postal authorities established Yulupa post office 5.5 miles southeast of Santa Rosa—but not at this site along the railroad—in 1892 and discontinued it in 1897 (Salley, p. 245).

Yulupa Creek [SONOMA]: *stream,* flows 2.5 miles to Sonoma Creek 2.5 miles south of Kenwood (lat. 38°22'45" N, long. 122°33'05" W). Named on Kenwood (1954) 7.5' quadrangle.

— Z —

Zem Zem: see **Zim Zim Creek** [NAPA].

Zim Zim Creek [NAPA]: *stream,* flows 6.25 miles to Eticuera Creek 5.5 miles south-southeast of Knoxville (lat. 38°45'15" N, long. 122°17' W; near SE cor. sec. 34, T 11 N, R 4 W). Named on Knoxville (1958) 7.5' quadrangle. Morgan Valley (1944) 15' quadrangle shows Zim Zim ranch at the mouth of the stream. According to Gudde (1949, p. 399), the creek is named for the ranch, and the ranch and creek names should have the form "Zem-Zem." Postal authorities established Zem Zem post office 14 miles north of Monticello in

1869 and discontinued it in 1890; the name is from a well in Mecca (Salley, p. 246).

Zinfandel [NAPA]: *locality,* 2 miles north-north-west of Rutherford along Southern Pacific Railroad (lat. 38°28'55" N, long. 122°26'30" W). Named on Rutherford (1951) 7.5' quadrangle. The place first was known as Pine Station, and later as Bell Station (Hoover, Rensch, and Rensch, p. 245).

REFERENCES CITED

BOOKS AND ARTICLES

Allen, E.T., and Day, Arthur L. 1927. *Steam wells and other thermal activity at "The Geysers," California.* Washington: Carnegie Institution of Washington, 106 p.

Anderson, Winslow. 1892. *Mineral springs and health resorts of California.* San Francisco: The Bancroft Company, 347 p.

Archuleta, Kay. 1977. *The Brannan saga.* (Author), 116 p.

Bailey, Edgar H. 1946. "Quicksilver deposits of the western Mayacmas district, Sonoma County, California." *California Journal of Mines and Geology,* v. 42, no. 3, p. 199-286.

Bancroft, Hubert Howe. 1886. *History of California, Volume II, 1801-1824.* San Francisco: The History Company, Publishers, 795 p.

_____1888. *History of California. Volume VI, 1848-1859.* San Francisco: The History Company, Publishers, 787 p.

Becker, Robert H. 1964. *Diseños of California ranchos.* San Francisco: The Book Club of California, (no pagination).

_____1969. *Designs on the land.* San Francisco: The Book Club of California, (no pagination).

Bradley, Walter W. 1915. "The counties of Colusa, Glenn, Lake, Marin, Napa, Solano, Sonoma, Yolo." *Report XIV of the State Mineralogist.* Sacramento: California State Mining Bureau, p. 173-370.

Brewer, William H. 1949. *Up and down California in 1860-1864.* (Edited by Francis P. Farquhar.) Berkeley and Los Angeles: University of California Press, 583 p.

California Division of Highways. 1934. *California highway transportation survey, 1934.* Sacramento: Department of Public Works, Division of Highways, 130 p. + appendices.

Cardwell, G.T. 1958. *Geology and ground water in the Santa Rosa and Petaluma Valley areas, Sonoma County, California.* (United States Geological Survey Water-Supply Paper 1427.) Washington: United States Government Printing Office, 273 p.

Clar, C. Raymond. 1974. *Out of the river mist.* (Second edition.) Santa Cruz, California: Forest History Society, 135 p.

Cowan, Robert G. 1956. *Ranchos of California.* Fresno, California: Academy Library Guild, 151 p.

Coy, Owen C. 1923. *California county boundaries.* Berkeley: California Historical Survey Commission, 335 p.

Crawford, J.J. 1894. "Report of the State Mineralogist." *Twelfth report of the State Mineralo-*gist, *(Second Biennial,) two years ending September 15, 1894.* Sacramento: California State Mining Bureau, p. 8-412.

_____1896. "Report of the State Mineralogist." *Thirteenth report (Third Biennial) of the State Mineralogist for the two years ending September 15, 1896.* Sacramento: California State Mining Bureau, p. 10-646.

Davis, Fenelon F. 1948. "Mines and mineral resources of Napa County, California." *California Journal of Mines and Geology,* v. 44, no. 2, p. 159-188.

Davis, William Heath. 1962. *Seventy-five years in California.* San Francisco, California: John Howell—Books, 345 p.

Durst, David M. 1916. "Physiographic features of Cache Creek in Yolo County." *University of California Publications in Geography,* v. 1, no. 8, p. 331-372.

Frickstad, Walter N. 1955. *A century of California post offices, 1848 to 1954.* Oakland, California: Philatelic Research Society, 395 p.

Goodyear, W.A. 1890a. "Napa County." *Tenth annual report of the State Mineralogist, for the year ending December 1, 1890.* Sacramento: California State Mining Bureau, p. 349-363.

_____1890b. "Sonoma County." *Tenth annual report of the State Mineralogist, for the year ending December 1, 1890.* Sacramento: California State Mining Bureau, p. 672-679.

Gudde, Erwin G. 1949. *California place names.* Berkeley and Los Angeles: University of California Press, 431 p.

_____1969. *California place names.* Berkeley and Los Angeles: University of California Press, 416 p.

Hanna, Phil Townsend. 1951. *The dictionary of California land names.* Los Angeles: The Automobile Club of Southern California, 392 p.

Hanna, Warren L. 1979. *Lost harbor, The controversy over Drake's California anchorage.* Berkeley, Los Angeles, London: University of California Press, 459 p.

Hansen, Harvey J., and Miller, Jeanne Thurlow. 1962. *Wild oats in Eden, Sonoma County in the 19th century.* Santa Rosa, California: (Authors), 147 p.

Heig, Adair. 1982. *History of Petaluma, A California river town.* Petaluma, California: Scottwall Associates, 166 p.

Higgins, Chris T. 1983. "Geology of Annadel State Park." *California Geology,* v. 36, no. 11, p. 235-241.

Hine, Robert V. 1983. *California's utopian colo-*

nies. Berkeley, Los Angeles, London: University of California Press, 209 p.

Hoover, Mildred Brooke, Rensch, Hero Eugene, and Rensch, Ethel Grace. 1966. *Historic spots in California.* (Third edition, revised by William N. Abeloe.) Stanford, California: Stanford University Press, 642 p.

Jackson, Walter. 1976. *Bridgeport, Mendocino County, California.* Ukiah, California: Mendocino County Historical Society, *Inc.,* 16 p.

Kroeber, A.L. 1916. "California place names of Indian origin." *University of California Publications in American Archæology and Ethnology,* v. 12, no. 2, p. 31-69.

Laizure, C. McK. 1926. "San Francisco field division (Marin County)." *Mining in California,* v. 22, no. 3, p. 314-365.

LeBaron, Gaye, and others. 1985. *Santa Rosa, a nineteenth century town.* (No place): Historia, Ltd. 224 p.

Mason, Jack. 1976. *Early Marin.* (Second revised edition.) Inverness, California: North Shore Books, 228 p.

Menefee, C.A. 1873. *Historical and descriptive sketch book of Napa, Sonoma, Lake and Mendocino.* Napa City: Reporter Publishing House, 356 p.

Miller, Jeanne Thurlow. 1967. *Seeing historic Sonoma today.* Santa Rosa, California: The Miller Associates, 50 p.

Mullen, Barbara Dorr. 1974. *Sonoma County crossroads.* San Rafael, California: C M Publications, (no pagination).

Perez, Crisostomo N. 1996. *Land grants in Alta California.* Rancho Cordova, California: Landmark Enterprises, 264 p.

Salley, H.E. 1977. *History of California post offices, 1849-1976.* La Mesa, California: Postal History Associates, Inc., 300 p.

Schwartz, Harvey. 1979. "Fort Ross, California, Imperial Russian outpost on America's western frontier, 1812-1841." *Journal of the West,* v. 18, no. 2, p. 35-48.

Shepherd, Forest. 1851. "Observations on the Pluton Geysers of California." *American Journal of Science and Arts* (series 2), v. 12, no. 35, p. 153-158.

Teather, Louise. 1986. *Place names of Marin.* San Francisco, California: Scottwall Associates, 96 p.

Trask, John B., 1856. *Report on the geology of northern and southern California.* (Sen., Sess. of 1856, Doc. No. 14.) Sacramento: State Printer, 66 p.

Tyson, Philip T. 1850. "Report of P.T. Tyson, esq., upon the geology of California." *Report of the Secretary of War, communicating information in relation to the geology and topography of California.* (31st Cong., 1st Sess., Sen. Ex. Doc. No. 47.) Washington: Government Printing Office, p. 3-74.

United States Board on Geographic Names (under name "United States Geographic Board").

1933. *Sixth report of the United States Geographic Board, 1890 to 1932.* Washington: Government Printing Office, 834 p.

_____(under name "United States Board on Geographical Names"). 1942. *Decisions of the United States Board on Geographical Names, Decisions rendered between July 1, 1940, and June 30, 1941.* Washington: Government Printing Office, 89 p.

_____(under name "United States Board on Geographical Names"). 1943. *Decisions rendered between July 1, 1941, and June 30, 1943.* Washington: Department of the Interior, 104 p.

_____1949. *Decision list no. 4903, March 1949.* Washington: Department of the Interior. 26 p.

_____1950. *Decisions on names in the United States and Alaska rendered during April, May, and June 1950.* (Decision list no. 5006.) Washington: Department of the Interior, 47 p.

_____1957. *Decisions on names in the United States, Alaska and Hawaii, Decisions rendered from May 1954 through March 1957.* (Decision list no. 5701.) Washington: Department of the Interior, 23 p.

_____1959. *Decisions on names in the United States, Decisions rendered from January, 1959 through April, 1959.* (Decision list no. 5902.) Washington: Department of the Interior, 49 p.

_____1962a. *Decisions on names in the United States, Decisions rendered from September through December 1961.* (Decision list no. 6103.) Washington: Department of the Interior, 75 p.

_____1962b. *Decisions on names in the United States, Decisions rendered from January through April 1962.* (Decision list no. 6201.) Washington: Department of the Interior, 72 p.

_____1967. *Decisions on geographic names in the United States, July through September 1967.* (Decision list no. 6703.) Washington: Department of the Interior, 29 p.

_____1970. *Decisions on geographic names in the United States, April through June 1970.* (Decision list no. 7002.) Washington: Department of the Interior, 20 p.

_____1977a. *Decisions on geographic names in the United States, January through March 1977.* (Decision list no. 7701.) Washington: Department of the Interior, 32 p.

_____1977b. *Decisions on geographic names in the United States, July through September 1977.* (Decision List No. 7703.) Washington: Department of the Interior, 25 p.

_____1978. *Decisions on geographic names in the United States, January through March 1978.* (Decision list no. 7801.) Washington: Department of the Interior, 18 p.

_____1979a. *Decisions on geographic names in the United States, January through March*

1979. (Decision list no. 7901.) Washington: Department of the Interior, 27 p.

_____1981. *Decisions on geographic names in the United States, October through December 1980.* (Decision list no. 8004.) Washington: Department of the Interior, 21 p.

_____1984. *Decisions on Geographic names in the United States, April through June 1984.* (Decision list no. 8402.) Washington: Department of the Interior, 22 p.

_____1986. *Decisions on geographic names in the United States, October through December 1986.* (Decision list no. 8604.) Washington: Department of the Interior, 22 p.

_____1991. *Decisions on geographic names in the United States.* (Decision list 1991.) Washington: Department of the Interior, 40 p.

_____1992. *Decisions on geographic names in the United States.* (Decision list 1992.) Washington: Department of the Interior, 21 p.

Wagner, Henry R. 1968. *The cartography of the Northwest Coast of America to the year 1800.* (One-volume reprint of the 1937 edition.) Amsterdam: N. Israel, 543 p.

Waring, Gerald A. 1915. *Springs of California.* (United States Geological Survey Water-Supply Paper 338.) Washington: Government Printing Office, 410 p.

Wheat, Carl I. 1959. *Mapping the Transmississippi West.* Volume One. San Francisco: The Institute of Historical Cartography, 349 p.

Whitney, J.D. 1865. *Report of progress and synopsis of the field-work from 1860 to 1864.* (Geological Survey of California, Geology, Volume I.) Published by authority of the Legislature of California, 498 p.

Wilkes, Charles. 1958. *Columbia River to the Sacramento.* Oakland, California: Biobooks, 140 p.

Williamson, R.S. 1857. "General report." *Reports of explorations and surveys, to ascertain the most practicable and economical route for a railroad from the Mississippi River to the Pacific Ocean.* Volume VI, part I. (33d Cong., 2d Sess., Sen. Ex. Doc. No. 78.) Washington: Beverly Tucker, Printer, 134 p.

MISCELLANEOUS MAPS

Bancroft. 1864. "Bancroft's map of the Pacific States." Compiled by Wm. H. Knight. Published by H.H. Bancroft & Co., Booksellers and Stationers, San Francisco, Cal.

Beechey. 1827-1828. "The harbor of San Francisco, Nueva California." By Captn. F.W. Beechey, R.N.F.R.S.

California Division of Forestry. 1945. "Sonoma County." (Used as base for plate 22 *in* Honke and Ver Planck.)

California Division of Highways. 1934. (Appendix "A" *of* California Division of Highways.)

California Mining Bureau. 1909. "Sonoma, Marin, Napa, Yolo, and Solano Counties." (*In* California Mining Bureau Bulletin 56.)

_____1917. (Untitled map *in* California Mining Bureau Bulletin 74, p. 164.)

Cardwell. 1958. "Geologic map of the Santa Rosa and Petaluma Valley areas, California, showing location of wells." (Plate 1 *in* Cardwell.)

Davis. 1948. "Map of Napa County, California, showing locations of mines and mineral deposits." (Plate 22 *in* F.F. Davis.)

Durst. 1916. "Sketch map of northwestern Yolo County." (Plate 37 *in* Durst.)

Eddy. 1854. "Approved and declared to be the official map of the State of California by an act of the Legislature passed March 25th 1853." Compiled by W.M. Eddy, State Surveyor General. Published for R.A. Eddy, Marysville, California, by J.H. Colton, New York.

Gibbes. 1852. "A new map of California." By Charles Drayton Gibbes, from his own and other recent surveys and explorations. Published by C.D. Gibbes, Stockton, Cal.

Goddard. 1857. "Britton & Rey's map of the State of California." By George H. Goddard.

Jefferson. 1849. "Map of the emigrant road from Independence Mo. to St. Francisco, California." By T.H. Jefferson.

Postal Route. 1884. (Map reproduced in *Early California, Northern Edition.* Corvalis, Oregon: Western Guide Publishers, p. 34-43.)

Ringgold. 1850. "General chart embracing survey of the Farallones entrance to the Bay of San Francisco, Bays of San Francisco and San Pablo, Straits of Carquines and Suisun Bay, and the Sacramento and San Joaquin Rivers to the cities of Sacramento and San Joaquin, California." By Cadwalader Ringgold, Commander, U.S. Navy. 1850.

Trask. 1853. "Topographical map of the mineral districts of California." Being the first map ever published from actual survey. By John B. Trask. Lithog. and Published by Britton & Rey. San Francisco.

Wilkes. 1849. "Map of Upper California." By the best authorities.

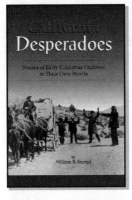

CALIFORNIA DESPERADOES
Stories of Early California Outlaws in Their Own Words
by William B. Secrest

> "*Fascinating...*"
> — John Boessenecker,
> author of *Gold Dust and Gunsmoke*

$15.95
Printed two-color throughout
Many rare photographs & illustrations
Bibliography • Index
272 pages • 6" x 9" • ISBN 1-884995-19-5

FROM MUD-FLAT COVE TO GOLD TO STATEHOOD
California 1840-1850
By Irving Stone
With a foreword by Jean Stone

> Irving Stone "...one of America's foremost
> literary figures and its greatest story teller."
>
> "...a fascinating book for high school students and adults."
> —*The Bookhandler*

$12.95
176 pages • 6" x 9" • ISBN 1-884995-17-9

THE NEWHALL INCIDENT
America's Worst Uniformed Cop Massacre
by Chief John Anderson with Marsh Cassady

> "*Not since Truman Capote's* In Cold Blood *has there been a
> true crime story that so intimately captures the lives of
> killers, victims and police.*"
> — Ted Schwarz, author of *The Hillside Strangler*

$14.95
With never-before published CHP photographs
192 pages • 6" x 9" • ISBN 1-884956-01-7

SAN JUAN BAUTISTA
The Town, The Mission & The Park
by Charles W. Clough

> "*Highly recommended.*"
> —*The Bookwatch*

$18.95
175 historic photos, maps and other illustrations
Bibliography • Index
144 pages • 8½" x 11" • ISBN 1-884995-07-1

Available from bookstores, on-line bookstores or by calling 1-800-497-4909

ABOUT THE AUTHOR

Many years ago in connection with his more than three-decade-long career as a geologist with the United States Geological Survey, David L. Durham often needed to know the whereabouts of some obscure or vanished place in California. He searched for a suitable gazetteer to help him locate these features but found no such volume. To meet his needs he began compiling his own gazetteer for part of the state and, as his interests expanded, so did his gazetteer.

For the first twelve years of his retirement, Mr. Durham compiled information for the gazetteer nearly full-time. Eventually he extended coverage to all of California. The definitive gazetteer of California, *California's Geographic Names: A Gazetteer of Historic and Modern Names of the State* is the result. The Durham's Place-Names of California series, of which this volume is one, contains the same information as *California's Geographic Names* but in thirteen regional divisions.

Mr. Durham was born in California, served as an infantryman in France and Germany during World War II and holds a Bachelor of Science degree from the California Institute of Technology. He and his wife Nancy have two grown children.

CALIFORNIA'S GEOGRAPHIC NAMES
A Gazetteer of Historic and Modern Names of the State

Compiled by David L. Durham

"The quantity and value of the information included in this work are simply staggering...a boon to historians, genealogists and outdoor folk of all kinds."

— Robert C. Berlo, Secretary of the California Map Society

"I am impressed! California's Geographic Names is the new standard."

— Robert J. Chandler, Wells Fargo Historian

The definitive gazetteer of California.

Hardcover • 1,680pp • 8½" x 11"
Bibliography • Index
ISBN 1-884995-14-4

Available from bookstores, on-line bookstores or
by calling 1-800-497-4909